SUBMARINES
& DEEP-SEA VEHICLES

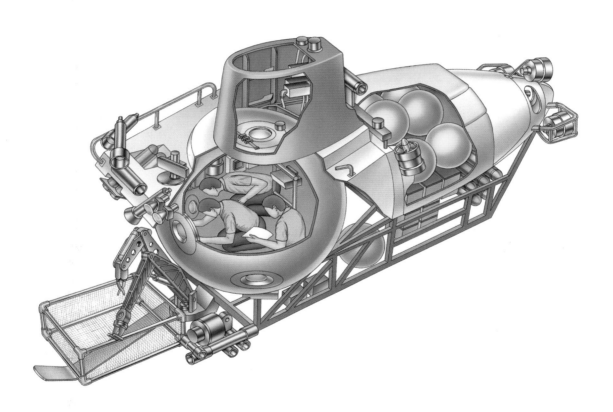

SUBMARINES
& DEEP-SEA VEHICLES

JEFFREY TALL

THUNDER BAY
P·R·E·S·S

San Diego, California

THUNDER BAY
P·R·E·S·S

An imprint of the Advantage Publishers Group
5880 Oberlin Drive, San Diego, CA 92121-4794
www.advantagebooksonline.com

Editorial and design by
Amber Books Ltd
Bradley's Close
74–77 White Lion Street
London N1 9PF
England

ISBN 1-57145-778-X

Library of Congress Cataloging-in-Publication Data available upon request.

Printed in Italy.

1 2 3 4 5 06 05 04 03 02

Project Editor: Naomi Waters
Designer: Zoë Mellors
Picture research: Lisa Wren and Debbie Corner

Note on Specification Boxes
Where two displacements and two performances are quoted for submarines,
the first applies to the surface condition and the second as submerged.

CONTENTS

EARLY PIONEERS

The most prophetic remark in history concerning the submarine and underwater attack was made in 1805 by Earl St Vincent, the British First Sea Lord. On hearing that his Prime Minister had allowed Robert Fulton's *Nautilus* submersible to be demonstrated to the Admiralty's 'torpedo committee', he remarked that 'Pitt is the greatest fool that ever existed to encourage a mode of warfare which they who command the seas do not want, and which, if successful will deprive them of it'.

Sir Herbert Richmond defined 'sea power' as 'that form of national strength which enables its possessor to send his armies and commerce across those stretches of the sea and ocean that lie between his country or the countries of his allies, and those territories to which he needs access in war; and to prevent his enemy from doing the same'. It is from this that 'command of the seas' derives. Throughout history, sea power has been exercised through the possession

Left: Robert Fulton's most famous submarine design was the *Nautilus*; here is another one of his designs, which operated on the same principle of using sail power while on the surface. The illustration is taken from his *Drawings and Descriptions*, the original drawings of which held are now in the New York Public Library.

Above: Admiral Sir John Jervis (later Earl St Vincent) defeated the numerically superior Spanish at the Battle of Cape St Vincent in February 1797. On that day, Horatio Nelson was knighted and promoted. Submarines? Never!

exploit its cloak of secrecy and surprise against an unwitting enemy. It was to be a struggle that lasted many centuries. Skin divers of Ancient Greece armed with knives as weapons to cut blockading ships' anchor cables – whose efforts lasted only minutes – were the human ancestors of modern nuclear-powered submarines of virtually unlimited endurance, the weapons of which can fly many thousands of miles with the capability of destroying enemy cities.

This is the story of those submarines, and we will see how they also stimulated man's desire for underwater exploration for peaceful and commercial purposes. Before telling that story, however, it is essential to understand the challenges posed by the physical properties of the depths that the pioneers had to overcome. It is important to appreciate that once these challenges had been met (to 'float') it was necessary to develop an underwater fighting machine that fulfilled the other two principles of a warship, to 'move' and to 'fight'. There were several underwater challenges.

PROVIDING AIR

A fish can extract oxygen from the water without a mechanical contrivance, but man cannot, so he needs a renewable source of fresh air to sustain activity underwater. Air can be supplied through a spare 'lung' for relatively short periods or an environment providing a large volume of air for longer operations. In addition, air has to be replenishable in order to keep it from being saturated with carbon dioxide, the by-product of breathing. Exertion creates a high demand for oxygen by the body, so the less the physical demand through strenuous activity, the longer the air will last.

COMBATING PRESSURE

For every 0.609m (2ft) descended in water, pressure increases by $0.07kg/cm^2$ (1psi). A simple experiment in the deep end of a swimming pool is sufficient to demonstrate how eardrums are affected, so it is easy to

of strong surface navies; what underwater warriors did was to pursue a mode of warfare that was regarded as 'unfair' and 'sneaky', since it ran in the face of honourable 'eyeball to eyeball' confrontation. In short, underwater warfare gave a weaker power the opportunity to redress the balance of maritime military might represented by *Armadas* and Grand Fleets.

So it was the stimulus of war that led to man's struggle with the deep in order to

imagine what the effect would be at 9.1m (30ft), when the pressure reaches 2 atmospheres. Being exposed to pressure for any length of time plays havoc with the human physiology, causing a build-up of nitrogen in the blood, the cause of bends.

ANCIENT ORIGINS

Contrary to the generally conceived idea that submarine warfare is one of the newer phases of naval conflict, underwater attack is one of the most ancient modes of disabling an enemy's warship. It all started with free-swimming divers armed with knives, whose favourite targets were the anchor ropes of their opposition's galleons. Without this security of attachment, besieging vessels became victims of wind and tide, and could easily be driven to destruction. Indeed, Alexander the Great suffered such an experience during his siege of Tyre in 332 BC. It is said that this prompted his expedition beneath the waves in a glass bottle to investigate what was going on.

OVERCOMING BUOYANCY

When a body is placed in a liquid, it sinks until it has displaced its own weight (density) of that liquid. Objects that are denser than water will sink. Density is calculated by dividing mass by volume. Density can be affected by a number of factors. Taking a whale, for example, its large size, its lung capacity (trapped air), and blubber content all influence its mass/volume ratio and give it positive buoyancy (i.e. it floats). Sharks, however, because of their bone structure and compact shape, are denser than water and would sink to the bottom unless they swam, so they have negative buoyancy. In a fish's swim bladder, the amount of air (volume) can be varied with depth without altering its mass (weight) so that it maintains neutral buoyancy. The human body with air in the lungs is neutrally buoyant a few feet below the surface, so, like the shark, swimming is necessary to stay afloat, but weights are required to get that inflated body into the depths.

1 The submarine at full buoyancy, sitting on a cushion of air in the ballast tanks.

2 Main vents open; air rushes out, water rushes in and destroys positive buoyancy.

3 The submarine sinks and achieves neutral buoyancy. Main vents are shut.

4 High-pressure air is blown into the ballast tanks and expels the water.

5 The submarine, now lighter (less dense), begins to rise.

6 The submarine is back on the surface, fully buoyant.

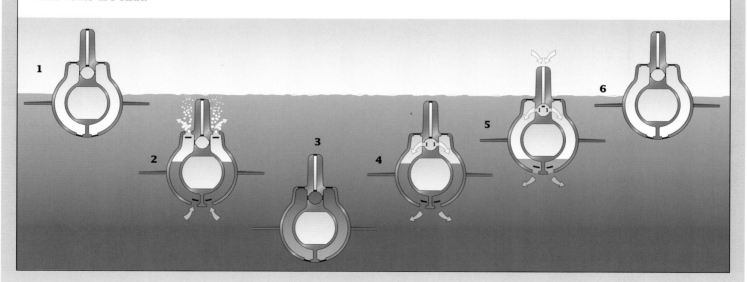

Friar Roger Bacon, one of the first modern scientists, referred to apparatus that allowed people to walk about underwater 'without danger to life or limb', as early as the 13th century.

Refinements to simply cutting cables followed in 20 BC, when the use of augers to bore holes in hulls to let the water in was suggested by Philon of Alexandria. Early in the Christian era, at the siege of Byzantium by Septimus Severus in AD 196, we see cable-cutting again being utilized by the free-swimming defenders; however, this time it was carried out with the added accomplishment of hijacking the galleons by dragging them away from their consorts.

We now leap forwards to 1190, when a German poem entitled *Salman and Morolf* discusses how Morolf built a diving boat of leather and used it to hide at the bottom of the sea for no less than 14 days, during which time he supplied himself with air through a long tube. In fact, this would not have been a practical proposition because without a positive, pumped supply of air, Morolf would have suffocated! It is not possible for human lungs to power air through a tube that is longer than twice the length of the human trachea (windpipe) without causing an overwhelming build-up of carbon dioxide.

Friar Roger Bacon (1214–92), recognized as one of the first modern scientists, does, however, allude to apparatus that enabled people to walk about underwater 'without danger to life or limb'. There is little doubt, too, that the great artist-engineer, Leonardo da Vinci (1452–1519) produced ideas for underwater work. He did not disclose details of his plans because he felt that the product was too destructive and he did not trust 'the evil nature of men who practice assassination at the bottom of the sea'.

WILLIAM BOURNE'S DIVING SUBMARINE

After a thousand years, any developments there had been in underwater activity had been inspired by salvage and exploration. It was not until an English gunner William Bourne, who had served with the Elizabethan Admiral Sir William Monson, wrote, in 1578, his *Inuentions and Deuices – Very necessary for all Generalles and Captaines, or Leaders of Men as wel by sea as by land,* that we see the first treatise on what we might recognize as a submarine.

Being a gunner, Bourne was probably inspired by the appealing idea of not being shot at by the enemy! In detailing his 'eighteenth devise' he offered the first lucid description of why a ship floats – by displacing its weight of water – and then described a mechanism by which, through decreasing its volume, it would sink. This reduction was achieved through winding in watertight greased leather pads: in effect, creating ballast tanks. Winding these pads out again made the craft lighter by increasing its volume, making it rise. There

Right: An interesting but suicidal form of underwater apparatus, designed by Leonardo da Vinci. Because the breathing tube is more than twice as long as the breather's trachea, he would have been overwhelmed by carbon dioxide.

WILLIAM BOURNE'S *INVENTIONS AND DEVICES ...* (1578)

'It is possible to make a shippe or boate that may goe under the water unto the bottom, and so come up again at your pleasure. Any magnitude of body that is in the water, if that qualitie is biggnesse, having alwaies but one weight, may be made bigger or lesser, then it shall swimme when you would, and sinke when you list: and to make anything doo so, then the jointes or places that make the thing bigger or lesser must be of leather; and in the inside to have skrewes to wind it in and also out againe; and for to have it sinke, they must winde the thing in to make it lesse, and then it sinketh unto the bottom: and to have it swimme, then to winde the sides out again, to make the thing bigger, and it will swimme according unto the body of the thing in the water ... And to make a small shippe or barke, or boate, do this, the barke being made of purpose, let there be a good store of ballast in the bottome of hir, and ouer the ballast, as low as may be, let ther be a close orloppe and that being done, then you must have one mast, that must bee of sufficient bignesse that it must have a hole bored through the one end unto the other, as a pompe hath: and that done, then when that you list to sinke, then you must sound the deepness of the water, and forsee that the water will not rise higher than the top of the mast, for the hole that goeth through the mast must give you ayre, as men cannot live without it.'

is no evidence that Bourne ever put his theory into practice, but to him goes the ancestral honour of being the first submarine designer.

CORNELIUS VAN DREBBEL AND HIS 'MOVING SUBMARINE'

The honour of building the first working submarine goes to Dr Cornelius Van Drebbel, appointed as 'court inventor' by King James I of England. The inspiration for his invention, it is said, occurred one night in 1623 when he was strolling by the River Thames and saw fishermen dragging heavy baskets of fish behind their boats. When their lines grew taut, the boats sank low in the water. When they slackened, the boats rose to the surface.

The physics of this phenomenon fascinated Van Drebbel, and he wondered whether a boat could be held underwater by forward motion when propelled by oars. His concept won the support of his monarch, and he proceeded to build his submarine by adding a wooden framework over a fishing vessel hull and covering the whole lot with layers of greased leather. Port and starboard oars protruded through collars in the leather covering, and the holes were made watertight with metal straps. The process worked when he demonstrated the craft to King James on the River Thames in 1626, with the downward-sloping foredeck acting as a diving plane, assisted perhaps with goatskin ballast tanks, taking the vessel to 3.65m (12ft) below the surface. Above all else, Van Drebbel had offered one solution to the second principle of a warship: using oarsmen to move!

THE ARK OF NAVIGATION

In 1648, John Wilkins, Oliver Cromwell's brother-in-law, a founder member of the Royal Society and later Bishop of Chester, took great interest in what he called 'An Ark of Navigation', which he discussed in his *Mathematical Magick*. He went further than anyone else hitherto in the potential applications of a submarine craft. 'Private, a Man may thus go to any Coast of the World invisibly without being discovered or

VAN DREBBEL'S SUCCESS

Van Drebbel's demonstration is referred to by no less than the distinguished mathematician Sir Robert Boyle when, in 1662, he remarked on:

'A Conceit of that deservedly Famous Mechanician and Chymist Cornelius Drebbel who among other strange things that he performed is affirmed (by more than a few credible persons) to have contrived for the late learned King James a vessel to go under water; of which trial was made in the Thames with admirable success the vessel carrying twelve Rowers besides passengers; one of which is yet alive and related to an excellent Mathemetician that informed me of it.'

prevented in his journey.' Wilkins said that 'such a vessel was 'safe from the Uncertainty of the Tides and the Violence of Tempests', but most significantly that 'it may be of very great advantage against a Navy of Enemies, who by this means may be undermined in the water and blown up'. Wilkins rather spoils his well-reasoned paper by suggesting that it might be possible in time for generations of humans to live beneath the sea and bring their children up without ever seeing land!

DE SON AND HIS 'FIGHTING SUBMARINE'

Six years after Wilkins's eulogy on the submarine, a boat was built in Holland in 1653 by the Frenchman Monsieur De Son, which one contemporary observer described as 'the Rotterdam ship that would kill the English underwater'. The shape of this impressive vessel was that of a nearly cubicle box extended forward and aft by long, rectangular pyramids. Running through her middle was a massive girdle of

Right: This wonderful lithograph by G.W. Tweedale depicts an anxious-looking Dr Cornelius Van Drebbel demonstrating his underwater craft to King James I of England on the River Thames in 1626. The congested background shows London's waterfront before the Great Fire; note the shape of St Paul's Cathedral in the centre.

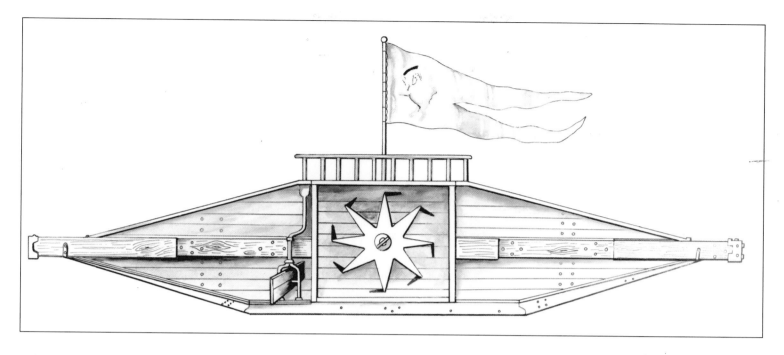

timber faced with iron, and she was propelled by a paddle-wheel housed in the centre of the vessel. The purpose of the girder was to ram an opponent just below the water-line, thereby sinking it. To have been effective she would have had to muster some speed, but in the event her driving mechanism was so ineffectual that she failed all her trials. Despite the failure, De Son had firmly established the third principle of a warship as it applied to submarines: she was built to fight!

BORELLI AND SYMONS

In 1680, a wealthy Italian, Giovanni Alfonso Borelli, added a further continental flavour to submarine invention when he published another list of *Devices*. His concept was very similar to Van Drebbel's, in that he planned to use an inverted rowing boat with its cockpit planked over. Once again it was to be oar driven, with the added refinement that the blades of the oar were to open and shut like the fin of a fish, so that when thrown back they would close up and pass easily through the water, but would open to their full extent as soon as the rower pulled forwards.

More importantly, for the first time, Borelli documented his intention to use large leather bottles fastened to holes in the bottom of the boat. These would act as as internal ballast tanks to control the displacement of the craft, determining whether it should sink or float. There is controversy as to whether the drawing of the craft that appeared in June 1749 was that of Borelli's design or actually that of a design by Nathaniel Symons, an English carpenter of Harbeston in Devon. Unlike many designers, Symons actually built a craft in 1729 and regularly demonstrated it on the River Dart near Totnes. He was hoping to make a profit out of his invention, but never collected more than 'twenty shillings', equivalent to about £1 (US$1.39), much less than his investment, and he disappeared into obscurity.

THE FIRST SUBMARINE CASUALTY

In 1774, we come across the first recorded casualty in submarine history. In this year, another Englishman, this time a wheelwright by the name of John Day, followed up an earlier submerged endurance experiment by building a submerged craft under the sponsorship of a gambler called Christopher Blake. Blake wagered that Day would sink a ship in the sea with himself in

Above: De Son's paddle-wheel was intended to be driven by a spring. It must have been successful in dock, otherwise the craft would never have been completed. During sea trials, however, it was a complete disaster, indicating that the inventor did not understand the principles of water resistance.

The *Turtle*'s attack on Lord Howe's flagship *Eagle* in New York Harbour in September 1776 established a number of principles of attack that were to dominate thinking by other submarine pioneers for the next hundred years.

it, to a depth of 30.5m (100ft), and remain in it for 12 hours without any communication, and at the due time rise up in the vessel. Day used a converted 50.8-tonne sloop, inside of which was 10.1 tonnes of ballast. Attached to the ballast were two quick-release 10.1-tonne weights, the slipping of which would ensure the craft bobbed to the surface. Helpers would add a further 20.3 tonnes of ballast once Day was locked in.

He climbed onboard his vessel in Plymouth Sound, England, having boarded with a hammock, a candle, some biscuits, and a supply of water. His helpers added the required additional ballast, and Day and his sloop were never seen again! This intrepid pioneer proved that a little knowledge is a dangerous thing, as he had grossly miscalculated his 'trim'.

TURTLE ATTACKS THE EAGLE

Two years after the Day débâcle, life began to get more serious in underwater warfare when the first submarine attack in history took place. On 6 September 1776, when the American Patriots' *Turtle* attacked Lord Howe's flagship *Eagle* in New York Harbour. It is worth dwelling on this episode because the *Turtle*'s creator, David Bushnell, established a number of principles of attack that were to dominate thinking by other submarine pioneers for the next century.

It all started when a brilliant young American scientist, David Bushnell, began to experiment with ways of getting gunpowder to explode underwater. His efforts resulted in the invention of a submarine mine, triggered by a clockwork mechanism. During the American War of Independence, Bushnell was determined to 'do his bit', so he translated his invention into a weapon of war to be delivered against the British Fleet.

The delivery vehicle for his 68kg (150lb) mine was to be a submarine, which Bushnell constructed on an island in the Connecticut River in total secrecy. Because of its shape (an inverted egg), it was dubbed *Turtle* and was 2.3m (7ft 6in) long, 2.4m (8ft) deep, and 1.2m (4ft) wide. It was made from tightly fitting oak planks bound by iron hoops, and a beam inside the hull that doubled as a seat further strengthened the frame. It was just large enough to carry a single 'navigator' and contained enough air to sustain him underwater for 40 minutes. The navigator looked through a porthole to see where he was going when *Turtle* was awash, and he had a compass, 'rendered visible by means of phosphorous', to steer by when fully submerged. The air could be replenished by the *Turtle* bobbing to the surface, when ventilators came into play.

To destroy the craft's positive buoyancy, Bushnell added 408.2kg (900lb) of lead

'THE STRANGE SHIP BUILT AT ROTTERDAM ...'

A manuscript in The National Library at Paris describes De Son's vessel thus:
    'The true and perfect forme of the Strange Ship built at Rotterdam A 1653. The inuentor of it doeth undertake in one day to destroy a hondred Ships: can goe from Rotterdam to London and back againe in one day, and in 6 Weekes to goe to the East Indiens, and to run as swift as a bird can flye: no fire, nor Storme, or Bullets, can hinder her, unless it please God. Although the Ships meane to bee safe in their hauvens, it is in vaine, for thee shall come to them in any place. It is impossible for her to be taken, unless by treacherie, and then cannot be governed by any but himselfe. The length is 72, the heighte 12 foote, the breadth 8 foote [22m x 3.6m x 2.4m].'

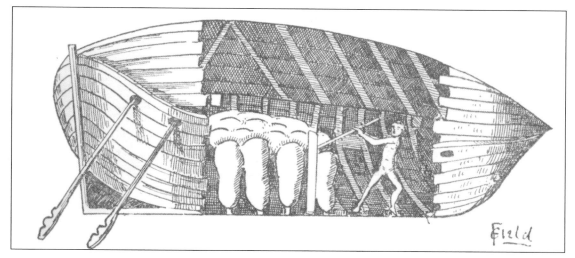

Left: Expelling water from goatskin ballast tanks to get back to the surface was no easy matter! It would seem that the invention shown in this drawing of 1749 is that of Borelli, as Symons's boat, according to contemporary description, was joined in the middle by a leather belt. When this was shortened in like a concertina, increasing the craft's density, it sank.

ballast, a chain weighing 90.7kg (200lb) that could be slipped in an emergency, and a small internal ballast tank of water. The ballast tank's valve was operated by a footpedal for letting water in and two brass forcing-pumps for expelling it. For horizontal and vertical movement, the *Turtle* was equipped with two hand-cranked propellers, one facing forwards and the other pointing upwards. To steer the submarine in a straight line (or go round corners!), there was a hand-operated rudder bar.

The principle of an attack with the *Turtle* was to approach the target awash taking care not to be seen, and, once lined up on the target and noting the course to steer, to admit enough ballast water to become completely submerged. Once underneath the target, the *Turtle* would be lightened so that she rested against the enemy's hull. A wood-screw which passed through a metal tube at the top of the submarine would then be turned so that the screw drove into the wooden planks of the target. Once firmly secured, this screw – which was connected by rope to the 'mine' – would be detached internally, leaving the operator free to make his escape before the explosion. The mine, which floated on the surface adjacent to the water-line of the target, was initiated by a time-controlled fuse, and the damage its 68kg (150lb)

charge caused would create a hole large enough to flood the ship's hold and cause it to sink.

As can be imagined, given the physical challenge of cranking propellers, operating valves, steering the craft, and finally implanting the screw into the target, it would take an enormously strong man to undertake the mission. To Bushnell's regret, he was not up to it, so he recruited 27-year-old Sergeant Ezra Lee, who had recently returned from the hazardous duty of operating fire-ships against the British Fleet blockading New York Harbour.

Soon after Washington's defeat at the hands of Lord Howe during the Battle of Long Island, the Patriots decided that something must be done to seize the initiative, so it was decided to attack Lord Howe's flagship *Eagle*. Under the cover of darkness, Lee approached his target, only to discover that someone had miscalculated the tide, and he spent over an hour trying to make ground towards his objective. He eventually succeeded and slipped underneath the British flagship.

He began cranking the screw, but soon realized to his chagrin that he had ended up against iron strappings supporting *Eagle*'s rudder hinge, so it failed to bite. By now the adventurous Lee was exhausted and his air was running out, so he was left with little option but to make good his

THE *TURTLE*

The details of this illustration are taken from a study made in 1875 by a Lieutenant F.M. Barber of the US Navy.

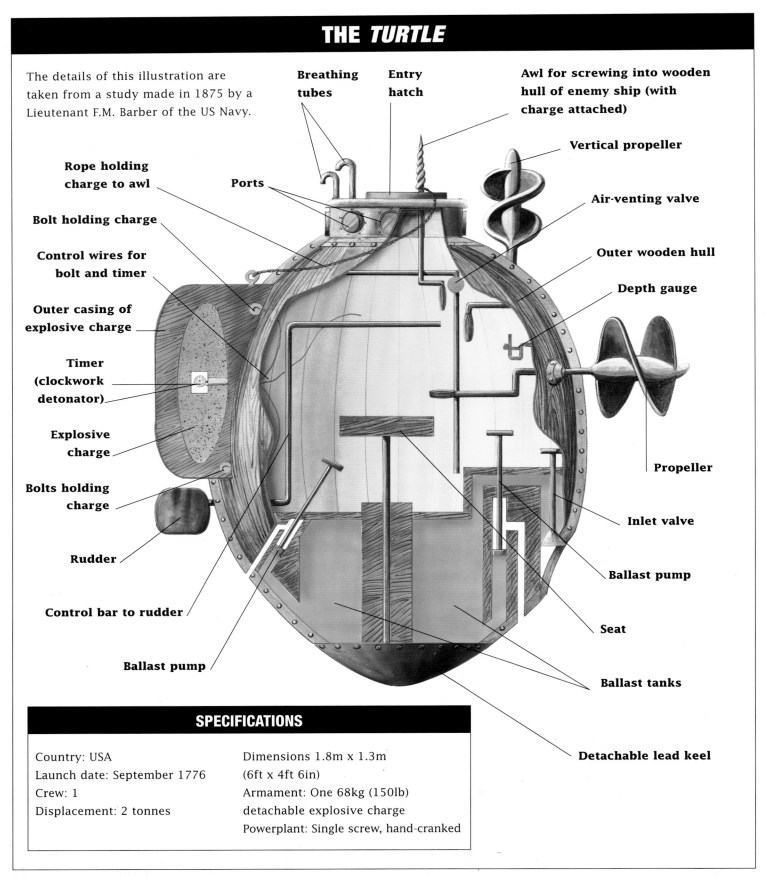

Breathing tubes

Entry hatch

Awl for screwing into wooden hull of enemy ship (with charge attached)

Vertical propeller

Air-venting valve

Outer wooden hull

Depth gauge

Ports

Rope holding charge to awl

Bolt holding charge

Control wires for bolt and timer

Outer casing of explosive charge

Timer (clockwork detonator)

Explosive charge

Bolts holding charge

Rudder

Control bar to rudder

Ballast pump

Propeller

Inlet valve

Ballast pump

Seat

Ballast tanks

Detachable lead keel

SPECIFICATIONS

Country: USA
Launch date: September 1776
Crew: 1
Displacement: 2 tonnes

Dimensions 1.8m x 1.3m
(6ft x 4ft 6in)
Armament: One 68kg (150lb)
detachable explosive charge
Powerplant: Single screw, hand-cranked

escape. It was now daylight, and the strange craft was seen by one of the boats pulling guard around the British Fleet, which gave chase. Lee slipped under the waves and released the mine, which soon afterwards blew up, to the great astonishment and consternation of the pursuing 'bluejackets'. Although Lee failed tactically in that he did not sink the *Eagle*, he nevertheless achieved a major strategic coup in that he scattered the British Fleet and weakened the blockade. The submarine attack had come of age.

ROBERT FULTON AND *NAUTILUS*: THE FIRST METAL SUBMARINE

The next exponent of the submarine was another remarkable American, Robert Fulton, who, being attracted to the principles of the French Revolution in the 1780s, eventually based himself in France. This artist-turned-engineer produced an entire series of ingenious projects and inventions that included a steamboat, an ironclad, a panorama, and numerous patents for flax-spinning, rope-making and canal equipment. Fulton made no secret of the fact that he was driven by the 'mighty dollar', but he is also credited with having the altruistic dream that the submarine – the ultimate weapon – could create such a stalemate in maritime warfare that nations would have no option but to live peaceably together, an early form of the deterrence policy adopted by the West during the Cold War! To fulfil this dream, it was necessary for at least one country to adopt his idea. Fulton targeted France and, in 1797, sent plans of his *Nautilus* to the French Directory. They turned him down on at least two occasions, but, finally, in the face of his unrelenting argument and reasoning, he was given permission to build his submarine at the Perrier Dockyard in Rouen.

The boat we know was in fact his second effort, and she was highly ingenious and 'top of the range' in technological terms for her age; being built of copper on iron frames, she was also the first metal submersible. The *Nautilus* was shaped like a cigar and had a dome-like conning tower

Left: Sergeant Ezra Lee's abortive attack on HMS *Eagle* in 1776 demonstrated beyond doubt that a submerged covert attack could well be a weaker power's trump card against a more powerful opponent. The British 'Bluejackets' must have wondered what they were chasing!

17

NAUTILUS

Designed by Robert Fulton, *Nautilus* was the first submarine to be built under government contract. Her hull comprised an iron framework covered with copper sheets, and buoyancy was controlled by hand pumps. *Nautilus* was propelled by sail when on the surface, and by hand-cranked propeller when submerged. During trials in Le Havre harbour, *Nautilus* remained underwater at a depth of 7.6m (25ft) for one hour.

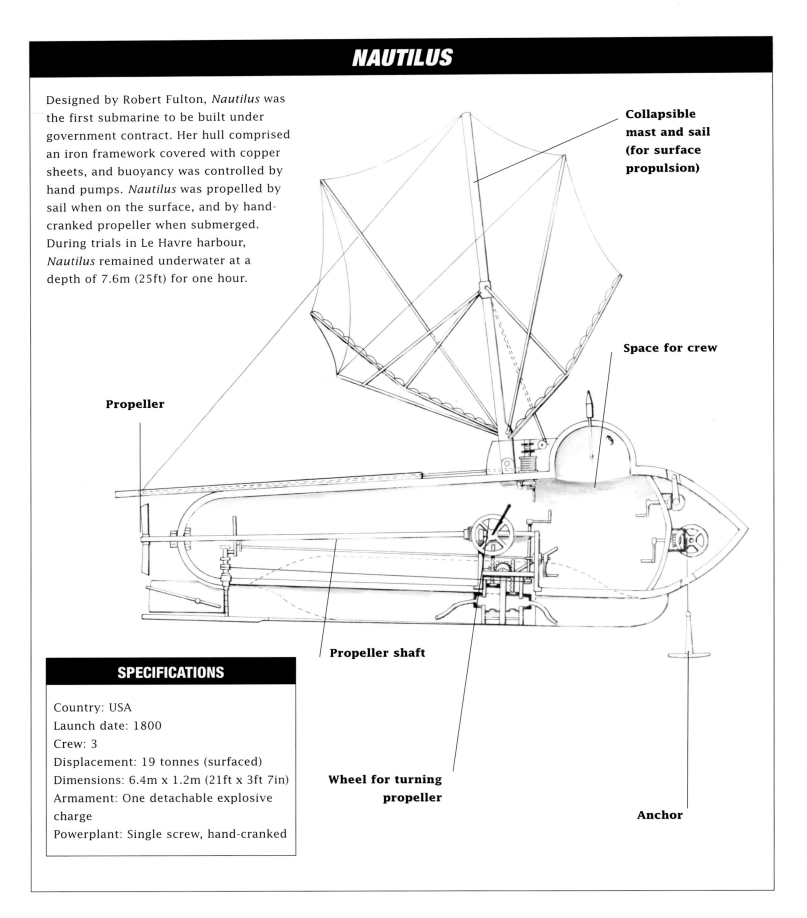

Collapsible mast and sail (for surface propulsion)

Space for crew

Propeller

Propeller shaft

Wheel for turning propeller

Anchor

SPECIFICATIONS

Country: USA
Launch date: 1800
Crew: 3
Displacement: 19 tonnes (surfaced)
Dimensions: 6.4m x 1.2m (21ft x 3ft 7in)
Armament: One detachable explosive charge
Powerplant: Single screw, hand-cranked

with glass scuttles. Just abaft this tower was a mast that was erected for surface passage. It was 6.4m (21ft) long and 1.8m (6ft) in diameter. Operated by three men, she was propelled by a hand-crank situated in the middle of the vessel that turned a propeller at the stern. A hollow iron bar served as both the keel providing stability and ballast tanks for controlling buoyancy. Her principle of operation was very similar to that of the *Turtle*, and her weapon was on exactly the same lines as that invented by Bushnell, except that the mine was initiated by a lanyard operating a percussion cap, rather than a clockwork timer.

After a number of successful demonstrations, Fulton felt that he had done enough to make his point and began to press for some financial return for his efforts. It was then that he began to run into serious difficulty and to come up against philosophical objections within the French naval hierarchy. Admiral Decres, the French Minister of Marine, had earlier described the invention as 'fit only for Algerines and Pirates', and his view began to be echoed throughout the corridors of power. In the end, Napoleon decided that Fulton was a charlatan and an adventurer and would have nothing to do with him.

Fulton swallowed his altruistic pride and slipped across the Channel to England, lured by the promise of a warmer reception – and money – for his ideas. In fact, despite the personal enthusiasm of the Prime Minister, William Pitt, Fulton's submarine scheme came to nothing. However, he did become heavily involved with the production of 'carcasses', floating mines capable of devastating a fleet at anchor. Britain was on the back foot, and under the threat of invasion by the French, so it could be argued that Pitt showed extraordinary vision in exploring any way he could of keeping the enemy at bay.

In 1804, a raid was mounted against the French Fleet in Boulogne using catamarans towing 'carcasses' that were almost certainly designed by Fulton. These catamarans were reminiscent of the 'human torpedoes' that played such an effective role during World War II in that they consisted of two pieces of timber about nine feet (2.7m) long and nine inches (23cm) square, placed parallel to each other at such distance as to receive a man to sit between them on a bar, which admitted of his sinking nearly flush with the water, and occasionally immersing himself, so as to prevent his being seen in the dark or by moonlight. The person who had charge of this notable contrivance was a sailor clad in black geurnsey, waistcoat and trousers with a black cap that covered his face; he was furnished with a paddle, and, being seated in this marine car, it was intended that he should take the clock-machine in tow. This instrument consisted of a copper case about 18 feet (5.5m) long, and something similar in shape to a coffin: its interior was furnished with combustibles, which were to explode by striking of a clock within, which was to run a certain number of hours. The sailor in the catamaran, under cover of the night, dropping silently down with the tide, was to attach the machine to the cable of the enemy's vessel, and thus the projector hoped that the sleeping and unsuspecting crew would be instantly destroyed.

The raid turned out to be a fiasco, and, when news of it and its methods crept out, it was greeted with horrified disgust by the general public as 'cowardly', even against the hated French. Despite a successful demonstration of an improved mine during the following year against the brig *Dorothea*, Fulton's flirtation with the British was brought to an end by the implacable hostility of Earl St Vincent to his ideas. Additionally, Horatio Nelson's victory at the Battle of Trafalgar had removed the threat of invasion, so the completely frustrated inventor returned to his native America, where he found fame and success with steamboats. The world

Bauer realized that the only way to escape was to flood water into the craft in order to equalize the internal pressure with the outside so that the hatch could be opened. His crewmates thought that he was mad and stopped him opening a sea-valve ...

was simply not ready for Fulton's brilliance and radicalism, even though he is rightly regarded as one the great pioneers in submarine navigation.

THE FIRST SUBMARINE ESCAPE

Every decade had its submarine enthusiast, and, in 1850, it was the turn of an ex-woodworker–turned–artillery corporal in the German Army, William Bauer. Bauer was a member of the Prussian constabulary based in Kiel to quell an insurrection in Schleswig-Holstein. When conditions suited them, the Danish Navy would blockade Kiel harbour and mount amphibious raids. Bauer advised his superiors that he would happily build a submarine to counter these raids, and, as Germany had no navy, the idea appealed to local commanders.

The *Brandtaucher* (*Sea Diver*) was the result of his efforts. Built of iron sheets, she was 7.6m (25ft) long, 1.8m (6ft) wide, and 2.7m (9ft) deep. She was propelled by two huge wheels which, when spun, drove a four-bladed screw propeller. She had side ballast tanks for determining buoyancy, and, for trim (fore-and-aft stability), she had a large weight that ran on a track down the centreline of the boat. All was ready for Bauer and two other crewmembers to take on the Danish fleet single-handedly, and they slipped from Kiel and headed for the Danes. As the *Brandtaucher* had no weaponry, it is not clear exactly what Bauer intended to do once he engaged the enemy; however, in the event, the Danish sailors saw this weird and wonderful contraption heading towards them and immediately stood out to sea. On return to harbour, Bauer and his colleagues were hailed as heroes!

However, the cautious and wary Danes crept back and resumed their marauding raids, so it was necessary for Bauer and his intrepid assistants to conduct a second 'attack'. This time fate took a hand and *Brandtaucher* went out of control during the dive and became stuck on the bottom.

After four hours of fruitlessly attempting to open the hatch – which at 18.2m (60ft) would have had 8.43kg/cm^2 (120psi) acting on it and therefore several tons of weight – Bauer realized that the only way to escape was to flood water into the craft in order to equalize the pressure with the outside so that the hatch could be opened. His crewmates thought that he was mad, and stopped him opening a sea-valve.

As breathing became increasingly untenable inside the stricken submarine, however, they finally let him have his way. Bauer opened the sea-valve and water rushed in, but it was not until it had reached the level of the men's chests, with breathing all the more difficult by that point because of the increase in carbon dioxide build-up, that Bauer ordered the hatch to be opened. This was done with relative ease, and water rushed in. Bauer and his companions were whisked up in a bubble of air and popped to the surface like champagne corks. Once again, they were hailed as heroes, but Bauer's experiment with the Germans – despite being the first man in history to escape from a sunken submarine – was over.

He left the army and touted his ideas around Europe. He got a significant nibble from the Austrian Government until the treasury stepped in, and, after further disappointment in Britain, in 1854 he took his ideas to her opponent during the Crimea War, Russia. Here the Grand Duke Constantine provided funds for Bauer to build 'the single most devastating naval weapon known to man – the underwater boat known as *Le Diable Marin* (*Sea Devil*)'. At 15.8m (52ft) long, 3.6m (12ft) wide, and 3.3m (11ft) deep, she was driven by four men walking a treadmill. Unlike the *Brandtaucher,* she was armed with a 227kg (500lb) bomb on her bow, which was fused and deployed against the target by a seaman who stuck his arms through long rubber gloves that protruded from the craft. She was operated highly successfully

INTELLIGENT WHALE

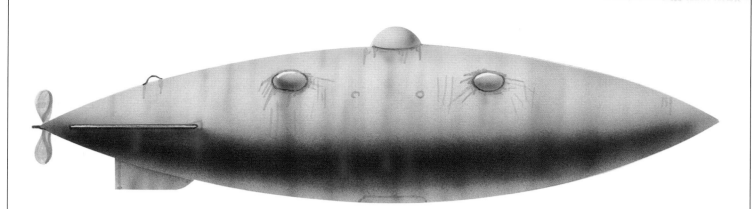

Intelligent Whale was the first submarine constructed for the Union Navy from a design by Halstead and was built in response to Confederate vessels of a similar type. Shaped like a whale, her form may have influenced the designs of J.P. Holland. She had promise, but was all too often swamped and is reputed to have drowned 35 men before she was finally abandoned in 1872. *Intelligent Whale* was then put on display at the Washington Navy Yard.

SPECIFICATIONS

Country: USA	(31ft x 8ft 6in x 8ft 6in)
Launch date: 1862	Armament: Mines
Crew: 13	Powerplant: single screw,
Displacement: Not known	hand-cranked
Dimensions: 9.4m x 2.6m x 2.6m	Performance: 4 knots

during trials by her 13-man crew; during 1856, she made 134 dives, on one occasion reaching 45.7m (150ft) in depth.

On 6 September 1856, Bauer achieved another first when, in honour of Tsar Alexander's coronation, he dived his submarine in Kronstadt harbour with a four-piece orchestra, and soon after the strains of the Russian national anthem could be heard wafting across the harbour.

Despite the obvious strength of the hull, *Le Diable Marin* never saw action, and it was with some considerable satisfaction that the traditionalists in the Russian Imperial Navy witnessed the craft come to an inconspicuous end during a demonstration attack in front of its royal sponsor. It ran into a sandbank and had to be abandoned.

So ended yet another contribution to the development of the submarine. Bauer notched up a number of 'firsts', and, even though none were of a warlike nature, more importantly he had alerted a number of nations around Europe to the potential of the craft.

A SUBMARINE SINKS A WARSHIP

We have seen how war continued to be the stimulus for submarine development in Europe, and it was even more so during the American War between the States (the Civil War). By the winter of 1864, it had entered its third bitter year; the Confederate forces were having to resort to desperate measures in order to survive. Charleston, the port vital to the Confederates, was being strangled by the effective blockade of Admiral Dahlgren's

Housatonic **earned the doubtful distinction of being the first ship in history to be sunk in a submarine attack. The *Hunley* did not return and was found many years later lying close to her victim. The blast had fatally stricken both vessels.**

Below: CSS *Hunley* finally realized the dreams of all early submarine pioneers – she had sunk a ship! But it was at a heavy human price, and it is ironic that, within two years of her attack, Robert Whitehead had invented the locomotive torpedo.

fleet. The previous October, Lieutenant W.T. Glassell had succeeded in damaging the Federal Ironclad *New Ironsides* in a steam-driven semi-submersible, *David*, thereby pointing a way to potential success against the stranglehold. A Confederate naval officer, Captain Horace L. Hunley, took it upon himself to design and fund an extension of the idea through his craft that could run completely submerged for the short distance needed to complete a surprise attack. The transition from awash to fully submerged was achieved by a pair of horizontal rudders. The *Hunley* was a 12.1m (40ft) long, 1.4m (4ft 6in) in diameter boiler tube with a hand-crank for eight men to operate running through its middle. It had internal ballast tanks at either end, a breathing tube in the middle, and two observation towers. Its weapon was a 9.1m (30ft) long spar, at the end of which was 63.5kg (140lb) of gunpowder encased in a copper container.

During trials, the *Hunley* had not been a lucky craft and had sunk three times,

killing in all 23 Confederate sailors, including its inventor. But rallying to a plea by Charleston's commander, General Beauregard, and perhaps further enticed by the promise of a huge reward for sinking an enemy ship, Lieutenant George E. Dixon and eight soldiers of the 21st Regiment of the Alabama Light Infantry volunteered for a mission to attack the Union blockaders.

They sailed on the evening of 17 February 1864, their target a Union frigate, thought to be the *Wabash*, some 19.3km (12 miles) distant. The submarine could make about four knots, but, even with a following tide, it was extraordinarily hard work for the sweating soldiers. Nevertheless, just before 2100 hours, Dixon lined the torpedo spar towards a dimly visible motionless Union ship. It was the new 1284-tonne frigate *Housatonic*. The heavy charge exploded against the target's starboard side and she rapidly settled by the stern, heeling over as she went. As she touched bottom in the shallow water, the *Housatonic* earned the doubtful distinction of being

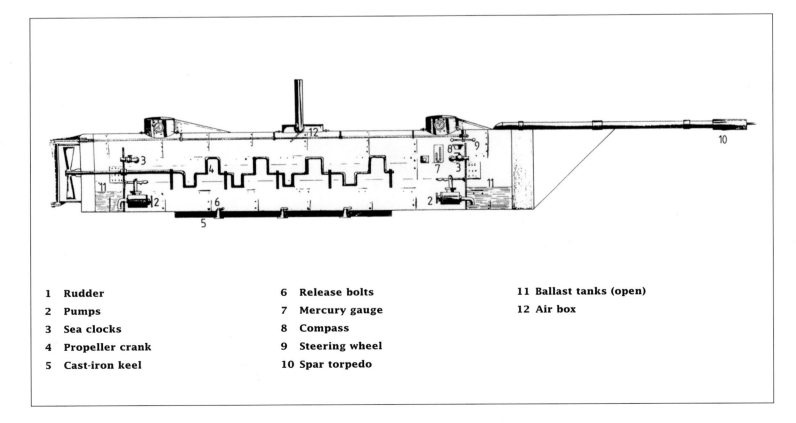

1	Rudder	6	Release bolts	11	Ballast tanks (open)
2	Pumps	7	Mercury gauge	12	Air box
3	Sea clocks	8	Compass		
4	Propeller crank	9	Steering wheel		
5	Cast-iron keel	10	Spar torpedo		

LE PLONGEUR: THE FIRST MECHANICAL SUBMARINE

The principal reason why submarines had advanced so little between Van Drebbel's fifteenth-century device and the *Hunley*, both of which relied on men's muscle-power, was that there was very little advance in the crucial area of propulsion. However, in typical fashion, it was the French who came up with the next idea: that of propelling a submarine using an air-turbine. *Le Plongeur* was

commissioned into the French Navy in 1863, and she was nothing short of a monster. Displacing 426 tonnes and measuring 42.6m (140ft) in length, she was in effect one enormous reservoir of air. However, given her relative lack of power (she only had an 81.1mhp (80hp) engine) and her great length, she was almost uncontrollable when dived, and her experiment was soon abandoned.

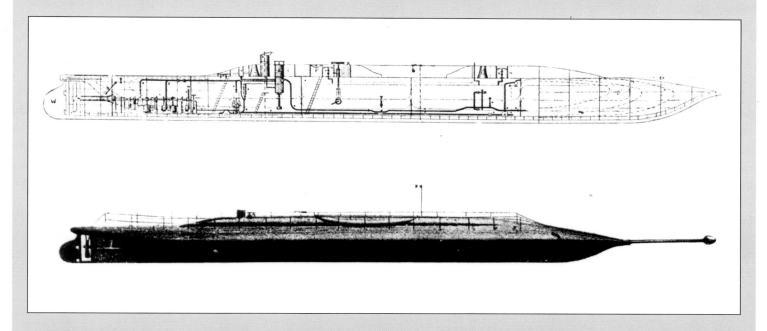

Above: The British followed the development of *Le Plongeur* with great interest. Such were the reports of her instability when dived, however, that the Royal Navy continued to sail the seas unperturbed.

the first ship in history to be sunk in a submarine attack.

The crew did not return, and the *Hunley* was found many years later lying close to her victim. The blast obviously mortally wounded both vessels, but the *Hunley*'s place in history, and that of her gallant crew, was sealed forever.

GARRETT, *NORDENFELT* AND STEAM SUBMARINES

Steam had come of age early in the nineteenth century and drove machinery, railway engines, and steamships, but it was not until the 1870s that an engine suitable

in size and performance for a submarine appeared. Such an engine was the Lamm engine, which was used on London's Underground Railway, and one of the first to exploit it was the English cleric, the Reverend George William Garrett of Birkenhead, England. In 1879, he designed the *Resurgam*, a 30.4-tonne cigar-shaped submarine. Having sealed the fires, the latent heat from the boiler turned the water in the boiler into steam when the throttle valve was opened, and this made *Resurgam* one of the first mechanical submarines in history. The steam held out for three to four hours, and the return connecting-rod

Right: Simon Lake was a brilliant inventor who worked his way up to submarines via bicycle steering gear and can tops. He was inspired by *20,000 Leagues under the Sea*, which he had read as a boy. Although always pipped at the post by J.P. Holland for military designs, he built some fine working submarines.

Opposite: G.W. Garrett with his young son on *Resurgam*. His relationship with Swedish industrialist Nordenfelt was disastrous for both of them, as their boats became bigger and longer, and the atmosphere inside them more dangerous.

cylinder engine provided propulsive power for two or three knots.

In practice, *Resurgam* never fulfilled her inventor's dream and ignominiously sank while under tow to a demonstration to a wider audience. However, two important relationships were established as a result of Garrett's efforts. The first was between him and the Swedish machine-gun manufacturer Nordenfelt, and the second was between the submarine and the torpedo.

Garrett's ability to 'bottle up' steam appealed to Nordenfelt, and, in 1885, he produced his first submarine, *Nordenfelt 1*, a 61-tonne submarine, which he built in Landskrona in Sweden. The submarine was revolutionary in that it was the first to be equipped with the Whitehead torpedo, fired from an internal tube. Her trials were attended by a most distinguished audience that included the British Prince of Wales,

PIONEER

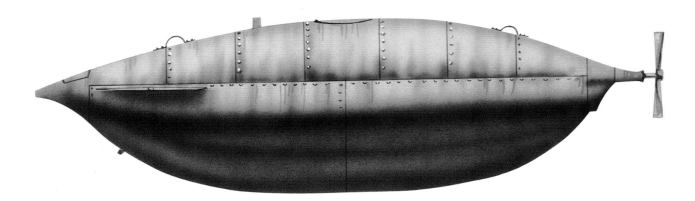

In the American Civil War, the Confederacy was interested in any development which might break the Union maritime blockade. In 1862, *Pioneer*, the only privateer submarine ever built, was issued with a Letter of Marque which licensed her to sink Union warships; her crew would collect a bounty of 20 per cent of the estimated value of their victim. In 1952, she was moved to the Louisiana State Museum.

SPECIFICATIONS

Country: Confederate States
Launch date: February 1862
Crew: 3
Displacement: 4 tonnes

Dimensions: 10.3m x 1.2m x 1.2m
(34ft x 4ft x 4ft)
Armament: One spar torpedo
Powerplant: Single screw,
hand-cranked

NORDENFELT I

SPECIFICATIONS

Country: Greece
Launch date: 1885
Crew: Not known
Displacement: 61 tonnes
Dimensions: 19.5m x 2.7m (64ft x 9ft)
Armament: One 355mm (14in) gun; one
25.4mm (1in) gun (fitted later)
Powerplant: Single screw, compound engine
Performance: 9 knots/4 knots

the King and Queen of Denmark, and the Czarina of Russia. Naval and military officers from almost every country in Europe and from Japan and Brazil were also present, and no submarine in history had such a distinguished 'send-off'. In fact, the boat did not perform badly, and she was bought by the Greek Government for further trials.

Perhaps unsurprisingly, the *Nordenfelt II* was built for the Sultan of Turkey and underwent comprehensive trials off Constantinople, at the end of which the

Sultan declared himself satisfied and completed the purchase. The true performance of the submarine beneath the surface was in fact appalling, particularly when she attempted to fire her torpedo, discharge of which turned the craft into an uncontrollable bucking bronco. The Turks made no use of her whatsoever. They were unable to find the engineers to operate her, her crew deserted as fast as they were appointed to her, and she was eventually left to rust away in the arsenal at Constantinople. The *Nordenfelt III*, a much

bigger boat of 38.1m (125ft) and 249 tonnes, was built at Barrow-in-Furness in England for the Russian Government. Although her motive power had been increased to 15 knots on the surface and 5 knots when dived, she suffered from the same inherent lack of horizontal control as her predecessors, induced by her length. Despite her evident deficiencies, she was despatched to Russia, but foundered on the coast of Jutland on 8 September 1888. A disillusioned Garrett emigrated to the USA, where he died penniless.

THE WHITEHEAD TORPEDO: 'THE DEVIL'S DEVICE'

Robert Whitehead was the manager of an engineering firm in Fiume, Austria, one of whose primary customers was the Austrian Navy. In 1865, he was approached by a naval officer, Captain Luppis, who wanted his advice on a design for a locomotive torpedo, i.e. not a 'bullet', but a weapon that was self-propelled. What Luppis had in mind was a steam- or clockwork-propelled device, controlled by the 'shooter' by wires in order to keep in a straight line towards

Above: Whitehead's brilliance lay in 'The Secret' – a depth-keeping mechanism based on a hydrostatic valve opposed by a spring that could be regulated for the desired depth. He added contra-rotating propellers in 1875 to keep his torpedoes upright, but it was not until 1895 that he applied the gyroscope to achieve accuracy in azimuth (direction).

CSS *HUNLEY*

SPECIFICATIONS

Country: Confederate States
Launch date: 1863
Crew: 9
Displacement: 2 tonnes
Dimensions: 12m x 1m x1.2m (40ft x 3ft 6in x 4ft)
Armament: One spar torpedo
Powerplant: Single screw, hand-cranked
Performance: 2.5 knots (surfaced)

The *Hunley* was the first true submersible craft to be used successfully against an enemy, sinking the Union frigate *Housatonic* in 1864 during the American Civil War. The craft had a nine-man crew, eight to turn the hand-cranked propeller and one to steer. Years later, when the wreck was located on the sea bed, the skeletons of eight of the crew were discovered, still seated at their crankshaft.

Below: The *Gymnôte* being rolled out ready for launch in September 1888. Her inventor, Dupuy de Lôme, had great fertility of imagination for the possible applications of submarines in war, including that of carrying troops to invade Britain. He died before many of his concepts left the drawing board, but his legacy remained an inspiration to other forward-thinking French submarine designers.

THE TORPEDO

'A torpedo may be defined as an explosive case, which may be fired automatically by concussion, or at the will of the user, and which is stationary underwater or travels through the water. Some travelling torpedoes are moved by being towed, others by working of independent machinery concealed within them, others by being at a boat's bow, or pushed; and yet others by a controlling power worked from shore or from some other fixed station.' (Laird Cowes, c. 1890.)

This contemporary description of exactly what a torpedo was indicates that it was the term was applied to anything that could cause an underwater explosion. The stationary torpedo was reclassified as a mine; those that were pushed (i.e. the spar torpedo used by CSS *Hunley*) rapidly became obsolete and the description is now reserved for weapons 'that travel through the water'.

the target. Such an arrangement had several obvious drawbacks, so Whitehead got to work and within a year had produced a revolutionary torpedo. At 35.5cm (14in) in diameter, it was propelled by high-pressure air and carried a charge of 8.1kg (18lb) of high explosive at 6 knots for 183m (200yds).

By 1870, when Whitehead was invited to demonstrate his weapon to the British Admiralty, this performance had improved to a range of 914m (1000yds) at a higher speed and with a much bigger warhead. In 1872, Whitehead built a torpedo factory, and over the years further improvements

Above: The *Gymnôte* with an improved conning tower in 1898. She was also fitted with drop collars for torpedo discharge.

GYMNÔTE

SPECIFICATIONS

Country: France
Launch date: September 1888
Crew: 5
Displacement: 30 tonnes/31 tonnes
Dimensions: 7.3m x 1.8m x 1.6m
(58ft 5in x 6ft x 5ft 6in)
Armament: Two 355mm (14in) torpedo tubes
Performance: 7.3 knots/4.2 knots

Gymnôte's electric power was provided by 204 cells spread along the lower part of the hull. Ordered in 1886, she made over 2000 dives in all. *Gymnôte*, along with *Gustav Zédé*, were the last French submersibles to depend on electric motive power alone. They had proved the concept of its use, but also that it did not provide the whole answer. From now on, thinking would turn increasingly to a combination of diesel and electric power.

Below: The crew of the *Gustav Zédé* sit comfortably on the surface; however, when she dived, she became a bit like a bucking bronco. She had a lot of free water in her tanks, probably causing her instability. She was nonetheless evolutionary, most notably because she was made from bronze. She also had an effective periscope and a bridge on which the Officer of the Watch could stand. Yet, even after six years of trials, she never worked properly.

were made to his torpedoes' depth-keeping qualities, range and explosive power. When he introduced the 'Obry Gear' gyroscope, the weapon became extraordinarily accurate.

The torpedo was snapped up by many navies around the world, and there was a proliferation of surface torpedo-boats, but it took 15 years before its potential for underwater work was seen. From *Nordenfelt* onwards, there was an inevitability about the engagement, and the course was set for the weapon to unlock the submarine's potential to a stunning extent on maritime warfare. The marriage of the 'devil's device' with the 'underhand' vessel was to cost thousands of lives in the future, but in the

mid-1880s there was still some inventive distance to be travelled to find a platform that could be easily controlled and efficiently propelled.

THE ELECTRICAL BOATS

The realization that submarines were necessary as part of a balanced fleet came late to every maritime nation in the world except France. From 1879, under the influence of Admiral Aube, later the Minister for the Navy, the French recognized the potential of the torpedo in *guerre de course* (the systematic destruction of an opponent's merchant marine) and it was but a short mental hop to

appreciate that the best torpedo-boat was a submarine. So, unlike the extreme reticence met by the English inventor J.F. Waddington when he demonstrated his *Porpoise* – an advanced electrically driven submarine – to representatives of the British Government in 1885, the *Gymnôte* was hailed in France as a triumph.

She was launched in September 1888 following three years of developmental work, first by Depuy de Lome and, after his death, by Gustav Zédé. She was a 18m (59ft) long, 30.4-tonne metal cigar, driven by a 55.7mhp (55hp) motor which derived its power from 564 accumulators. She was also revolutionary in that she was fitted with a periscope. Despite her perfection, no further submarines were built along her lines, although she did remain in commission until 1907.

The successful experiment with the *Gymnote* persuaded the French to build a bigger boat, and at 48.5m (159ft) long and displacing 270 tonnes, the 1893 *Gustav Zédé* was a comparative monster. In addition to her greatly increased size and power, she carried innovations such as an internal torpedo tube and room for two Whitehead torpedo reloads. For all that, however, she proved to be a huge disappointment to her designers. Her great length made her horizontally unstable, and

The torpedo was snapped up by many navies around the world, and there was a proliferation of surface torpedo-boats. It took another 15 years, however, before its potential was seen for underwater work.

Right: The French submarine designer Maxime Laubeuf. His steam- and electricity-driven, double-hulled *Narval* won an open competition in 1896. She was the first true submersible in that she could recharge her batteries while at sea. The French believed that steam propulsion was both safer and cheaper than the petrol engine, but their fascination with it would cost them their lead in submarine design.

she was inclined to 'yaw' violently, throwing her crew around. This factor, combined with the obnoxious fumes given off by her accumulators, made her a most undesirable craft in which to go to sea. Although she was modified a dozen times over the course of six years, the *Gustave Zédé* was never a success.

THE FRENCH *NARVAL*: THE FIRST RECHARGEABLE SUBMARINE

But still the French persevered. After an open competition in 1898 for a submarine that could make reasonably high speed on the surface over a considerable distance and run submerged for a comparatively short period, diving for only long enough to carry out a sneak attack, the Laubeuf-designed *Narval* was selected to be built. She was a submersible torpedo-boat, and she became the first submarine in history capable of recharging her battery at sea. Hitherto, the greatest drawback of the straightforward electrically powered submarine was that it was cripplingly short of range and relied on shore power to recharge the accumulators. *Narval* carried her own power station – a steam engine – which she used in the dual role of propulsion when on the surface and as a battery charger. Unlike internal combustion engines that were still in their infancy and considered somewhat risky, steam engines were well advanced. Hence they were almost a natural choice as the means of developing sufficient power for good surface performance, the overriding consideration for most naval tacticians of the time. However, steam submarines had their vulnerabilities when applied to submersibles: they were hot for a considerable period after being shut down and made conditions uncomfortable for the crew; they required funnels which were vulnerable to damage in rough weather; and they were extremely slow to dive because it took more than 20 minutes to douse the boiler. Nevertheless, France was

to maintain her obsession with steam until after World War I, and this was to cost her navy its lead in submarine warfare.

In addition to her charging capability, *Narval* was revolutionary in another respect in that she was double-hulled. She had an outer hull that looked very much that of a conventional torpedo-boat and an inner hull that was capable of withstanding pressure. The gap in between housed the ballast and fuel tanks.

JOHN PHILIP HOLLAND AND THE FIRST PRACTICAL SUBMARINE

Just as the French believed that steam was the way forwards for submarine propulsion, so John Philip Holland believed that the key to success lay in the internal combustion engine. Holland was an Irish-American schoolteacher, an inventive genius, and an Anglophobe, and was obsessed by the idea that submarines were the ideal platform to attack the hated British Royal Navy. He entered the submarine 'game' in the 1870s, and, despite chronic misfortunes, Holland remained steadfast, learned many lessons as he went along, and emerged towards the end of the nineteenth century as the father of the modern submarine.

Holland's first financial backing came from the Irish Fenian Society in America,

FENIAN RAM

SPECIFICATIONS

Country: USA
Launch date: May 1881
Crew: 3
Displacement: 19 tonnes
Dimensions 9.4m x 1.8m x 2.2m
(31ft x 6ft x 7ft 3in)
Armament: One 228mm (9in) gun
Powerplant: Single-screw petrol engine

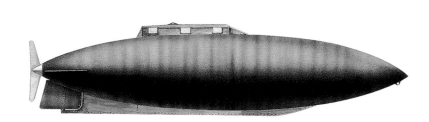

whose dream was to humble mighty Britain, a country almost at the zenith of her Victorian era during the late nineteenth century. The tactics the society advocated were hit-and-run terrorist attacks that would intimidate and sap the morale of an enemy too powerful to confront openly. The idea of a submerged gunboat thus had tremendous appeal to them, and they happily provided $6000 (about £4320) to Holland from their skirmishing fund. In fact, this prototype proved a dismal failure in practical terms, and her primitive combustion engine barely sparked, but her inventor added greatly to his theoretical knowledge during lengthy

trials and was ready to move on to greater things. His second submarine, again funded by the Fenians – who dreamed of shipping many such craft across the Atlantic Ocean in the holds of a 'Trojan horse' mother ship to create mayhem in British ports – was a dramatic advance on his first.

She was the legendary *Fenian Ram*; 9.4m (31ft) long and displacing 19.3 tonnes, she was powered by a 15.2mhp (15hp) Brayton engine. It was in the *Fenian Ram* that Holland overcame the problem that had plagued many of his predecessors, that of horizontal stability. Instead of ballasting her to 'zero buoyancy' to submerge, he kept his

Right: Like all good engineers, J.P. Holland undertook the most comprehensive trials possible for his revolutionary little craft, the *Fenian Ram*. It was his pursuit of perfection that eventually led his backers, the Fenian Society, to lose patience and hijack the craft. In their turn, they demonstrated the folly of amateurs meddling with a science they do not understand.

HOLLAND I

SPECIFICATIONS

Country: USA
Launch date: 1878
Crew: Not known
Displacement: 2.2 tonnes
Dimensions: 4.4m x 0.9m (14ft 6in x 3ft)
Armament: None
Powerplant: Single-screw, petrol engine

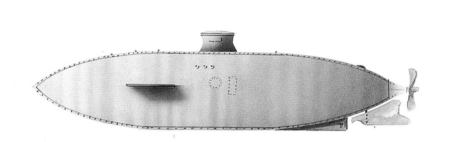

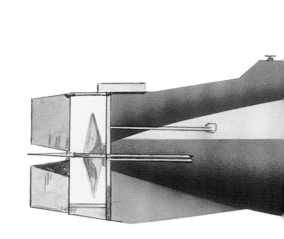

Below: J.P. Holland, the father of the modern submarine, was more than an engineer, he was a thinker. He battled against the US Navy's lethargy and occasional antagonism towards the submarine. In 1886, he wrote an article entitled 'Can New York be bombarded?', pointing out how a few submarines could significantly counter this threat. Somewhere in the bowels of the Navy Building, something stirred, and submarines were back on the agenda.

craft slightly positively buoyant, so that to get down she had to be driven down and would be held on depth by her diving rudders. While it was by no means the perfect solution, for the first time man controlled his machine, rather than the other way round.

The Brayton engine provided motive power both on the surface and when dived, with the air inside the boat being replenished from compressed air bottles, and the exhaust fumes were expelled through a hull valve. The *Fenian Ram* was armed with a 3.35m (11ft) long pneumatic gun with a 23cm (9in) bore. This gun could be loaded with a 1.8m (6ft) long projectile that was fired out through the bow by a blast of 181kg (400lb) of compressed air.

Holland VI was the first modern American submarine and became the prototype for British and Japanese submarines which combined petrol engine and battery power with hydroplanes. Her petrol engine developed 45hp and her electric motor 75hp when submerged. Diving depth was 22.8m (75ft). She served as a training boat until 1905 and was scrapped in 1913.

In 1881, her first sea trials for diving and propulsion on the Hudson River went perfectly, and her 9-knot surface speed greatly impressed the watching journalists. She was by now barely a secret weapon! The *Ram* was ready for her weapon-system trials, and Holland accepted the offer of underwater torpedoes from Captain John Ericsson – formerly skipper of the *Monitor* that had fought in the Civil War – for the purpose of demonstrating that his submarine was ready to do damage. In fact, far from remaining underwater, both firings saw the projectiles soaring high into the air, and the only damage they did was to the peace of local fishermen! Before Holland had the chance to sort out this problem, his backers, anxious to advance their terrorist cause and having run out of patience, hijacked the *Ram* and made off

HOLLAND VI

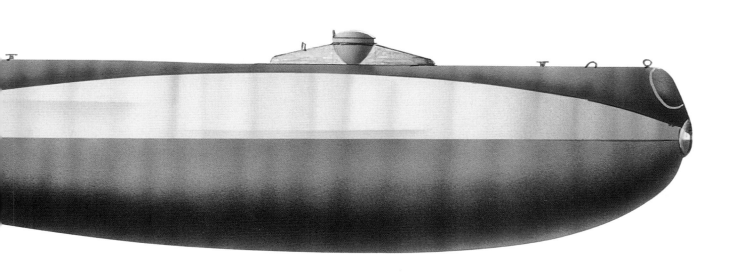

SPECIFICATIONS

Country: USA	Displacement: 64 tonnes/76 tonnes	Armament: One 457mm (18in) torpedo tube
Launch date: May 1897	Dimensions: 16.3m x 3.1m x 3.5m	Submerged range: 74km (40nm) at 3 knots
Crew: 7	(53ft 3in x 10ft 3in x 11ft 6in)	Performance: 8 knots/5 knots

with her. During this operation, she sank; the next time the *Ram* made her appearance, it was as a tourist attraction. So ended in 1883 a furious Holland's first foray into submarine construction, and it was to be another five years before he found a reason to re-enter the frame.

In 1886, he collaborated with an artillery officer called Zalinsky to build a submerged gunboat that threw out a dynamite charge, but this sank as it was being launched. In 1888, he entered a government-inspired competition for a submarine boat, and, while his design was the preferred option, it did not meet the over-ambitious staff requirements, and the issue was shelved. In 1893, yet another competition was launched, and again Holland was the winner, but it took two years before an appropriation of $150,000

was made to get the project under way. Holland set to work to meet the once again unrealistic demands and produced the *Plunger*, a 24.3m (80ft) steam/battery machine which, in his heart of hearts, he knew would never work.

The determined inventor then committed an extraordinary act of faith to his own genius and, with private financial backing, built a submarine that he presented to the government as a *fait accompli*. Happily, this last throw of the dice worked, and, when *Holland VI* was demonstrated to them in March 1898, even self-interested staff officers in the US Navy could not fail to recognize that they had seen the first successful submarine in history!

The boat was 16.4m (54ft) long and 3.12m (10ft 3in) at the beam. Her displacement was 64 tonnes on the surface and 75 tonnes

Before Holland received his just rewards from the US Government, the inventor's business acumen failed him, and his company was absorbed by the Electric Boat Company. His name, however, remained well respected, and he had truly made his mark on history.

Right: In 1895, Holland won an open competition worth $200,000 to build the 15-knot, steam-driven *Plunger*, pictured here. Holland was never comfortable with the design, recognizing the limitations of steam as a mode of propulsion and its adverse effects on habitability. What he really wanted to build was his ICE/battery-driven *Holland VI*, and by the time that *Plunger*, as expected, failed her sea trials in 1897, he had his brain-child ready.

dived, and her design, construction, and general arrangements would be very familiar to modern submariners. In particular, the boat's layout of ballast tanks for diving and compensating tanks for torpedo fire and fine-tuning for bodily weight showed that Holland's understanding of submarine control was highly advanced. Propulsion on the surface and for recharging the battery was provided by a four-cylinder Otto gasoline engine that developed 46mhp (45hp). This provided a maximum speed on the surface of about 7 knots, and a 51mhp (50hp) electric motor provided about 5 knots when dived. A tail clutch and an engine clutch permitted the engine to drive the propeller direct or to recharge the battery by using the motor as a generator. She carried enough fuel to give her a range of about 1609km (1000 miles).

ARGONAUT

Argonaut was built by Simon Lake as a salvage vessel for inshore waters. Successful trials led to a number of export orders but by that time Lake had lost the initiative to John Holland in the eyes of the US Navy, whose senior officers were not impressed by the idea of a wooden-hulled craft trundling along the sea bed.

SPECIFICATIONS

Country: USA
Launch date: 1897
Crew: 5
Displacement: 60 tonnes (submerged)

Dimensions: 11m x 2.7m (36ft x 9ft)
Armament: None
Powerplant: gasoline engine
Performance: 5 knots/5 knots

The diving rudders on either side of the propeller were controlled by a mechanical-linkage from a position at the base of the conning tower. The main armament was an 46cm (18in) torpedo tube, with two reload torpedoes, and there was an inclined pneumatic gun fitted above the torpedo tube.

Before Holland received his just rewards from the US Government, there followed a year of further trials and refinements to the submarine, during which time the inventor's business acumen failed him, and his Holland Boat Company was absorbed by the Electric Boat Company, the president of which was Isaac Rice. Rice was an astute businessman and soon swallowed other companies associated with the production of ancillary equipment to drive the submarine; slowly but surely Holland's influence in the company dwindled. He was retained as manager, but when he finally left in 1904, he held no more than one-half of one per cent of the company's stock. His name, however, remained well respected, and he had well and truly made his mark on history.

In the meantime, in November 1899, *Holland VI* completed her sea trials. After an impassioned report by the senior naval captain present at the trials, Captain John Lowe USN, the US Navy bought her on 11 April 1900. USS *Holland (SS-1)* joined the Fleet, and other navies sat up and took notice!

COMING OF AGE

The worst news for the Royal Navy was the announcement that the United States had adopted the submarine, because now the weapon of the weaker power had come of age and could no longer be ignored. Until 1900, the British Admiralty, while keeping an eye on developments across the Channel, had done their best not to encourage the progress of the submarine; indeed, they had gone out of their way to belittle the threat.

These early submersible craft required extremely deft handling, which, according to Lieutenant Arnold-Foster RN, the first captain of the Royal Navy's *Holland I*, was beyond the capabilities of most early submariners: 'The ingenious designer in New York evidently did not realize that the average naval officer has only two eyes and two hands; the little conning tower was simply plastered with wheels, levers and gauges with which some superman was to fire the torpedoes, dive and steer, and do everything else at the same time!' But there was a growing weight of evidence that these tiny experimental craft could indeed threaten the might of the most powerful navy

Left: British submarines lined up alphabetically from 'A' to 'E' alongside Fort Blockhouse, with the Floating Dock in the background. The idiosyncratic numbering system applied to these early submarines confused both friend and foe alike.

the world had ever seen, a navy that underpinned Britain's maritime access to her colonies, providers of the raw materials for her huge industrial appetite, and her trading partners. Despite the railings of vociferous detractors of the submarine and those who manned them – 'underhand, unfair and damned un-English'; 'no occupation for a gentleman'; 'any submariner captured in war should be hanged as a pirate' – wiser heads realized that the time had come to act.

Having taken the decision to respond, their Lordships went for the best and ordered five *Holland* boats from the Electric Boat Company to be built under licence by Vickers Sons and Maxim at their yard in Barrow-in-Furness, England. The order was placed in November 1900 at a price of £35,000 (US$48,650) per hull. In fact, despite the outward vestiges of prevarication and their insistence that the *Holland*s were experimental, once the Admiralty had committed itself down the submarine path, Britain soon made up for lost time and the improved *A*-class quickly came off the drawing board.

However, before then there was the inevitable problem for all nations new to submarines: where were they going to find the quality of men to make up the crews? By great fortune, a 'man for his time' appeared on the scene to find such men and lead the embryonic flotilla through its first hesitant steps. He was Captain (later Admiral Sir) Reginald Bacon. A major incentive was the payment of 'hard-lying money' – six shillings (about 30 pence (US$0.42) a day for officers and two shillings (about 10 pence (US$0.14)) for able seamen. With this money, plus the allure of a relaxed discipline, Bacon soon gathered around him a nucleus of enthusiasts who were prepared to put up with the most appalling living conditions. They all lived cheek by jowl, and, for the first time, officers actually got oil under their fingernails! The most primitive of human needs also had to

be shared in a common bucket, and the Royal Navy witnessed the greatest social revolution in its history. These very early pioneers, despite a number of close calls and often unreliable machinery, never lost a man, and they quickly learned from their mistakes. Through their efforts and successes during exercises, an often sceptical hierarchy began to take note, but it took a visionary such as Admiral Jackie Fisher, the First Sea Lord, to ram the message home when he wrote in 1904: 'It is astounding to me, perfectly astounding, how the very best among us fail to realize the vast impending revolution in Naval warfare and Naval strategy that the submarine will accomplish ... it is enough to make your hair stand on end!'

Fisher saw the submarine not just as the weapon of the weaker power, but he realized that it could be of great value to the stronger power as well. He set in train a scheme to rid all British ports of short-range shore batteries and controlled minefields and replace them with torpedo-boats (surface torpedo-boats by night and submarines by day), thereby extending the defensive shield for both ports and the east coast.

The technical development of the submarine made the possibility of extended operations possible, but the limit had been reached with the *Holland* type of boat. What emerged from the drawing board was the diesel-electric powered *D*-class. She was 508 tonnes in weight and had external ballast tanks which improved her reserve of buoyancy; twin shafts to improve her reliability and performance;

Above left: The crew of *Holland No. 1*: William Waller, the Submarine Service's first Coxswain is seated. Submarine ratings had to be of impeccable character and superior performance, as well as long experience. Clay pipes can be seen in abundance!

ON DISCOMFORT

'The discomforts in submarines cannot be exaggerated; in my own experience I have found the old Yarrow Torpedo Boats entail a certain amount of discomfort unless the weather was fine, but compared with a submarine it is luxurious. Clothes cannot be dried, fires are not permissible, in cold weather it is difficult to keep reasonably warm, the amount of fresh water precludes any attempt at personal cleanliness and the roar of the Engines is all over the boat and though the Officers and men are nominally in watch and watch there is no certainty in the watch off. To many the smell inside a submarine after she has been a short time at sea, which is absolutely peculiar to itself, is most revolting. All food tastes of it, all clothes reek of it, it is quite impossible to wear any clothes again after they have been used in it.'

Captain S.S. Hall, Inspecting Captain of Submarines, 19 May 1910

Above: Admiral Lord Jackie Fisher, exponent of the submarine. He was famous for the three 'R's – Ruthless, Relentless, Remorseless.

Below: In August 1916, HMS *B10* became the first RN submarine to be lost to air attack when she was bombed by Austrian aircraft while in dock in Venice.

and a battery capacity that enabled her to remain dived throughout daylight hours. This class was now equipped to conduct offensive operations and provided the basis of a design that would prevail through two world wars. The days of close blockade were over, and from now on Britain only built 'overseas' submarines.

In 1914, the Royal Navy had 75 boats in commission with 28 building. Of the former, only 20 were the capable *D*- and *E*-classes, with the remainder being made up of the coastal-capable *Holland* type *A*-, *B*- and *C*-classes. Additionally, the Royal Navy had a number of rising stars in its ranks of commanding officers who had trained themselves with great imagination and as much realism as possible. They were ready to go, albeit in uncomfortable surroundings.

GERMAN SUBMARINE DEVELOPMENT

Fisher's message about the potential of the submarine was also being heard loud and clear in ominous places beyond the shores of Britain. In 1904, Admiral Tirpitz, despite his unrelenting pursuit of building up the Imperial German High Seas Fleet, allowed himself a sideways glance at three submarines being built for Russia by Krupp-Germania. Tirpitz had earlier convinced himself that 'Germany did not need submarines', but, noting that Britain was building them, he realized that Germany had to follow if she was to keep up in the arms race. In July 1904, he authorized the laying down of *U1*, a truly momentous decision. Because Germany had little coastline to defend, German naval planners came to the early conclusion that the submarine could be an offensive weapon as well as carrying out their traditionally held role as defensive coastal craft, and their submarine designs over the coming years reflected this. Indeed, their *Naval and Military Record* in 1908 declared: 'we are building big submarines, the only ones that can carry out the work we want them to do; they will be capable of acting on the offensive in the North and Baltic seas'.

U1 was commissioned in 1906, and there followed another 27 before 1914, each one bigger and more capable than its predecessor. From *U19* onwards (completed in 1913), all U-boats were equipped with diesel, rather than paraffin, engines; and at 64m (210ft) in length and 850 tonnes in weight, they were poised to play their part as stealthy adjuncts of the battlefleet,

EARLY BRITISH SUBMARINES

The *B*- and *C*-classes were in the Holland design of petrol-driven coastal submarines, although each successive class grew bigger and more seaworthy. Despite their short range and low endurance, both classes saw war service in a number of theatres. The *D*-class, diesel driven, twin shafted, and fitted with saddle tanks, was the first RN submarine capable of extended overseas patrols.

B1 SPECIFICATIONS

Launch date: October 1904
Crew: 16
Displacement: 284 tonnes/319 tonnes
Dimensions: 41m x 4.1m x 3m (135ft x 13ft 6in x 9ft 10in)
Armament: Two 475mm (18in) TTs
Powerplant: Single-screw petrol engine, electric motor
Surface range: 2799km (1500nm) at 8 knots
Performance: 13 knots/7 knots

C25 SPECIFICATIONS

Launch date: 1909
Crew: 16
Displacement: 295 tonnes/325 tonnes
Dimensions: 43m x 4m x 3.5m (141ft x 13ft 1in x 11ft 4in)
Armament: Two 457mm (18in) TTs
Powerplant: Single-screw petrol engine, one electric motor
Surface range: 2414km (1431nm) at 8 knots
Performance: 12 knots/7.5 knots

D1 SPECIFICATIONS

Launch date: August 1908
Crew: 25
Displacement: 490 tonnes/604 tonnes
Dimensions; 50m x 6m x 3m (163ft x 20ft 6in x 10ft 5in)
Armament: Three 457mm (18in) TTs; one 12-pounder gun
Powerplant: Twin-screw diesel engines, electric motors
Surface range: 2038km (1100nm) at 10 knots
Performance: 14 knots/9 knots

FRIMAIRE

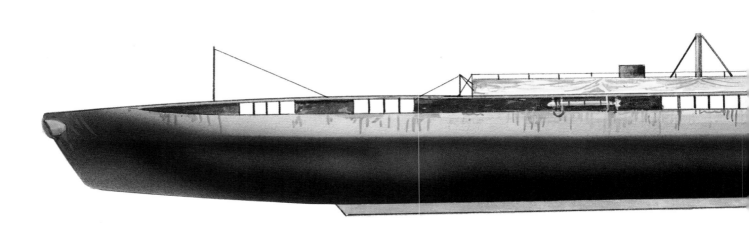

Frimaire was one of the *Brumaire* class of 16 submarines launched between 1911 and 1913. All 16 boats operated in the Mediterranean during Word War I. One of them, *Bernouilli*, infiltrated Cattaro harbour on 4 April 1916 and torpedoed the Austrian destroyer *Csepel*, blowing off her stern, and another, *Le Verrier*, accidentally rammed the German *U47* on 28 July 1918 after an unsuccessful torpedo engagement. *Frimaire* survived World War I and was stricken from the Navy List in 1923. The boats of this class were named after the months of the French Revolutionary calendar.

SUBMARINES IN OTHER NAVIES OF THE WORLD

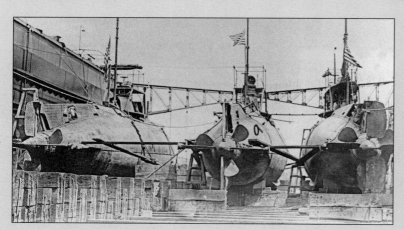

Above: Three US Navy *A*-class submarines in the 'Dewey' drydock at Olongapo, circa 1911. Like the Japanese, the US Navy submarine service was to sit out World War I. These boats ended their careers in the Far East as targets.

The two navies of the Adriatic were to end up on different sides in World War I. Austria had only six boats with two building, but it was an effective service based on German technology and training methods. Italy, on the other hand, had 21 boats with seven under construction, but of the former, few could be considered operational. Austria was ready; Italy was far from being so. Turkey had neither a modern Navy nor any submarines; however, she was to play a significant role during World War I and deserves a mention at this point. The United States had 30 submarines in service, with 10 on the building blocks, while Japan had 13 in service and three building. The submarines of these navies that were to play such important, but contrasting, roles during World War II were only spectators during World War I. So, as the storm clouds of war gathered over Europe, we see the two submarine services of Great Britain and Germany ready – but ready for what?

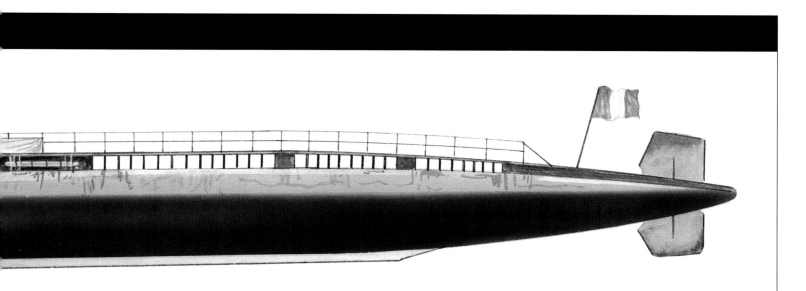

SPECIFICATIONS		
Country: France	Dimensions: 52.1m x 5.1m x 3.1m	Surface range: 3150km (1700nm) at
Launch date: 26 August 1911	(170ft 11in x 17ft 9in x 10ft 2in)	10 knots
Crew: 29	Armament: Six 450mm (17.7in) TTs	Performance: 13 knots/8 knots
Displacement: 403 tonnes/	Powerplant: Two-shaft diesel engines,	
560 tonnes	electric motors	

capable of reconnoitring enemy harbours and anchorages, and to give early warning of enemy movements.

As a result of this measured approach to submarine design, in 1914, Germany had a smaller but far more capable underwater arm than her by now deadly rival, the British Royal Navy. This small and elite corps had also prepared itself well and was ready to go. By 1913 in Britain, anxious eyes were being cast over the German capability, with the prophecy that the 'submarine is the coming type of vessel for sea fighting' and was more than capable of undermining British naval might.

FRANCE LOSES ITS EARLY LEAD

After galloping into an impressive lead in submarine development in the late 1890s, the French fixation on coastal and harbour defences and an over-academic approach as to whether boats were submarines (all

electric) or submersibles (steam-/electric-propelled torpedo-boats) made them slip further and further behind in both design and tactical thinking. Although they had 76 boats listed in their order of battle in 1914, they lacked a proper sea-going design that would be of some value in conflict. In short, in submarine terms, because they had ignored the internal combustion engine, the French were ill equipped and poorly prepared for the war when it came.

RUSSIA ILL-PREPARED FOR CONFLICT

After a disaster in 1903 with their home-built petrol-driven *Delfin* of 203 tonnes, the Tsarist Navy went abroad; by 1914, they had a varied collection of 36 British, American, French, and German-built boats scattered east, west, and in the middle (the Black Sea). The majority were involved in Army–Navy operations, and some may have been adept at minelaying, but the stark truth is that the

British Royal Navy submarine captains, members of this infant branch, would win Victoria Crosses, representing huge personal initiative, heroism, and skill. Neither was it expected that from the ranks of both submarine services should emerge some of the most influential figures of World War II.

THE DAWNING OF A NEW ERA

The German High Seas Fleet got off to an inauspicious start when it lost *U13* through accident and *U15* when, on 11 August 1914, she was rammed and cut in half by HMS *Birmingham,* as it reconnoitred for the Grand Fleet. She became the first submarine in history to be lost through an enemy attack. By way of revenge, *U21* (Hersing) sank HMS *Pathfinder* off the Firth of Forth, Scotland, three weeks later, and the latter became the first ship under way to be sunk by a submarine. This tit-for-tat battle was soon to take on a much more significant tone, which finally alerted both sides to the potential of a craft that had been so long regarded as a mere adjunct to the important elements of the navy and certainly not one that could influence the battle for the seas.

Above: The Russian petrol-electric *Delfin* was launched in 1903. She suffered a fatal accident in June 1904 when, with 22 trainees on board in addition to the crew of 10, she was swamped on the surface by the wash of a passing tug. The fact that the Captain had not turned up for the training session speaks volumes about the state of training in the Imperial Navy.

Tsar's submarines were in a very poor state of readiness; in particular, their sailors suffered a life of almost abject misery, being poorly fed, poorly led, and ill-trained. They were to under-achieve in an almost spectacular fashion in the coming conflict.

WORLD WAR I: THE SCALE OF CONFLICT

It was never in the Schleiffen plan that, by 1918, 372 German U-boats would sink 4837 merchantmen totalling over 11.17 million tonnes of Allied merchant shipping, losing 174 of their number in the process to all causes. Nor was it ever intended that five

U21

SPECIFICATIONS

Country: Germany
Launch date: 8 February 1913
Crew: 35
Displacement: 660 tonnes/850 tonnes
Dimensions: 64.2m x 6.1m x 3.5m
(210ft 6in x 20ft x 11ft 9in)
Armament: Four 508mm (20in) TTs; one 86mm (3.4in) gun
Powerplant: Two shafts, diesel-electric motors
Surface range: 9265km (5500nm) at 10 knots
Performance: 15.4 knots/9.5 knots

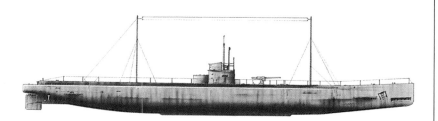

The *U21* was one of a class of four boats, built at Danzig and completed in 1913. They were the first German submarines to use diesel engines, German engineers previously having preferred to use smellier but safer kerosene fuel. *U21* foundered in the North Sea on 22 February 1919, as she was sailing to surrender.

THE GERMAN GRAND PLAN

The war on land was started by Germany against the Triple Entente of Britain, France, and Russia to underpin the ailing continental Austro-Hungarian Empire, and it was always intended to be a short, sharp affair. Indeed, a protracted war, dominated by activities of attrition, was not covered by any military manual at that time. Germany did not have the raw materials to sustain such a war, nor could she acquire them through conquest, so to win, she would have to import them. To import, she required 'command of the sea'.

However, at the outbreak of war in 1914 that power lay in the hands of the British Royal Navy; being outnumbered by three capital ships to two, the German High Seas Fleet could not risk a full-scale engagement. It had, therefore, to rely on a strategy of using locally superior force against elements of Britain's Grand Fleet, until it was so weakened that it could be taken on in a 'Trafalgar' style battle and defeated. This strategy in turn relied on the British taking offensive action and straying into hostile waters. It fell at the first hurdle because the Royal Navy had no intention of risking its ships in waters potentially littered with mines and submarines. In a sense, the moment the Grand Fleet established its distant blockade of the Heligoland Bight and the Skaggerak, 'Germany's arteries were subjected to an invisible pressure which never relaxed'.

However, Germany did have three cards to play in an otherwise very weak hand. The first was the importation of iron ore across the Baltic Sea from neutral Sweden; the second was the opening up of a trade route from Asia Minor with the help of her ally, Turkey; and the third, a powerful ace, was the blockade of Britain and her allies' merchant traffic by submarines. Blockade had always been a recognized part of German naval strategy, but it was intended to be conducted by her cruisers and destroyers, so in effect this submarine 'ace' was up the Germans' sleeve without them at first realizing that they had it.

Left: Emperor Willem II with his admirals von Tirpitz and von Holtzendorf in 1910. Tirpits initally played down the value of the submarine because he wanted no rival to the build-up of his surface fleet. By 1905, however, he had withdrawn his objections, and, indeed, he produced submarines in numbers for the express purpose of using them against British ships.

A defining moment in history happened in the North Sea on 22 September 1914, when the paraffin-driven *U9* under the command of Kapitanleutnant Otto Weddigan sank the old cruisers *Hogue, Aboukir*, and *Cressy*. These ships were widely known by the sadly prophetic nickname of the 'live bait squadron' because of their age and vulnerability to attack. Steaming line abreast in a straight line at 10 knots, they were unescorted by destroyers. Because of their obsolescence, they simply could not achieve the laid-down minimum patrol speed of 15 knots imposed after the *Pathfinder* sinking, and they were not zig-zagging (another recommended countermeasure), as there was no intelligence to suggest that U-boats were active in their area. At 0625 hours, Weddigan struck by firing a single torpedo which hit *Aboukir* and sank her. Her two consorts then attempted to pick up survivors, and both paid the price as Weddigan finished off his 'turkey-shoot' – the incident, which only lasted a little over an hour and a half, became known as 'three before breakfast'. In total, 1459 men died.

On 20 October, *U17* struck an equally ominous note when she sank SS *Glitra* off southern Norway under 'prize rules' and became the first submarine in history to sink a merchantman. This was followed, on 26 October, by a sinking that was singularly more sinister, when *U24* sank *Admiral Ganteaume* as she carried Belgian refugees across the Channel, without warning and in contravention of the 'prize rules'. This went without reprimand and heralded the next phase of submarine employment.

In November 1914, *U18* set another precedent when she succeeded in penetrating the Grand Fleet's 'lair' in Scapa Flow in the Orkney Islands off Scotland. Although she was spotted by a trawler and a destroyer, who turned in to ram her and drove her onto rocks, her gallant effort sent the Grand Fleet scurrying for cover to Queenstown until Scapa was reinforced with anti-submarine measures. This action was never to be forgotten!

THE FIRST UNRESTRICTED SUBMARINE CAMPAIGN

As Britain tightened the blockade of Germany, U-boats were at a severe disadvantage against commerce under the conditions of 'prize regulations'. They did not carry sufficient crewmembers to provide a 'prize crew'; they had no room to carry prisoners; and they were themselves at risk of ramming or being fired upon during the process of challenge. In short, to be effective, they had to break international law and sink without warning. This policy carried huge risks, not least that of dragging the United States into the war, which would have proved disastrous. Nevertheless, on 4 February 1915, Germany declared the waters around Great Britain and Ireland, including the English Channel, a war zone. All British shipping would be sunk on sight and the safety of neutral

Below: The German *U35* cruising by moonlight in the Mediterranean in April 1917. The number of crew enjoying the fresh air indicates the low level of threat expected, a confidence supported by the 'happy time' against lightly escorted targets enjoyed by U-boats operating in this arena.

THE SUBMARINE INTERNAL COMBUSTION ENGINE

Admiral of the Fleet Lord Fisher had always been perceptive about the impact the submarine would have on naval warfare. In 1913, he wrote: 'The vital qualities with which the oil engine has endowed the submarine are as follows:

(a) The ability to start at once (like a motorcar) from the engine cold. It is simply impossible to exaggerate the fighting advantage of this characteristic.

(b) Absence of smoke, so that invisibility can be maintained while their initial approach is being made on the surface.

(c) Ability to stop on the surface and instantly dive, then proceeding by electrical power when submerged.

(d) The increase in their radius of action; their possibilities in this direction being due to their not expending fuel when lying about in wait of their enemy, while at the same time their readiness for instant action remains unimpaired.'

Above: 'It's one of ours!' If it were not, then these two U-boats rendezvousing in presumably friendly waters could be in for a nasty shock. The stockade on the front of the approaching *UB*-class boat was for mine-wire cutting and dispersion.

'Germany's decision to employ U-boats as commerce raiders must rank as by far the most important event in the First World War ... it ended once and for all the distinction between combatant and civilian.'
Edward Horton

vessels could not be guaranteed. In short, if Germany could dissuade neutral countries from conducting trade with Britain, or if she could sink tonnage faster than it could be replaced, she would then balance the effect that the Royal Navy's blockade had on her population.

Despite protests from the United States following the German declaration, a respectable score began to be notched up by the small number of U-boats on patrol (about 10 at a time). This figure steadily increased as Germany's crash-building programme was instituted; by February 1915, another 43 boats had been ordered. However, on 7 May, an incident occurred that will remain in the annals of submarine infamy for ever.

THE SINKING OF THE *LUSITANIA*

Lt. Cdr. Walther Schweiger was coming to the end of a patrol in *U20* to the south of Ireland. In the preceding two days, he had sunk three ships. Now, with fuel running low and having only three torpedoes left, he decided to return to his base on Heligoland Island. At about 1330 hours, he sighted the black exhaust from the four red funnels of a transatlantic liner, later

recognized as either the *Lusitania* or the *Mauritania* of the Cunard Line. Schweiger manoeuvred himself into the perfect firing position 732m (800yds) on its starboard beam and fired a single torpedo that struck *Lusitania* almost amidships. The percussion of the torpedo then caused a sympathetic explosion of coal dust that ripped a huge hole in the passenger liner's side. Within 20 minutes this 34,545-tonne ship had sunk, taking with her 1198 passengers and crew, including 94 children and 128 Americans.

The fall-out from this outrageous act was swift and significant. It induced a telegram of protest from President Woodrow Wilson of the United States, and it sickened the rest of the world. What heightened the aura of barbarism surrounding the sinking was the German reaction to it, with newspaper proclamations such as 'With joyful pride we contemplate the latest deed of our Navy and it will not be the last' (*Kölnische Volkszeitung*), and a private medal was struck that showed Cunard as the death-dealer. The isolationist camp in the United States – until that point staunchly opposed to entering what they saw as a purely

UB4

SPECIFICATIONS

Country: Germany
Launch date: April 1915
Crew: 14
Displacement: 129 tonnes/144 tonnes
Dimensions: 28m x 2.9m x 3m (92ft 3in x 9ft 9in x 10ft)
Armament: Two 457mm (18in) torpedo tubes
Powerplant: Single-screw, diesel-electric motors
Surface range: 2778km (1599nm) at 5 knots
Performance: 6.5 knots/5.5 knots

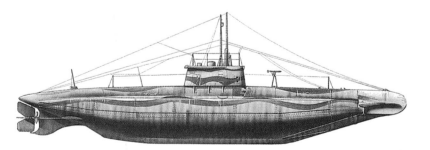

Construction of the small *UB* coastal boats was begun in 1914. Upon completion, the majority of these were sent by rail in sections to Antwerp in Belgium, which was in German hands, or Pola, the Austro-Hungarian port on the Adriatic, where they were assembled and made ready for deployment.

U-BOAT MINING

Having declared waters around Britain a war zone, in addition to its more overt attacks on ocean-going merchant traffic, the German U-boat arm invested heavily in mining offensively anticipated trade routes in the North Sea. The tiny *UB*-class and *UC*-class had already engaged in defensively mining the Heligoland Bight and entrances to the Baltic Sea, but now their activities were spread further afield, including the Dover Strait. As a measure of their effectiveness, German mines sank 94 merchant ships during 1915, and mines were also to take a heavy toll on British submarines when they attempted to carry the war to the enemy.

Left: The small German *UC*-class (185 tonnes) and even smaller *UB*-class (140 tonnes) were purpose-built minelayers. It was with a torpedo, however, that *UB20* raised American blood pressure when, in March 1916, she severely damaged the cross-channel ferry *Sussex*, killing 25 Americans.

European war – was further weakened, and the United States stepped closer to entering the war. The Imperial Navy now had to tread very carefully indeed!

THE U-BOAT 'HAPPY TIME' IN THE MEDITERRANEAN

Following the uproar caused by the *Lusitania* incident, U-boat captains were instructed not to attack large passenger ships, thereby strapping one hand behind their backs, but even so, they still had plenty to keep them busy, and the tonnage they sunk began to rise steeply. Indeed, in August 1915 – the first anniversary of the start of the war – at 188,400 tonnes, British

tonnage lost exceeded her replacement capacity. Then, in August 1915, south of Ireland, *U24* (Schneider) torpedoed the White Star liner *Arabic* of 16,053 tonnes, mercifully without huge loss of life. The sinking resurrected outrage, however, and this time US President Wilson's protest was even sharper.

Germany was now in desperate straits. Being denied the rich hunting grounds of the chokepoint in the South West Approaches that carried transatlantic traffic, she therefore turned her attention to the Mediterranean, an American-free zone.

Through this inland sea, with its artery of the Suez Cannel to the east and its

Above: Captain Wilson, a King's Messenger, was picked up by *U35* (right) from one of her victims. Hoping that Wilson's capture meant something of an intelligence coup, von Arnauld quickly transferred him to a smaller U-boat for passage home.

narrow exit of the Gibraltar Strait to the west, passed vast amounts of mercantile traffic carrying goods and men from India, Australia, and New Zealand. Not as strategically significant as the goods arriving from the United States and Canada, this trade route was still very important to Britain, as every ton of trade-carrying shipping lost had to be replaced from ever-diminishing resources.

It was in this theatre that three of the German top-scorers were to make their mark: Lother von Arnauld de la Periere of *U35* and *U139* (10 patrols, 406,420 tonnes), Walther Forstmann of *U12* and *U39* (16 patrols, 386,099 tonnes), and Max Valentiner of *U38* and *U157* (17 patrols, 304,815 tonnes). These three 'aces' were able to go about their business with astonishing ease.

THE ZIMMERMANN TELEGRAM

In early 1916, U-boats had crept back into the Channel and North Sea. They were operating under hazy restrictions, but managed to avoid any headline blunders. This changed in March when the French cross-Channel packet *Sussex* was torpedoed without warning. She was carrying a number of Americans, and the incident elicited the strongest protest yet from the Americans, with the threat of severance of diplomatic relations. On went the clamps once again, to the chagrin of those who realized that Germany's only hope was to accelerate the demise of Britain's struggling war effort. There were also those who realized that America's entry into the war was becoming just a matter of time, so what had Germany to lose, as there was the very real possibility that Britain was herself close to starvation and she may sue for peace before the arrival

of United States's overwhelming might? The inconsequential Battle of Jutland in early June, while a tactical success for the German Imperial Navy, reinforced the Royal Navy's supremacy at sea, leaving little option but to 'unleash the dogs of war'.

It all came to a head in January 1917 when British cryptographers deciphered a telegram from German Foreign Minister Arthur Zimmermann to German Minister to Mexico, von Eckhardt, offering United States territory to Mexico in return for joining the German cause. David Kahn, author of *The Codebreakers*, wrote: 'No other cryptanalysis has had such enormous consequences ... never before or since has so much turned upon the solution of a secret message.' The American press published news of the telegram on 1 March, and, on 6 April 1917, the United States Congress formally declared war on Germany and her allies.

Below: The British introduced the casing-mounted gun in 1910. It was used when a victim was not deemed worth a torpedo and accounted for many small, lightly armed targets. Shell cases can be seen being off-loaded from *U35* after another stunningly successful patrol in 1917.

THE CONVOY SYSTEM

Despite the fact that British convoys had been employed at sea since time immemorial, there was huge opposition to their introduction during World War I by both the Admiralty and Merchant Masters themselves. Earl Jellicoe, Commander of the Grand Fleet, claimed that convoys 'offered too big a target'. In December 1916, an Admiralty Memorandum stated that there were too many destinations to which to convoy and too many vessels to organize; convoys had to travel at the speed of the slowest vessel; convoying denied vessels 'prize rules' protection.

Much of the Admiralty's reluctance was founded on the belief that it would be impossible to marshal the 5000 or so movements that took place in British ports every week, a figure issued by HM Customs at the beginning of the war. Deeper investigation in 1917 revealed that this figure included every movement of every vessel, whether it be fishing smack or troop-carrying liner. The Prime Minister personally took a hand in April (a terrible month for losses), and, when a deeper investigation stripped the dross away, the true figure was found to nearer 300 inward and outward movements per week, an eminently manageable figure. With the help of the recently appointed Admiral Beattie, who relieved Jellicoe as Commander of the Grand Fleet, David Lloyd-George finally had his way and the convoy system was instituted, albeit rather reluctantly with only a tiny number of destroyer escorts being provided.

The advantages of the convoy, however, far outweighed Jellicoe's assertion that a group of ships presented 'too big a target'. A convoy:

(a) allowed a concentration of escorts. Instead of trying to protect a sea lane that had more holes in it than a kitchen colander through which a U-boat might slip, nippy and unpredictable escorts provided both a deterrent and combined strength if a submarine was detected. At a minimum, their presence could cause a submarine to dive to evade, thereby denying it a leisurely acquired fire-control solution.

(b) was harder to find than a number of individual ships scattered all over the ocean.

(c) presented a submarine with a single shot as the convoy passed *en bloc*, rather than a series of opportunities for engagement presented by single ships.

As the system began to prove itself as a genuine method of protecting against the U-boat menace, more and more escorts were made available for the duty. Rear Admiral William Sims of the US Navy provided much encouragement by allocating 80 of his destroyers to the escort role. Indeed, during the last 12 months of the war, less than 0.5 per cent of shipping was lost in convoys (fewer than 500 out of 100,000), while 12 times this number was lost in independent sailings, a truly staggering comparison. This reduction was also achieved despite growing numbers of U-boats being maintained on patrol, up from an average of 30 to 40 at any one time.

Left: Lother von Arnauld of *U35* with his crew. He was the most successful submarine skipper of World War I. Germany had some 400 submarine captains during the war, but more than 60 per cent of the damage they inflicted was accomplished by just 22 of those 400 officers.

DEUTSCHLAND

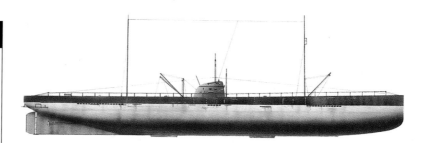

SPECIFICATIONS

Country: Germany
Launch date: March 1916
Crew: 56
Displacement: 1536 tonnes/1905 tonnes
Dimensions: 65m x 8.9m x 5.3m (213ft 3in x 29ft 2in x 17ft 5in)
Armament: None
Powerplant: Twin-screw diesel engines, electric motors
Surface range: 20,909km (11,284nm) at 10 knots
Performance: 12.4 knots/5.2 knots

Before America's entry into the war in 1917, the Germans were quick to recognize the potential of large, cargo-carrying submarines as a means of beating the blockade imposed on Germany's ports by the Royal Navy. *Deutschland* made two commercial runs to the United States before America's entry into the war brought an end to the venture.

In the first nine weeks of unrestricted submarine warfare, Britain lost more than 1.1 million tonnes of shipping, and the life-expectancy of an ocean-going merchant ship was down to four return voyages (compared with 16 in 1914), so even with USA's entry into the war, she was staring disaster in the face. Desperate measures were called for.

THE LAST THROW OF THE DICE

Whilst the German U-boats sank an average of 203,210 tonnes of Allied shipping, the figure was a long way short of what was needed to persuade Britain and her new ally to sue for peace. In the meantime, U-boat losses grew in number, and Britain's relentless blockade was generating misery in Germany, with a growing disaffection amongst their military and civilian populations alike. However, during the last nine months of the war, the United States was to receive its first taste of submarine-induced damage. This damage was carried across the Atlantic in U-cruisers; large submarines of almost 2540 tonnes submerged which were capable of long-range and extended patrols.

The forerunner of the class had been the *Deutschland*, an unarmed merchant-manned submarine which had visited Baltimore amidst great acclaim in June 1916. She and her six sisters (*U151–157*) were converted into warships with the addition of torpedo tubes and guns, and two purpose-built 'cruisers' were added to the order of battle (*U139* and *U140*). These submarines carried out one patrol each off the eastern seaboard of the American continent, as well as roaming throughout the Atlantic Ocean; through torpedoes and mines they were to sink 174 ships of nearly 375,939 tonnes, a not insignificant haul, given their late arrival on the scene.

In October 1918, crews of the High Seas Fleet mutinied, spelling the end of the surface war, but the loyal submarine arm kept going to the bitter end and, in a final act of defiance, *UB16* (Emsmann) once again entered Scapa Flow. Emsmann was heard on defensive seabed-mounted hydrophones, and, as he passed over a line of mines, they were activated from ashore and the submarine was destroyed. Emsmann's act of bravado was in sharp contrast to the activities of the mutineers

Above: The American *SS-47*, which, because she was fitted with two 76mm (3in) guns, was designated a 'monitor' submarine. Like a number of other classes of submarine being considered by the US Navy, she was not a great success and was sold in 1922.

who ultimately brought the conflict at sea to an end. The U-boats were not defeated, but, following the Armistice, 176 U-boats surrendered, and a further 200 building were destroyed where they lay.

ANTI-SUBMARINE MEASURES

At the start of World War I, naval staffs had simply not addressed the issue of anti-submarine measures and, through naivety and false assumptions, had paid a heavy price. They failed to advise the simple precautions of using speed and frequent alterations of course (zig-zagging) to make the opposing submariners' lives more

difficult. Nor was 'convoy' – which, when combined with zig-zagging, was by far the most effective protection for merchant ships – introduced until the end of the battle, by which time the German submarines had almost conquered, with Britain, at her nadir, down to her last six weeks of food stocks.

In addition to deploying hundreds of small patrol craft to deter submarines from surfacing, two other physical measures against the U-boat were deployed from the outset. The first was the mine, laid in two huge barrages across the English Channel and the northern entrance to the North Sea.

Left: The British also used minelayers, although they were conversions rather than purpose-built. Eight mine-chutes replaced the beam torpedo tube in five of the *E*-class boats, one of which is being loaded here.

In all, in excess of 160,000 devices were laid. In fact, very few U-boats were destroyed by these measures.

It is an astonishing fact that out of the 400 or so U-boat captains, more than 65 per cent of tonnage sunk was achieved by five per cent of their number, proving that it is possible to have as many submarines as one likes, but, without effective crews to man them, they have little more than nuisance value. It can only be surmised what deterrent effect the mine in particular had on the remaining 95 per cent!

The second measure deployed against the U-boat was the depth-charge, a canister filled with high explosive which was triggered by a hydrostatic (depth) fuse. This device was developed in Britain in 1915, although not deployed in numbers until 1916. Both ramming and using the gun against a submarine careless enough to get itself caught remained the primary attack weapons against the U-boat for the majority of the war.

Another physical 'ploy' introduced by the British was the Q-ship. This was a merchant vessel whose false upperworks concealed guns. Manned by volunteer naval crews, the Q-ships' purpose was to present themselves as tempting targets and to lure a U-boat into a position where it was possible to get a certain shot at her. The fact that Q-ships were loaded with timber to help keep them afloat is indicative of the degree of danger that their crews were prepared to accept to achieve their aim. In all, 17 U-boats were sunk by Q-ships, at a cost of 24 of their number. On the downside, the arming of merchant ships in this manner helped the Germans to justify their 'no-warning' policy.

It is a measure of the desperation the British felt at the height of this helpless slaughter that fishermen were issued with canvas bags to pop over the top of

SUBMARINE. E.9.

Right: HMS *E9*, commanded by Lieutenant (later Admiral Sir) Max Horton, was the first British submarine to sink another ship when, in 1914, it destroyed the German light cruiser *Hela*. Horton was an ice-cool character who could out-drink and out-poker his Russian hosts when he operated in the Baltic Sea.

periscopes, seagulls were trained to perch on exposed periscopes indicating the presence of a submarine, and two sea lions were borrowed from a Glasgow circus to be trained for anti-submarine duties! Their names were Billikins and Queenie, and they were based at HMS *Dolphin*, the Alma Mater of the Royal Navy Submarine Service in Gosport, England. This unlikely experiment failed primarily because Billikins preferred frolicking with swimmers at the nearby beach at Lee-on-Solent than learning how to identify submarines.

The most scientific activity was centred on the development of the hydrophone. This was a listening device capable of picking up sound waves in the ocean, itself an excellent carrier of sound energy. It was very susceptible to self-noise and achieved little. However, where the hydrophone did have real value was in defended anchorages, as was demonstrated during the *UB116* incident.

THE U-BOATS THWARTED

In spite of the prodigious destruction wrought by the U-boats, the campaign failed to prevent the Allies from exerting their military strength through sea power wherever they wished; they maintained the British Expeditionary Force in France; they transported the US Army to Europe; they supplied Allied armies in the Middle East and elsewhere. The U-boats got close to, but ultimately failed at, reducing imports to the United Kingdom to an extent that wrecked her war effort. On the other hand, U-boats were thwarted, rather than defeated.

THE BRITISH CAMPAIGN

The British entered the war with a submarine flotilla which was dominated by small coastal submarines and a small number of overseas submarines. The coastal submarine was designed for and stationed as an integral portion of the defence of seaports, coasts, and overseas bases. The overseas submarines were vessels for use off the enemy's coasts and on the high seas between.

The first ever British war patrols were undertaken by two boats of the Eighth Flotilla based on the depot ship HMS *Maidstone* at Harwich, England, in August 1914. They were *E6* and *E8,* which were deployed to the Heligoland Bight for reconnaissance duties, and their first experience contained all the expected elements of finding few targets, having to avoid the attention of many patrol craft, and operating under the constant threat of enemy minefields close to their coasts. The first torpedoes fired by a British submarine in anger came from *D5* (Herbert of the later Baralong incident), against the German cruiser *Rostock*. Despite the cruiser being an easy target, *D5* missed because her torpedoes ran deep. It was discovered during later trials that the explosive warhead weighed 181kg (40lb) more than the practice head used in peacetime, causing the increase in running depth.

The first sinking in Royal Navy submarine history took place on 13 September 1914 when Lieutenant Max Horton (later Admiral Sir Max Horton DSO) in *E9* sank the German light cruiser *Hela* and, during his next patrol, sank the destroyer *S116* (it was as difficult as 'shooting snipe with a rifle'). Returning to harbour in triumph, and recalling Admiral Arthur Wilson's words about 'hanging submarine crews as pirates', Horton flew two small Jolly Rogers (the pirate flag) and started a tradition that persists to this day. The sinking of *S116* was to have even greater impact than the award of Horton's first DSO: Admiral Von Ingenohl declared, 'Submarines have entirely altered conditions in our operational bases in the German Bight: in this confined area we are exposed to continual danger and continual observation, which we have no means of avoiding.' He moved the High Seas Fleet into the Baltic, thereby establishing the ingredients of another classic encounter.

Despite these successes, from the British point of view it was becoming obvious that large-scale submarine operations in the Heligoland Bight were both dangerous and unproductive. *E3* became the first submarine in history to be sunk by another when, on 17 October, she was caught on the surface

Below: HMS *B11* was commanded by Lieutenant Norman Holbrook, who won the first of the Royal Navy's Submarine Service's 14 Victoria Crosses. He earned this highest award for gallantry when he penetrated the Dardanelles, with its minefields and treacherous currents, to sink the Turkish battleship *Messudieh*.

by *U27* (Wegener) off the River Emms. The defeat at Coronel at the hands of Admiral von Spee showed that the naval battle was going badly for the Royal Navy. On 30 October 1914, Admiral Jackie Fisher, at the age of 74, returned as First Sea Lord.

Just before Fisher's arrival, three submarines were despatched to the Baltic. The orders for *E1* (Noel Lawrence), *E9* (Max Horton), and *E11* (Nasmith) – what names to conjure with in the future! – were to pass into the Baltic, seek out the German Fleet at exercise, sink the battleships, and proceed to the Russian port of Libau to refuel. The operation was expected to last two weeks. *E1* and *E9* successfully penetrated the Baltic, but *E11*, having been delayed by engine trouble, ran into a swarm of German patrol assets and wisely turned back. *E1* and *E9* stayed considerably longer than two weeks!

DANGER IN THE DARDANELLES

Readers will recall that Turkey, with dreams of reviving the Ottoman Empire, had entered the war on the side of the central powers in 1914. Germany had 'sold' the battle-cruiser *Goeben* and the light-cruiser *Breslau* to their new allies, and as well as reviving nautical skills, they were also running the Turkish Army. Germany's intent was to seal off the Dardanelles, the passage through which passed over 95 per cent of Russian trade. The big naval guns and land-based invasion failed miserably and led to the Gallipoli fiasco; however, the British effort also entailed the use of submarines. Three tiny *B*-class submarines (*B9, B10,* and *B11*) had been based at Mudros on the Island of Lemnos from December 1914 and had begun to probe the Dardanelles narrows, a 56km (35-mile) long, 2.4km (1.5-mile) wide stretch of water leading into the Sea of Marmora. It was an extremely dangerous patch of water for a submarine. No fewer than five minefields traversed it; there was a continuously running outflow of current; there was a layer of fresh water at 18.3km (60ft) that made depth-keeping hazardous;

and Turkish guns ashore were waiting for anything on the surface. Despite these hazards, Lieutenant Norman Holbrook pulled off the magnificent feat of getting as far north as Charnak and torpedoing the 10,160-tonne Turkish battleship *Messudieh* at anchor, and getting back against all odds. For this, he was awarded the Victoria Cross, the first of 14 won by the Submarine Service.

Elsewhere at the start of 1915, patrol followed patrol for the Eighth Flotilla in the Heligoland Bight with rarely a glimpse of the enemy, but always with the constant strain of navigating accurately and staying clear of known minefields. For the coastal submarines, life was also extremely tedious, with their primary role being to guard against bombardment forays by units of the German High Seas Fleet.

The Baltic campaign restarted in April when the ice melted. Max Horton had taken *E9* to sea at the height of winter, much to the astonishment of his reluctant hosts, and had proved that the thick coat of ice that gathered on the casing of the submarine would melt once the submarine was dived. However, this foray was as much to relieve the tedium as for any true operational purpose because potential targets were also few and far between. Once off the leash, the newly promoted Commander Max Horton DSO RN – just 31 years of age – and Noel Lawrence became extremely active. Between them, they steamed 11,263km (7000 miles) in two months, and, although unreliable torpedoes caused more misses than hits, their successes convinced the Germans that a whole flotilla was engaged in operations. In July, Horton damaged the cruiser *Prinz Adalbert* and, in August, Lawrence damaged the battle-cruiser *Moltke*; noting these successes the Admiralty decided to reinforce the pair with *E19* (Cromie), *E18* (Robert Halahan), and *E8* (Goodhart). *E13* (Geoffrey Layton) was also intended to join them, but a compass failure caused the submarine to run aground inside Danish territorial waters.

Life was extremely tedious for the British coastal submarines operating in the Baltic, with their primary role being to guard against bombardment forays by units of the German High Seas Fleet.

Left: The art of effective submarine gunnery – to surface, surprise the enemy, get the shot away quickly and accurately, and dive with the minimum time on the surface – required constant practice. This over-dressed gun party is obviously conducting just such a practice.

> '[Submarines] have the power to fight or evade a fight at will; they can pick and choose their prey, and can remain for an almost indefinite time an omnipresent, constant and harassing menace to all surface craft, and at present there are no means for their destruction.'
>
> **Admiral of the Fleet Lord Fisher, May 1913**

Although protected under international law for 24 hours to complete repairs, and despite the courageous intervention of a Danish destroyer, two German escorts first attempted to torpedo *E13* and, when this failed, bombarded the submarine until it was a flaming hulk. Several British sailors were killed during this incident, which was described by the official historian as an 'outrage that was perpetrated in cold blood, by men under the control of their officers, upon a helpless wreck on a neutral shore. For a cumulation of illegality it would surely be hard to match in the annals of modern warfare'. This incident summed up the hatred and passion that the submarine could arouse in otherwise civilized men.

Soon afterwards, the Baltic squadron got into their stride and began to sink merchant ships in large numbers – all in accordance with the 'prize rules'. Cromie, in *E19*, sank no fewer than seven in one patrol! The end result was that not only was ore for Germany's steelworks severely stemmed, further adding to the blockade, but also valuable escorts had to be assigned for protection duties.

In the meantime, the Turkish response to *B11*'s incursion in late 1914 was to sow even more mines in the Dardanelles Strait and to move their heavy units further north to Constantinople. This put them outside the range of the *B*-class, so four *E*-class were despatched as reinforcements. While the British Army made their preparations for the ill-fated Gallipoli campaign, the Navy's submarines attempted to get into the Sea of Marmora to interdict the Turkish supply lines. The first to run the gauntlet was *E15* (T.S. Brodie) in April, but she fell victim to the treacherous currents and became stuck fast on the mud. She was close to a fort and was destroyed with heavy loss of life. The second attempt was by the Australian *AE2* under the command of Lt. Cdr. H.G. Stoker RN. He succeeded in getting into the Sea of Marmora, but the operation was unsuccessful in that his torpedoes failed to find any mark. Being forced to the surface because of a density layer, *AE2* fell victim to a Turkish escort's guns and was destroyed, and the crew went into a Turkish prisoner-of-war camp. It was to be third time lucky when, on 27 April 1915, *E14* (Boyle) succeeded in penetrating the strait, and, in the Sea of Marmora, he enjoyed considerable success, culminating in a successful return from patrol. Boyle was immediately promoted to Commander and was awarded the Victoria Cross.

A LEGENDARY CAREER

The next arrival was *E11* under Martin Nasmith. This highly experienced commanding officer (he had escaped from *A4* in 1905 and had fired the first submarine deck-mounted gun in *D4* in 1910) had been frustrated by his earlier failure to get into the Baltic and was thirsting for action. His exploits during three forthcoming patrols were the stuff of legend!

Nasmith's second patrol was just as successful as his first. The *E11* was now fitted with a gun, which Nasmith used against targets that did not warrant a torpedo, and he despatched 35,561 tonnes of enemy shipping, including the battleship *Barbarossa*. He also conducted the first-ever submarine-delivered commando raid by despatching his First Lieutenant, Guy D'Oyley Hughes – whose idea it was – to blow up a viaduct carrying the main Constantinople railway line. The sack of gun-cotton used as the explosive was floated on a raft, and Hughes swam ashore, towing it behind him. The daring raid was a complete success, and, in recognition of this act of extraordinary courage, he was awarded the DSO.

Nasmith's endeavours, combined with those of Boyle in *E14* (he, too, made three successful incursions into the Sea of Marmora), Bruce in *E12*, Cochrane in *E7*, and Stocks in *E2* (the last out), had almost succeeded in their quest to starve out the Turkish Fifth Army – but not quite. Despite this, Churchill was to write 'the Naval History

NASMITH'S FIRST PATROL IN *E11*

Between 19 May and June 1915, Nasmith wreaked havoc on the Turkish supply lines and completed one of the most successful patrols in British Royal Navy submarine history. One of his most outstanding feats was to enter Constantinople Harbour and torpedo a large transport, the *Stamboul*, moored alongside. To prove he had been there, he took a picture of the Grand Mosque by applying a box-brownie camera to his periscope, thereby inventing periscope photography and creating another first in submarine history. His feat was the equivalent of a U-boat turning up in the Pool of London! During the same patrol, Nasmith:

(a) captured a dhow and used it for disguise as he searched for targets;

(b) got into a fight with the Turkish gunboat which, before it sank, plugged a neat hole in *E11*'s periscope;

(c) got shot at by 50 Turkish Cavalrymen from the top of a cliff and took a bullet through his cap, but not before his own crew replied with their rifles;

(d) gave an interview to the American reporter Raymond Gram Swing of the *Chicago Herald*, who was taking passage in the munitions ship *Nagara*, before putting him into a lifeboat and blowing the ship sky-high;

(e) on two occasions recovered back into the submarine and re-prepped torpedoes that had missed the target;

(f) cooperated regularly with air reconnaissance patrols and established a new level of tactical interaction between two relative newcomers on the maritime scene;

(g) only withdrew from patrol after one engine totally failed, and then actually turned round in the narrow strait during his exit passage to go back and get a target he had spotted late through his periscope. Once again, his unerringly accurate evaluation of risk versus gain came into play when he sank a large transport off Moussa Bank;

(i) had the misfortune to hook a mine in his foreplanes once he had reversed again, which he then towed for miles through other minefields, not daring to slow down lest the horns touch his hull. His extraordinary nerve never failed him though, and, once clear, he surfaced and got rid of his unwanted passenger by going astern on his motors.

Above: During an approach to Constantinople, *E11* attacked the Turkish gunboat *Pelenk-I-Dria* and hit her with a torpedo. Before she sank, her crew manned the guns and returned fire, scoring a hit on the submarine's slender periscope, which was the only visible target. The periscope is now on display at the Royal Navy Submarine Museum, Gosport, England.

'The naval history of Britain contains no page more wonderful than that which records the prowess of her submarines at the Dardanelles.'
Winston S. Churchill

E11

Completed between 1913 and 1916, the *E*-class submarines ran to 55 hulls, the construction of which, once war was declared, was shared between 13 private yards. *E11*, under the command of the talented Lt. Cdr. Martin Nasmith, was arguably the most famous of them all; operating in the Dardanelles area, she scored many successes, including the sinking of the Turkish battleship *Hairredin Barbarossa*. Many RN submariners who rose to high rank learned their trade in *E*-class boats. For operations in the Dardanelles, the British submarines adopted a blue camouflage to conceal themselves in the clear, shallow waters.

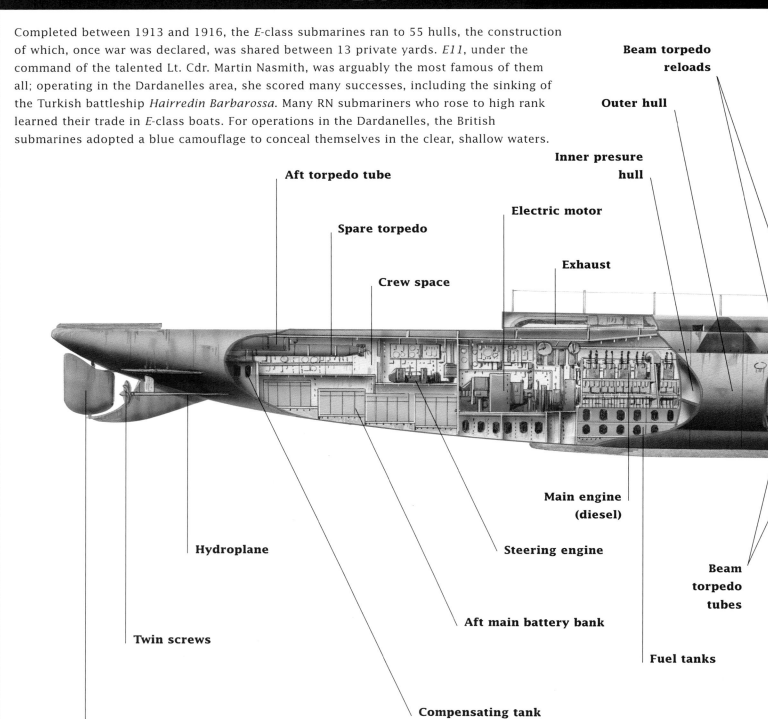

Beam torpedo reloads

Outer hull

Inner presure hull

Aft torpedo tube

Spare torpedo

Electric motor

Exhaust

Crew space

Main engine (diesel)

Hydroplane

Steering engine

Beam torpedo tubes

Aft main battery bank

Twin screws

Fuel tanks

Compensating tank

Rudder

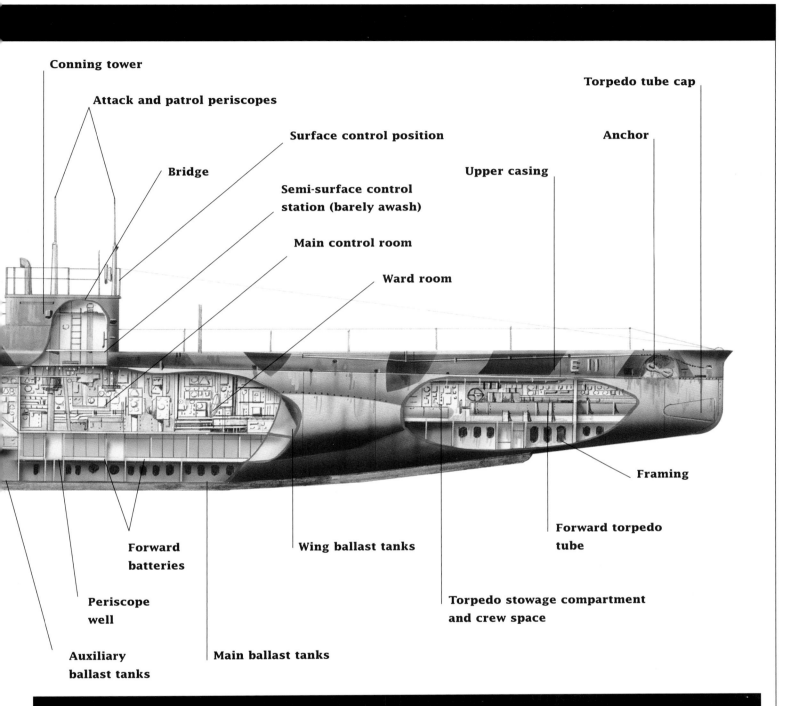

Conning tower

Attack and patrol periscopes

Torpedo tube cap

Bridge

Surface control position

Anchor

Semi-surface control station (barely awash)

Upper casing

Main control room

Ward room

Framing

Forward torpedo tube

Forward batteries

Wing ballast tanks

Periscope well

Torpedo stowage compartment and crew space

Auxiliary ballast tanks

Main ballast tanks

SPECIFICATIONS

Country: Great Britain
Launch date: 1913
Crew: 30
Displacement: 677 tonnes/
820 tonnes

Dimensions: 55.2m x 6.91m x 3.8m
(181ft x 22ft 8in x 12ft 6in)
Armament: Five 457mm (18in) TTs; one
12-pounder gun

Powerplant: Two twin-shaft diesel engines,
two electric motors
Surface range: 6035km (3579nm) at 10 knots
Performance: 14 knots/9 knots

THE *K*-CLASS

SPECIFICATIONS

Country: Great Britain
Launch date: 15 July 1916
Crew: 50–60
Displacement: 2174 tonnes/2814 tonnes
Dimensions: 100.6m x 8.1m x 5.2m
(330ft x 26ft 7in x 17ft)
Armament: Ten 533mm (21in) TTs;
three 102mm (4in) guns
Powerplant: Twin screws, steam
turbines/electric motors
Surface range: 5556km (3000nm) at 13 knots
Performance: 23 knots/9 knots

In 1915 the British Admiralty decided to design a class of exceptionally fast ocean-going submarines that could keep up with the battlefleet. The boats were a disaster, no fewer than five of the 18 built prior to 1919 being lost in accidents. It was hardly surprising that morale in the Submarine Flotillas to which the *K* boats were assigned was not high. In general, the *K* boats were relegated to anti-submarine patrols.

of Britain contains no page more wonderful than that which records the prowess of her submarines at the Dardanelles'.

LATER BRITISH SUBMARINE TYPES

When the Dardanelles campaign ended, there came the realization that the Royal Navy, with its *D*s, *E*s, *H*s – of US design at 457 tonnes and with four 53cm (21in) tubes – and *J*s – 1930-tonne submarines which were hard to handle, but also with 53cm (21in) tubes – had sufficient overseas submarines to fulfil every mission required of the service. Indeed, as their targets dried up, they were beginning to be employed on tasks for which they were never originally designed: minelaying, fleet escorts, shore bombarders, seaplane carriers, anti-submarine craft (some were fitted with depth-charges), and even anti-aircraft duties. So, from late 1915 onwards, orders were placed for 'specific to type' platforms.

Opposite: The torpedo tubes of an *E*-class submarine, with the tails of two 457mm (18in) Whitehead torpedoes protruding from them. These boats were also fitted with beam torpedo tubes to give the commanding officer another option when in close range of the enemy.

THE *R*-CLASS

SPECIFICATIONS

Country: Great Britain
Launch date: April 1918
Crew: 36
Displacement: 416 tonnes/511 tonnes
Dimensions: 49.9m x 4.6m x 3.5m (163ft 9in x 15ft x 11ft 6in)
Armament: six 457mm (18in) TTs
Powerplant: single screw, diesel/electric 1200hp motors
Surface range: 3800km (2048nm) at 8 knots
Performance: 15 knots/9.5 knots

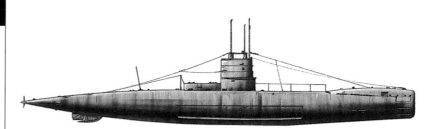

The *R*-class boats were part of an attempt to develop submarines to hunt other submarines, in this case, the German U-boats. They were a daring solution to a problem which nearly brought Britain to disaster, but they arrived too late to have any effect.

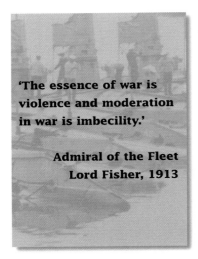

'The essence of war is violence and moderation in war is imbecility.'

Admiral of the Fleet Lord Fisher, 1913

Below: The diesel-driven *J*-class did not produce enough speed to accompany the fleet, so the Royal Navy turned to steam propulsion. Despite the lessons of others, it soon discovered that these large, unwieldy, and complex submarines caused a lot of trouble for little gain. Here, *K22* is seen lowering her funnels before diving.

The most significant in the short term was the *K*-class, which was designed as a fleet escort. In order to achieve the required 24 knots, the submarine had to be propelled by steam; however, undeterred by previous 'bad experiences', an order for 20 of the craft was placed with Vickers. Because it had never been imagined that submarines would fire at a target from a range greater than 457m (500yds) – a range from which a hit should be almost guaranteed – they had only been provided originally with a single tube, which was later increased to two. In fact, the average firing range was outside 914m (1000yds), and two torpedoes were simply not enough to generate a salvo that covered inaccuracies in the CO's firing assessment of range, course and speed of the target. A 1016-tonne overseas submarine fitted with four bow tubes was therefore ordered as the successor to the *E*-class: the *L*-class. A 30cm (12in) gun monitor submarine, the *M*-class, and the single-shafted, high-speed anti-submarine submarine *R*-class also joined the queue for building. Such were the demands placed on British shipyards that many of these designs only emerged towards the end of the war.

The *K*-class became known as the 'Kalamitous Ks' because of the vessels' unwieldiness, which made them highly accident-prone. Indeed, of the 18 completed during the war, nine were to suffer major disasters, including sinking through accidental flooding and ramming.

As the war drew to a close in a frustrating anti-climax, accidents were beginning to overtake actions, the misidentification of *H5* in the Irish Sea by the steamer *Rutherglen* being a typical example. Merchant ship captains were encouraged to ram any enemy submarines that threatened them, so it was without hesitation that *Rutherglen*'s captain put his wheel over against the unfortunate friendly submarine. On board was Ensign Childs of the US Navy, the first American submariner to lose his life in action. It is a matter of footnote that the usual bounty for sinking a U-boat was paid to *Rutherglen*'s crew, including a decoration for the captain, as it was considered essential that no doubts about taking immediate action should be allowed to enter merchant masters' minds, something that would surely have happened had *H5*'s true identity been revealed.

However, despite the drudgery of routine and uneventful patrols interspersed with only the occasional flurry of success, there was one more glorious page for the British to be recorded and that belonged to the tiny petrol-driven *C3*. Commanded by Lieutenant Richard Sandford and a crew of one other officer and four volunteer ratings, and crammed with high explosives, *C3* jammed

herself under the viaduct that connected the mole of Zeebrugge with the mainland. This task was an essential part of a joint operations raid to block the Belgian canal system used as a highway for U-boats breaking out into the North Sea and on to the Atlantic. Three of the six crew were badly wounded when making their escape, but bullets against the crew stopped when *C3* exploded with a mighty roar. For this outstanding feat of courage, Sandford was awarded the fifth and final submarine Victoria Cross of the war, his First Lieutenant (Lt Howell-Price) the DSO, and his four sailors the Conspicuous Gallantry Medal.

CONCLUSION

So ended a war during which submarines of all nations came of age. Never again would they be regarded as 'the weapon of the weaker power'. They had shown that, in the future, a power wishing to exercise 'command of the sea' would not only need a superior surface battlefleet to counter surface raiders, but would also have to provide a huge armada of anti-submarine vessels, aircraft, and mines, 10 times the size of a likely enemy submarine force. When used as a commerce raider, despite its relative infancy, the submarine had shown itself to be one of the decisive weapons of sea power.

Above: The *H*-class was a proven US design, and Britain needed more submarine hulls quickly. However, the US Government objected to supplying them on the grounds of its neutrality, so arrangements were made to have them built in Vickers's Canadian Yard.

Left: HMS *M1* was the only one of her class to conduct a patrol during World War I. The concept of the 'monitor' submarine armed with a 305mm (12in) gun was the idea of Commodore S.S. Hall, who observed that by 1916 no torpedo engagement had been effective outside 1000 yards. He argued that shells were cheaper than torpedoes and guns were longer ranged. His diagnosis was correct, but his treatment for the patient was not. The cure actually lay in larger salvoes of torpedoes.

THE INTER-WAR YEARS

'The U-boats had brought Great Britain nearer to defeat at sea in World War I than at any time since the Battle of Beachy Head in 1690. Although they now had the largest submarine fleet in the world ... the British believed that the submarine, in the hands of an enemy, was potentially so dangerous that it outweighed any advantage they themselves could gain from using it.' (Vice Admiral Sir Arthur Hezlet, 1967)

Britain was left debt-ridden and greatly weakened by World War I, and her now unsustainable naval supremacy ended at the Treaty of Washington in 1922. At that conference called by the United States (like Japan, the growing industrial power in the world) Britain was forced to accept a limitation proposal by the United States of a ratio of 5:5:3 in capital ship power. In return, she sought to have the submarine banned as a weapon of war, but both France and Japan vetoed this proposal. She did manage, however, to establish the protocol that submarines would not be used for unrestricted warfare against merchant shipping, although France refused to ratify this element of the declaration.

Left: HMS *Saracen* under way flying her Jolly Roger, the symbol of a successful war patrol adopted from World War I. In 1918, few would have believed that Germany would be able to rearm and be prepared to plunge the world into a second global conflict.

At the London Naval Conferences of 1932 and 1935, Britain continued to press for the banning of submarines, but without success, achieving only limitations on total tonnage (52,834 tonnes) and size (2032 tonnes). By the second conference, with Hitler in power in Germany and the rise of National Socialism (Fascism) rampant elsewhere, all thoughts of any limitations on an arms race had been ignored.

THE BRITISH SUBMARINE FORCE

At the end of World War I, Britain had forced herself to the fore of submarine design and tactical thinking. She had introduced the steam-driven fleet-submarine (the *K*-class); the big 30cm (12in) gun monitor submarine (the *M*-class); and the small, fast anti-submarine submarine (the *R*-class). The *K*-class had an unhappy history and left service in the 1920s, and the *R*-class always suffered from a lack of recharging capability and was another concept that withered on the vine. In 1925, Britain

investigated the concept of the 'cruiser' submarine through the construction of HMS *X1*, at that time the largest submarine in the world at 110m (363ft) long and weighing 3048 tonnes. She boasted four 13.9cm (5.5in) guns, making her more heavily armed than many surface ships! The *X1* was plagued by engine problems and spent more time in dockyard hands than at sea, and was eventually scrapped in 1937.

The concept of the big gun on a submarine emanated from Lord Jackie Fisher who, noting that torpedoes were ineffectively fired from outside 914m (1000yds) – too small a salvo to cover fire control errors – theorized that fitting a gun would allow a submarine to engage the enemy's major units from a significant distance of up to 8km (5 miles) and carry plenty of ammunition. It also provided the submarine with a significant shore-bombardment capability, and *M1* was tasked with such a mission against Istanbul in late 1918. *M2* was converted into a

Below: Built in 1921, HMS *X1* was a contradiction in terms: just at the time the British were moving against the submarine, they built this monster cruiser submarine. She was a mistake. Engine problems prevented her keeping up with the Fleet, and she was fit only for long-range commerce-raiding – not a British strategic intention.

At the London Naval Conferences of 1932 and 1935, Britain continued to press for a ban on submarines, but without success. By the second conference, with Hitler in power in Germany, all thoughts of any limitations on an arms race had been ignored.

submersible seaplane carrier and was the inspiration of the school of thought led by Max Horton, who believed (correctly) that the future of maritime power lay in the submarine and the aircraft. So, it was argued, why not combine the two capabilities into a single platform? *E22* had carried two Sopwith Pups on external rails after casing for Zeppelin engagement during World War I, so the concept was not totally outrageous. The thinking behind *M2* was that her catapult-launched 'Peto' aircraft could be used for reconnaissance.

The third of the class to be built, *M3*, (four were planned, but the last was cancelled) was converted into a minelayer, using the large after-casing as the mine magazine. In this respect, she was revolutionary, as submarine minelayers hitherto had used a few fixed tubes in ballast tanks. The British also developed a 'belt-driven' method of laying mines. The experiments with *M3* led to the development of the *Porpoise*-class of minelayers that provided outstanding service in a number of roles during World War II. It is sad to relate that both *M1* and

Above: The British experiment with HMS *M2* and her 'Peto' aircraft married the strengths of the submarine with air reconnaissance. A watertight hangar was fitted in place of her 305mm (12in) gun, and she was able to dive with her plane on board. She could surface, catapult the aircraft, and dive again in five minutes. *M2* was lost with all hands in 1936.

BASS

SPECIFICATIONS

Country: USA
Launch date: 27 December 1924
Crew: 85
Displacement: 2032 tonnes/2662 tonnes
Dimensions: 99.4m x 8.3m x 4.5m (326ft x 27ft 3in x 14ft 9in)
Armament: Six 533mm (21in) TTs; one 76mm (3in) gun
Powerplant: two-shaft diesels, plus electric motors
Surface range: 11,118km (6000nm) at 11 knots
Performance: 18 knots/11 knots

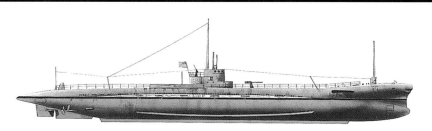

USS *Bass* was one of the three *Barracuda*-class submarines, the first post-World War I submarines to be built. They were partly re-engined before World War II. Their war service was limited to training, and plans to convert them to transport submarines were abandoned, although they might have proved very useful in this role.

After the *River* class, Britain decided that all future submarines would be built with internal fuel tanks. They also planned to build a medium-sized patrol type for operations in the North Sea, and a larger type for overseas operations. These decisions were made in the nick of time.

M2 met disastrous ends through collision and accident, and their achievements were written down, as they were deemed more useful to an enemy than to the Royal Navy.

THE FIRST POST-WAR DESIGNS

The first of the fully post-war designs was the long-range *Oberon*-class, designed to operate in the Far East, where war in the Pacific was a growing possibility, as the Anglo-Japanese treaty had not been renewed. There then followed the *P*- and *R*-classes which were slight improvements on the *O*s, and they were joined by three fast 'fleet' submarines of the *River*-class. In attempting to give them longer range, they had been provided with external fuel tanks, which all leaked, and it became obvious that it was time to consolidate and standardize designs. It was decided that all future submarines would

be built with internal fuel tanks and that there would be a medium-sized patrol type for operations in the North Sea and a larger type for overseas operations to replace the *O*s, *P*s and *R*s. These decisions were made in the nick of time.

The first of the standardized types became the *S*-class: 61.5m (202ft) long; 914 tonnes dived displacement, and six forward torpedoes, with one stern tube added later. They were a great success. The second was the outstanding *T*-class: 81.9m (269ft) long, and 1626 tonnes dived; eight forward and two stern torpedo tubes. In 1936, the idea of building an unarmed submarine for training surface ships emerged off the drawing board; by the time these vessels undergoing construction, the gloves on arms limitation were off, and four internal tubes were squeezed into their cramped interiors. This was the famous *U*-class of 57.9m (190ft) and about 609 tonnes dived – although this class of submarine was painfully slow at 11.5 knots on the surface, compared with the 15 knots of her bigger sisters.

The essence of these British designs was simplicity, with little compromise for crew comfort. There were no complicated fire-control aids and their Mk VIII torpedoes were straight running with only a contact fuse. This meant that Commanding Officers had to point the whole submarine down the intended direction of fire, having calculated the appropriate 'Director Angle' (aim-off) to achieve a hit against the target. Salvo fire to achieve a spread of torpedoes across the

Left: HMS *Triad* was the eventual derivative of the excellent *T*-class. The major limitation of the torpedo attack – small salvoes – revealed during World War I, had been well recognized, and these submarines were fitted with 10 torpedo tubes.

RADAR

In August 1940, the British revealed to the Americans their latest invention: radar (RAdio Direction And Ranging). This device was to have an enormous influence both at sea and on land and in the air because, when fitted to maritime patrol aircraft (MPA) with 'legs', it denied the U-boat its use of the surface, and, when fitted to asdic-equipped escorts, it provided the defending ship with eyes and ears above and below the surface of the sea.

Right: When Captain Karl Dönitz was appointed to command the new German U-boat service in 1935, he had no doubt whatsoever that its function was to expand and be ready to fight a new campaign against British commerce.

attack periscope (thin at the top to reduce tell-tale 'feather'). The periscopes contained graticules for estimating target range by measuring the angular distance subtended by the target. Their other primary sensor was asdic, the main purpose of which was to search for targets and to help evaluate their movements during a counterattack, and it also had an active search capability to hunt for mines.

Because it was expected that submarines would be operating in areas of enemy air superiority, they were quick-diving. The attack philosophy was to achieve a firing position at about 914m (1000yds) on the target's beam, having manoeuvred the submarine through the defensive screen. This called for high skill and extreme nerve. Their 'modus operandi' was to surface at night and recharge the battery (this was the time when a hot meal would be cooked) and to conduct any transit that was necessary. By day they would be dived, maintaining a periscope and asdic search for their enemy. Navigation, so essential to stay in area and avoid known minefields, was based on sun and star sights using a sextant. Britain entered the war with 58 submarines, many of which were the barely satisfactory early overseas classes, and the World War I vintage *H*- and *L*-classes, which

target track – to compensate for inaccuracies in determining target range, course or speed – was achieved either by using firing interval or individual aiming points. Every class had a medium-calibre gun on the casing, designed for use against lightly armed targets that did not warrant a torpedo. All submarines were fitted with both a binocular search periscope with a sky surveillance capability and a monocular

U2

SPECIFICATIONS

Country: Germany
Launch date: July 1935
Crew: 25
Displacement: 254 tonnes/302 tonnes
Dimensions: 40.9m x 4.1m x 3.8m
(133ft 2in x 13ft 5in x 12ft 6in)
Armament: Three 533mm (21in) TTs; one
20mm AA gun
Powerplant: Twin-screw, diesel-electric motors
Surface range: 1688km (912nm) at 10 knots
Performance: 13 knots/7 knots

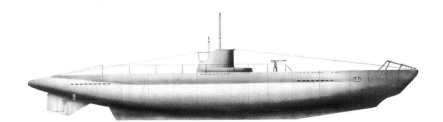

Under the terms of the Versailles Treaty, Germany was forbidden to build submarines, but during the 1920s she set up clandestine design teams in Spain, Holland and Russia. The first boat was built for Finland in 1927 and this was the prototype for *U2*, one of the first Type II submarines intended for coastal service.

were mainly used for training young commanding officers and other Anti-Submarine Warfare (ASW) forces.

THE RENAISSANCE OF THE U-BOAT ARM

The Versailles Treaty of 1918 banned Germany from owning submarines, but she nevertheless managed to keep her submarine design and building skills alive through an extraordinary web of skilful deceit. She was allowed to retain all the drawings of her World War I designs, and these she quietly nurtured in a building yard in neighbouring Holland! Finland, Spain, and Turkey were all to acquire boats from the yard of IvS in Rotterdam during the 1920s, and post-construction advice was provided by both serving and retired officers. It was necessary to build 'schools' to underpin this after-sales service, which kept alive submarine thought-processes and tactical thinking.

When Adolf Hitler came to power in 1933 he embarked immediately on a programme of building up his surface forces, re-establishing his air force and creating a standing army of half a million. Wary of 'spooking' the French and British governments, he did not introduce the submarine into his building programme until 1935 when, through supreme diplomacy, he actually achieved the approval of an appeasing British Government to reintroduce submarines into his order-of-battle to a limit of 45 per cent of British submarine tonnage. The equanimity with which Britain accepted the renaissance of the U-boat arm was undoubtedly influenced by the confidence they placed in asdic, which, according to the Admiralty, 'had virtually extinguished the submarine menace'. Nevertheless, the world was stunned when, barely three months after the signing of the Anglo-German Naval Pact, three new coastal submarines emerged in September 1935, and at their head was 44-year-old Captain Karl Dönitz.

Dönitz, a determined and brilliant staff officer with real charisma, probably achieved his selection in part through his experience in motor torpedo-boats (MTBs), which gave him clear ideas of how he would employ submarines. Whatever the reasons, he was an inspired choice. He trained his embryonic force with a zeal born of his experience as a defeated U-boat captain in World War I and briefly a prisoner of war, and brought

Above: The concession by Britain to allow Germany to build submarines following the London Submarine Agreement in 1936 was not seen as a high risk. Asdic was (erroneously) considered to have turned submarines into toys. The Type VII, shown here, would prove to be some toy, and the Atlantic Ocean its playground.

Below: This German torpedo
preparation shop is a
reminder of the importance
of weapon evaluation in
peacetime. Both the Germans
and the Americans suffered
from problems with their
torpedoes before the war;
however, because of
bureaucratic ineptitude, very
little was done to correct the
faults. This was to cost both
submarine services dear.

them quickly to a high state of readiness. He was convinced of the efficacy of the night surface attack, correctly assessing that asdic had no capability against a surfaced submarine, and during his time in command of MTBs had evolved tactics that allowed him to hold onto his target at the limits of visibility by day, creep up on his target at dusk, and press home his attack when darkness fell. He also appreciated that a submarine with its low freeboard and small fin would be extremely difficult to see, even by the most alert lookout. Should the opposition use flares to try to improve visibility, this would work to the submarine's advantage probably more than to the defenders'. He was also guided by the principle of meeting numbers with numbers.

GERMAN U-BOAT TYPES

Recognizing that British commerce would once again be the primary target, Dönitz successfully resisted the temptation to build large, unwieldy submarines, and advocated building smaller craft in numbers. He demanded 300 submarines in order to keep 90 on patrol at any one time. There were doubts among the rest of the Naval Staff about the relative value of the submarine against commerce in comparison with the mighty surface raiders being constructed, and they received priority; nevertheless, the overarching Plan Z, due to be instituted by 1943, did allow for the construction of those 300 boats, and at the outbreak of war this plan was accelerated.

Donitz, however, entered the war with only 65 boats, of which the most numerous was the Type VII. These were brilliantly designed 762-tonne submarines capable of a top speed of over 17 knots on the surface, and a range of 10,458km (6500 miles) at 12 knots. Fitted with four forward torpedo tubes and one at the stern, they carried between 11 and 14 torpedoes. They were extraordinarily reliable, although no better than the British boats in terms of habitability, and bore the brunt of the anti-convoy actions. Their bigger sisters, the 1016-tonne Type IX, although more heavily armed, were less reliable in the rugged conditions of the Atlantic and tended to be employed as singletons in the deep field.

The U-boats were armed with T1 (compressed air) and T2 (electric) torpedoes, the latter leaving no wake and therefore harder to detect and avoid. To back up the weapons, they were also fitted with an advanced fire-control system that transmitted target bearing and other characteristics to a computer that automatically calculated the DA. The bridge firing sight was known as the UZO. Additionally, the torpedoes' gyro-angles were constantly updated, and these could be ordered to steer up to 90 degrees from ship's head to intercept the target's track. They also carried a deck gun.

FIRST-RATE OVERSEAS SUBMARINES

In submarine terms, the Americans were largely insulated from the terms of arms-limitation conventions, and, because of their lack of operational experience, they were selective about the lessons learned from World War I. Soon after the war, building on design features observed in the submarines that they received as prizes of war from Germany, they focussed on the 'fleet escort' concept, then looked at the 'cruiser', neither of which options satisfied the operators. Even though the primary role for the submarine was seen as an adjunct to the surface fleet, it was realized that, in order to cater for the huge distances that had to be covered from US bases in both the Atlantic and the Pacific, submarines had to have long range, high speed, good habitability, and a large magazine of weapons, as they could not 'pop back' for a reload.

The first class to be built incorporating these design features was the *Barracuda*-class of 2032/2641 tonnes, increasing to 12,192 tonnes at 11 knots, followed by the *Tambor*-class of 1854/2448 tonnes, increasing to 11,582 tonnes at 11 knots, with a maximum speed of 20 knots plus; 24 torpedoes or 40 mines; deck gun and AA mounting. This class, and the *Balao*-class

that followed it, was an outstanding overseas submarine, designated 'fleet submarine' by the Americans, with first-class sea-keeping qualities and excellent conditions for the crew, including air-conditioning. The fact that these submarines were built was testimony to the excellent relationships established between Commander Lockwood and Commander Christie (both future admirals) and the US Bureau of Ships. They were equipped with the excellent TDC (Torpedo Data Computer) that provided a torpedo gyro-angling facility. The United States Navy also had in service a number of ageing *S*-class, which

Above: Despite development problems with their submarines, the Americans never stopped pursuing the highest quality in design. They sought a large fleet-submarine with a trans-Pacific endurance, and the result was the excellent *Sargo* and *Tambor* classes. Capable of 20 knots, they were magnificent warships of high performance.

S28

SPECIFICATIONS

Country: USA
Launch date: 20 September 1922
Crew: 42
Displacement: 864 tonnes/1107 tonnes
Dimensions: 64.3m x 6.25m x 4.6m
(211ft x 20ft 6in x 15ft 3in)
Armament: Four 533mm (21in) torpedo tubes; one 102mm (4in) gun
Powerplant: Two-shaft diesels
Surface range: 6333km (3420nm) at 6.5 knots
Performance: 14.5 knots/11 knots

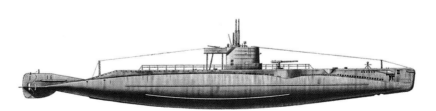

The *S*-class submarine was built in large numbers because it was the design then in production when the United States mobilised for World War I. As a result, these *S* boats formed the bulk of the US Submarine Service throughout the 1930s, and fought in substantial numbers in World War II. *S28* was lost during training in July 1944.

Japanese submarines were equipped with the Long Lance torpedo, unquestionably the most capable torpedo in the world. Propelled by oxygen, which made it wakeless, it could travel 11.2km (7 miles) at a speed of 50 knots.

they forward-based at Brisbane, Australia. These submarines had no air-conditioning and were manifestly unsuitable for the tropical conditions in which they operated, nor did they have the TDC facility. All submarines were armed with the Mk IV torpedo, an alcohol- and compressed air-driven weapon. They were all fitted with a sonar set (the equivalent to the British asdic). The United States entered World War II with 19 *S*-class and 73 *Tambor*-class in service or ordered.

THE RISE OF JAPAN

Japan was a growing industrial economy, and her tonnage 'allowance' under various declarations reflected her growing influence in the world. To establish her place on the international scene, she set out on a policy of expansionism in both political and military terms and, during the early 1930s, invaded Korea and Manchuria, with the longer term aim of dominating China and humbling the Soviet Union. Like Britain, Japan had few natural resources

Right: Despite the fact that they built large submarines, the Japanese, with typical disregard for comfort, curtailed crew endurance by failing to exploit the room available. They trained hard in peace, accepting losses in men and machines. Discipline was harsh, and physical punishment, in many cases abusive, was normal.

and relied heavily on imports; however, unlike Britain, she had no natural allies who might make up the deficiencies should she be subjected to a trade or physical blockade. So she matched her 'northern army strategy' with a 'southern naval strategy' – the domination of South-East Asia – in order to achieve economic self-sufficiency. The Navy she built up – once she had abandoned the 1936 protocol and before the West embargoed her supplies of oil and steel – was a phenomenal one, consisting of two gargantuan battleships, six fleet aircraft carriers and several light carriers (all carrying the impressive Zero fighter), and a multitude of supporting cruisers and destroyers. Its major draw-back was that its units were built for a single role and lacked technological sharpness in communications and asdic. The Japanese Navy was constructed for one single task – to win the 'grand battle' – and her strategists knew that they had to achieve victory quickly.

GIANTS AND MIDGETS

The Japanese, like many others, saw the submarine as an adjunct to the battlefleet whose purpose was to attrite an enemy fleet in its home waters to such an extent that the resultant 'big battle' was fought on favourable terms. The concept of attacking enemy merchant shipping (in the US case, off the Panama Canal) was considered to be a role unfit for 'warriors', so they concentrated on the construction of large, ocean-going submarines. There were three types: *B1*, a scout fitted with a seaplane to

DEPTH CHARGES AND HEDGEHOGS

The depth-charge had made its first appearance at the end of World War I, and the only improvement made since then was to incorporate variable depth settings to cover a bracket of potential depths adopted by an evading submarine. It was succeeded by the ahead-thrown 'Hedgehog' bomb, which overcame the inherent weakness of the escort having to steam over the position of its target, giving the evading boat a few vital seconds during which to alter course.

Below: Radar aerials on HMS *Unbeaten*. British development of radar started in 1935 with the historic 'Daventry Experiment' when an aircraft, flying in the beam of the BBC's 50m (164ft) shortwave station at Daventry, produced an echo in a receiver 13km (eight miles) away. Radar was fundamental in the defeat of the U-boat.

extend the range of reconnaissance; *A1*, a headquarters vessel, also fitted with a seaplane, but with extra accommodation and communications; and an attack variant, *C1*, with eight torpedo tubes and the capability of carrying midget submarines 'piggybacked' on the after-casing. The *I*-types were all were big submarines of more than 2032 tonnes, 107m (350ft) in length, capable of 23 knots on the surface, and with a range of more than 22,526km (14,000 miles) at the economical speed of

16 knots. Coastal submarines (*RO*-type) and a number of transport submarines also appeared in the order of battle.

All these submarines were equipped with the Long Lance torpedo, unquestionably the most capable torpedo in the world. Propelled by oxygen, which made it wakeless, it could travel 11.2km (7 miles) at a speed of 50 knots!

In addition to the 'traditional' submarine, the Japanese also built 'midgets' in large numbers. The most common, the *A*-type, were 23.7m (78ft) long and had two torpedo tubes protruding from the bow. They were battery driven and capable of speeds up to 19 knots dived to the extraordinary range of 29km (18 miles). It is fair to say that their two-man crews did not expect to return from their intended role of playing a decisive part in the 'big battle', having been launched from either a submarine or a mother ship.

AIR SURVEILLANCE

Another area of serious neglect between the wars was air surveillance. Airships and patrol aircraft had been used during the latter stages of World War I, yet their influence on forcing submarines to dive (thereby denying them the opportunity to attack or at least to spoil their fire control solution) had not been properly analysed. There was the further distraction within the airborne community of the birth of the Royal Air Force. This new organization was 'gung-ho' in outlook and, as well as denying the British Royal Navy any influence in post-war air strategy until the late 1930s, regarded anything 'defensive' in nature (which convoy protection was deemed to be) as second-class. As a result, Britain was woefully short of escort carriers at the beginning of World War II, and Coastal Command, with only medium-range aircraft, was very much the poor cousin. This left the huge 'Atlantic Air-Gap' for the first two years of the war, which, when combined with the short-sightedness of

ASDIC

Left: Just as the first equipment for radar was crude in the extreme, so the genesis of asdic appeared slightly prehistoric. Britain developed the listening hydrophone (seen here) through the 'Hawkshead Experiment' during World War I, and this was translated into an active and passive format during the 1920s.

At the end of World War I, Britain had established the Anti-Submarine Division Investigation Committee (ASDIC) to seek ways of building on her successes with both mobile and bottom-laid hydrophones (listening devices) during World War I. The greatest drawbacks of these early experiments had been the interference experienced by the listening ships from their own (self) noise and the lack of directional information on a contact if detected (i.e. inability to localize to attack). By 1920, the team of experts had devised the sonic beam emitted from a transducer housed in a dome under the bow of an escort, which sent out a 'ping' and received an echo back if it struck a solid object. Unfortunately, while it was a major step in being able to detect a submarine dived, it was not infallible because it could not distinguish between a submarine and a rock, or even a shoal of fish, nor could it detect a submarine on the surface. Regrettably, many in the British Naval Staff decided that the anti-submarine problem had been solved and, confident of the efficacy of the 1922 Declaration on the use of submarines in war, stuck their heads back into the sand, concentrating instead on battlefleet supremacy. This over-confidence on two fronts was to cost Britain dear yet again in the forthcoming conflict.

their fellow ostriches on the Naval Staff in failing to provide sufficient escort vessels, allowed the German U-boats a wonderfully 'happy time' for a significant, and very costly, period. Vice Admiral Sir Peter Gretton, a distinguished U-boat hunter during World War II, summed up the situation when later he wrote: 'we were criminally unprepared for the Battle of the Atlantic in 1939'.

Initially equipped with the medium-range Hudson bomber and Catalina flying boat, in June 1941, Coastal Command received her first Liberator (B24) long-range bomber. When fitted with additional fuel tanks and ASV radar, these were the only land-based aircraft capable of filling the 'mid-Atlantic' gap. They carried a formidable payload of 24 depth-charges. In addition to radar, maritime patrol aircraft (MPA) were eventually fitted with the

The Germans were unaware that the British could intercept their high-frequency transmissions, which carried heavy traffic when 'wolfpack' tactics were introduced. The plethora of 'chat' provided the Allies with positional and other invaluable information.

MERCHANT SHIP ORGANIZATION

After her experience in World War I, despite some continued reluctance, Britain was ready to go in terms of convoy organization. However, given the over-confidence in the capability of asdic, she was woefully short of escorts, being able to muster only 220, and quite a few of these received a mauling at Dunkirk. This resulted in her inbound convoys only picking up their protection at longitude 15W and outward bounders being similarly denuded at the same longitude. After that, there was the dreaded air-gap, and, until it was realized that Norway was firmly lost, even the accessible parts of the convoy routes received very little attention from Coastal Command.

Above: The German interpretation of international law was that ships in convoy could be attacked without warning. The 'liberal' ideals of war regulated by international treaty were dead in the water.

Leigh Light (a powerful searchlight), sonobuoys (listening hydrophones), and MAD (magnetic anomaly detector). The last two enabled the aircraft to locate a submarine which had gone deep.

Where Britain had not forgotten lessons were in the areas of control of merchant shipping – operated through the Naval Control Service (NCS), which had in place an NCS officer in every major port – and the value of intelligence, after the Zimmermann Telegram, generating the birth of the Naval Intelligence Division (NID).

ANTI-SUBMARINE INTELLIGENCE

The Government Code and Cipher School was given a new lease of life after the Abyssinian crisis of 1936, and its code-breaking activities were moved to Bletchley Park in England. Information from this organization was fed to the Operational Intelligence Centre (OIC), a subdivision of NID, under the command of Paymaster Lt. Cdr. Norman Denning. He pressed successfully for the establishment of a network of listening posts around the world which, in addition to providing signal intelligence (Sigint), provided the platform for radio-direction finding (RDF). The same signal received by a number of these posts could provide a 'fix' by triangulation on the source.

The Germans were unaware that the British could intercept their high-frequency transmissions which, because they were 'bounced' off the Earth's ionosphere, could travel very long distances. A refinement of these terrestrial listening posts was local intercept sets carried by convoy escorts known as Huff/Duff (high-frequency direction finding). This was a fatal flaw in German thinking because U-boats used the frequency band for their communications, which were by necessity heavy when 'wolf pack' tactics were introduced. The plethora of 'chat' provided the Allies with not only positional information, but eventually, when the 'Enigma' programme was fully in its stride, group intention and composition information as well.

By 1939, all the submarine and anti-submarine pieces of the jigsaw lay on the table waiting to be put together. It would not be long before the world saw how they would fit, in a conflict of global proportions.

Left: The depth-charge had proved an effective weapon during World War I, and it was believed that, in combination with asdic, it would prove to be the undoing of the submarine. Not only was the capability of asdic over-estimated, but another important fact was also overlooked in peacetime exercises. As the attacking ship had to steam over its target, the submarine had almost two minutes to evade the depth-charges that had been released.

WORLD WAR II

The German U-boats were quite unprepared for war with Great Britain in 1939. They totalled only 57 units, 30 of which were small and fit only for North Sea operations. The Germans considered that the first priority for the U-boat arm was to build up to the 300 submarines thought necessary to be decisive against the British convoy system.

In 1939, both the British and German submarine services began where they had finished in World War I, with British submarines pursuing warships and the Germans attacking commerce. In addition, it was recognized by the British that training anti-submarine warfare (ASW) platforms (frigates and aircraft) was an additional important role for submarines, and a number of the older submarines (H- and L-classes) were organized for this task.

The Royal Navy's greatest concern was to attempt to intercept those ships in which the Germans had made such heavy investment, the surface raiders *Deutschland*, *Graf Spee*, *Scharnhorst*, and *Gneisenau*. During exchanges in the 'Phoney War' period, there was 'blooding' by both sides. Royal Navy submarines were forward-deployed to the Heligoland Bight and off south-west Norway (areas where air superiority was not

Left: In addition to the torpedo, merchant ships also faced the threat of mines. This ship, the *Brisbane Star*, was part of a convoy to Malta in August 1942, and shows the damage that could be inflicted.

Above: The return of the *U47* to Germany on 25 October 1939, following the successful attack on the *Royal Oak* in Scapa Flow. Gunther Prien and his crew were fêted as national heroes. Churchill later described the raid as 'a remarkable exploit of skill and daring'.

enjoyed), and *Salmon* sank *U36* and damaged the cruisers *Leipzig* and *Nurnberg*. In return, the Germans sank three submarines in quick succession, even though the escorts were not yet fitted with asdic. *Triton* also torpedoed her sister *Oxley* after a mix-up in recognition signals, the first of five British submarines to be lost during the war in 'blue-on-blue' engagements between various elements of friendly forces. On the German side, Gunther Prien in *U47* penetrated Scapa Flow and sank *Royal Oak* with heavy loss of life, *U30* damaged the battleship *Barham*, and the battleship *Nelson* exploded a U-boat laid mine.

By November 1939, the Germans reverted to unrestricted submarine warfare against commerce, taking the view that even when not in convoy, a merchant ship that took any defensive measures whatsoever (including darkening ship at night or zig-zagging) forfeited its immunity under the conditions of 'prize rules'. However, when Lemp in *U30* sank the passenger liner *Athenia* on the first day of the war, he did it against orders and, like the *Lusitania* incident in World War I, it

did the German cause enormous harm overseas. It also had the effect of persuading the British to introduce the convoy system immediately. Nevertheless, the U-boat arm sank 762,037 tonnes of shipping (roughly five ships for every U-boat on patrol) in the first seven months of the war, and, by March 1940, all the battle-lines were drawn, although some tactics had yet to evolve.

At the outbreak of war, British ASW forces were very thin indeed. A mere 60 escorts and 40 Sunderland flying boats plus some short-ranged land-based reconnaissance aircraft were all that could be mustered. The British attempted to extend the range of air-coverage by deploying the two air-craft carriers *Courageous* and *Ark Royal* in the Western Approaches, but *U29* sank the former and *U39* very nearly got the latter, saved only by a 'premature' torpedo, so the idea was very quickly dropped. Like the Americans, the Germans employed an influence (magnetic) fuse that for a long time proved to be unreliable and prevented at least another 25 per cent of shipping being sunk. In return, 18 U-boats were lost (an exchange rate of 12.5 ships per loss), 11 to escorts and the rest to mines. What these initial skirmishes told the Germans (and the penny was dropping with the Royal Navy as well) was that asdic was not nearly as effective as both sides thought.

When France fell in June 1940, Germany lost no time in moving U-boat bases to the French coast, and Lorient was brought into operation in July. This was of enormous benefit to German submarines: passage time to the Atlantic was shortened, allowing 25 per cent more boats to patrols, rather than transit; they were spared the dangerous route of the North Sea with its mine and patrols; the short-legged Type II boats could be deployed in the Atlantic; and, finally, they also had the industrial capacity of the French to undertake repairs and maintenance.

THE START OF WOLFPACK TACTICS

These advantages now encouraged the U-boats to develop new tactics. Until now they had not enough submarines to employ wolf-pack tactics, Dönitz's brainchild, and

Left: The loneliness of command is well expressed in this photograph. The success of a submarine rested entirely on the shoulders and 'periscope eye' of the captain. A false move on his part could lead to the destruction of his ship and the loss of her crew.

TYPE IX

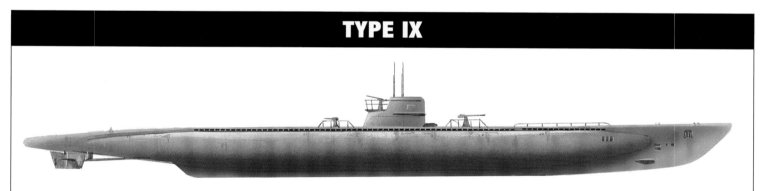

Nearly 200 of the large Type IX-boats were built in seven variants. They had an enormous range and endurance that allowed them to range as far away as the Indian Ocean without the need for a 'milch-cow'. In January 1942, these boats sank 58 ships totalling 300,000 tonnes, half of them valuable tankers.

SPECIFICATIONS

Country: Germany
Launch date: 1939
Crew: 48
Displacement: 1068 tonnes/ 2183 tonnes
Dimensions: 76.5m x 6.8m x 4.6m (251ft x 22ft 3in x 15ft)

Armament: Six 533mm (21in) TTs; one 102mm (4in) gun; one 20mm AA gun
Powerplant: Twin-screw, diesel-electric motors
Surface range: 13,993km (7552nm) at 10 knots
Performance: 18.2 knots/7.2 knots

U47

U47 was an early Type VIIB submarine, of which 24 were built (more than 600 Type VIICs were built). They were quieter, more reliable, and far more resilient against depth-charges than their predecessors. U47 was the submarine commanded by Lt. Cdr. Gunther Prien which, on 14 October 1939, sunk the battleship HMS Royal Oak inside Scapa Flow, one of the most daring submarine attacks of the war and a bitter blow to British prestige.

Radio aerial

Free-flood holes

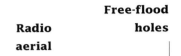

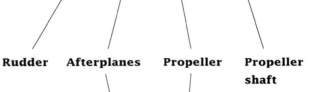

Bow torpedo tubes

Bow torpedo tubes

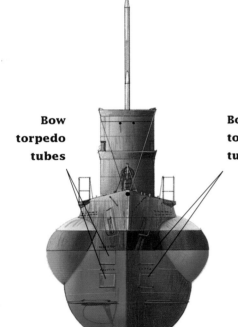

Rudder **Afterplanes** **Propeller** **Propeller shaft** **Saddle tank**

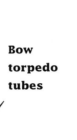

SPECIFICATIONS

Country: Germany
Launch date: 1938
Crew: 44
Displacement: 765 tonnes/871 tonnes
Dimensions: 66.5m x 6.2m x 4.7m (218ft x 20ft 3in x 15ft 6in)
Armament: Five 533mm (21in) TTs; one 88mm (3.5in) gun; one 20mm AA gun
Powerplant: Two-shaft diesel-electric motors
Surface range: 10,454km (5642nm) at 12 knots
Performance: 17.2 knots/8 knots

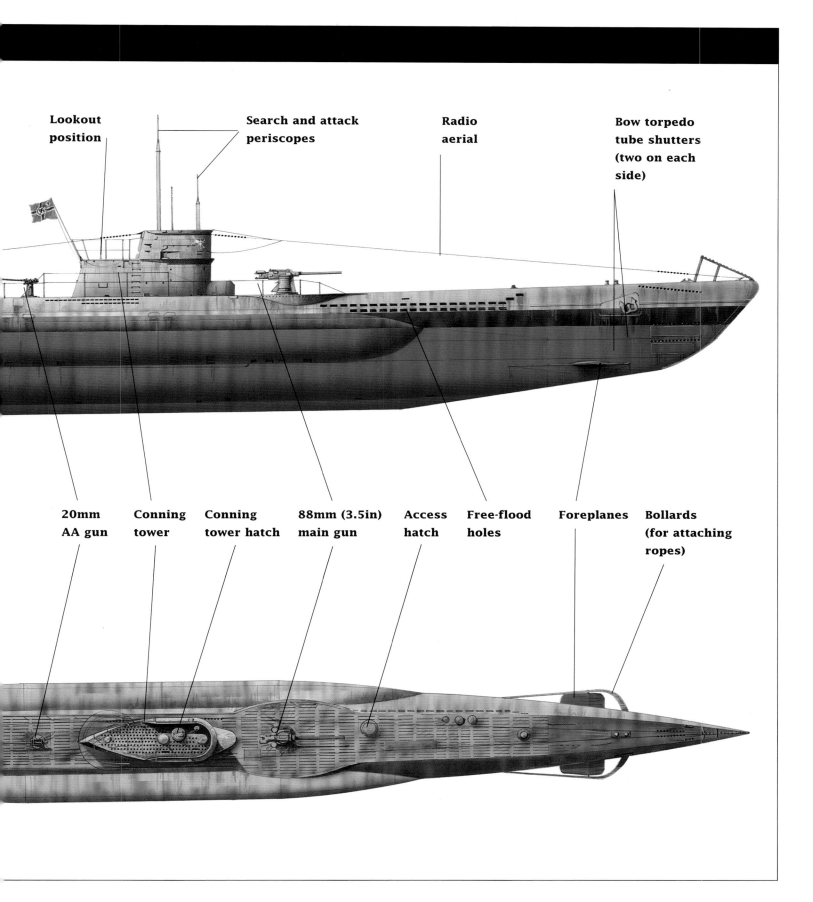

Lookout
position

Search and attack
periscopes

Radio
aerial

Bow torpedo
tube shutters
(two on each
side)

20mm
AA gun

Conning
tower

Conning
tower hatch

88mm (3.5in)
main gun

Access
hatch

Free-flood
holes

Foreplanes

Bollards
(for attaching
ropes)

he had already concluded that the best way to attack an escorted convoy was for his submarines to remain on the surface as long as possible, including the disengagement phase when it was necessary to reload their tubes, and to attack at night. In addition, as the first indication of a convoy's approach was usually ashore by signal intelligence, it was a relatively simple matter to line them up across the anticipated route. Once in contact, the U-boats were allowed to work individually. This ploy immediately reaped dividends, and, between June and October 1940, they sank 274 ships of 1.42 million tonnes. The winter months and bad weather, which slowed U-boat intercept speeds and made sighting a convoy much more difficult, slowed the massacre, but between February and June 1941 the pace picked up again, and they sank 400 ships of more than 2.1 million tonnes. U-boat building rates also increased to 10 a month, well ahead of losses, but significantly behind the 25 or so required by the original

Plan Z and well short of the numbers required to break Britain's 'tonnage bank'.

LEND-LEASE ESCORTS

Britain was alarmed, however, and stiffened her countermeasure programme. She obtained 50 obsolescent but nevertheless extremely valuable escorts from the United States under the Lease-Lend scheme, and 100 destroyers and 400 other escort vessels were ordered. Coastal Command's primary mission also fell into line, so, in March 1941, the Battle of the Atlantic was about to be properly engaged, with Iceland now being established as a forward airbase. The convoy system was extended to 35W, and the increased numbers of escorts allowed Canadian Escort Groups to meet their British counterparts in mid-Atlantic. Convoy HX129 in May 1941 became the first convoy to be escorted continuously across the 'pond'. In early 1941, there was still an air-gap of 480km (300 miles), but the presence of aircraft on the peripheries was beginning to

Below: It was the closing of the air-gap in the mid-Atlantic that began to swing the pendulum against the U-boat. Aircraft from USS *Bogue* (CVE-9) caught *U118* on the surface and conducted a depth-charge and gun attack on her. Her tracks indicate that she has been evading like fury, but to no avail.

TYPE XB

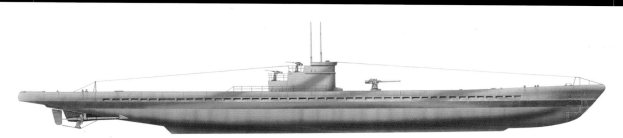

The eight Type XB minelayers were by far the largest submarines built for the Kriegsmarine. Their large size also made these boats suitable for use as supply boats, and *U116*, *U117*, and *U118* were regularly employed in this role. Towards the end of the war two boats, *U219* and *U234* were converted for use as long-range transports, to deliver men, equipment, and weapons to Germany's ally, Japan.

SPECIFICATIONS

Country: Germany
Launch date: 1941–43
Crew: 52
Displacement: 1735 tonnes/ 2143 tonnes
Dimensions: 89.8m 9.2m x 4.7m (294ft7in x 30ft 2in x 15ft 5in)

Armament: Two 533mm (21in) TTs; one 105mm (4in) gun; one 37mm gun; one 20mm AA gun
Powerplant: Twin-screw, diesel-electric motors
Surface range: 26,761km (14,450nm) at 12 knots
Performance: 16.4 knots/7knots

make itself felt, not least because they would slow U-boat progress on the surface by forcing them to dive to avoid detection. Additionally the coordination of wolf-pack operations required a huge amount of tactical voice traffic that gave away a lot of information to British listening stations. The Admiralty tracking-room never wasted an opportunity to determine where concentrations of U-boats existed, and re-routed convoys accordingly. Finally, defending British ASW forces achieved something of a coup in March 1941 when three U-boat aces were sunk off Iceland when attacking OB293 and HX112. The Germans had almost certainly suffered from overconfidence and paid a corresponding price.

Nevertheless, during this period and into early 1942, the U-boats continued to enjoy significant success, particularly against 'loners' in the South Atlantic when they patrolled off Sierra Leone and the Canary Islands. They sank 372 ships of 1.87 million

Left: The crew of a Type VII U-boat hauls in the fuelling line floated over to them from a *milchkuh* or tanker-submarine. Ten of these Type XIV supply boats were built, and each had the capacity to completely replenish four Type VIIs with everything except munitions.

'The Battle of the Atlantic was won because the Allies put an immense military, civil and scientific effort into it. They had to do this because the submarine, as a commerce raider, was a potentially decisive weapon of sea power ...'
Vice Admiral
Sir Arthur Hezlet

tonnes, including 81 independents, for the loss of only one of their number. This ratio of 81:1 should be compared with 6:1 for ships in convoy. However, the portents for the U-boat command were beginning to look much bleaker. Convoying was introduced into the South Atlantic route in July, and immediately the loss rate dropped to a ratio of 14:1 in all theatres. The United States formally entered the war in December 1941, and her shadow-boxing was now translated into solid punches. At about the same time, U-boats were used on a number of missions other than anti-commerce work, all of which weakened their effectiveness. Already used as weather-reporters and escorts for blockade-runners in the Bay of Biscay, in November 1941 they were ordered to render assistance to the naval effort in the Mediterranean. Italian submarine performance in the Atlantic had proved a great disappointment to their German allies, and

now they were failing to protect the supply lines of the Afrika Corps. This had the effect of bringing operations in the Atlantic to a complete halt for seven weeks. Indeed, during 1941, despite the fact that the U-boat arm had almost trebled in size, the capability of U-boats to sink more ships did not improve. Torpedo problems were still dogging Dönitz's submarines, they still had not woken up to the fact that they were having trouble finding convoys because of their plethora of radio signals, and they still had not found a way to alert submarines to the presence of radar, now being used with great effect by Allied escorts.

AMERICA ENTERS THE FRAY

America's entry into the war now offered the Germans another opportunity, however, as care no longer had to be taken against US-flagged ships and unrestricted warfare could be waged. The south-eastern coast of

TYPE XXI

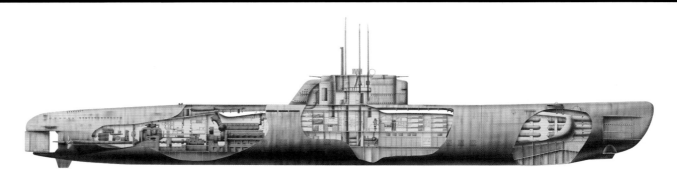

In 1943, Germany began to build submarines with an excellent submerged capability (the *Elektriko-U-boote*). Their ultimate quest was for the high-performance Walther-engine driven boat; however, until this could be perfected, they opted for the ocean-going, Schnorkel-fitted Type XXI and smaller Type XXIII. They had a dash speed of over 18 knots for an hour, or eight knots for nearly 24 hours. They arrived too late, however, to influence the course of the war.

SPECIFICATIONS

Country: Germany
Launch date: 1944–45
Crew: 57
Displacement: 1595 tonnes/ 1790 tonnes
Dimensions: 76.7m x 6.6m x 6.3m (251ft 8in x 21ft 8in x 20ft 8in)

Armament: Six 533mm (21in) TTs; four 20mm guns
Powerplant: Twin-screw, diesel-electric motors, silent creeping motors
Surface range: 17,934km (9678nm) at 10 knots
Performance: 15.5 knots/16 knots

the United States and the Caribbean were well within the range of the larger Type-IX (762-tonne) U-boats, and New York could be reached by the Type-VII, so Dönitz pressed for 12 boats to be despatched as quickly as possible before convoys were introduced. Initially, he was only allowed to send five, but they were soon in their stride, with *U123* sinking eight ships off Cape Hatteras in a 24-hour period! In their operational area between St Lawrence and the Cape, by February, 12 U-boats had sunk 508,025 tonnes of shipping, about half of it in tankers. The Americans (most notably the Anglophobe Admiral King, Chief of Naval Operations) obstinately refused to learn the British lesson of convoying from the outset, and these losses were little short of a scandal in ineptitude. Fortunately, there was an equally stubborn Führer who failed to press home his advantage by insisting that sufficient submarines be retained to guard against a re-invasion of Norway and so 20 potential attackers were withheld from the fray. In February and March, losses soared to unsustainable levels (1.52 million tonnes – exchange rate 198:1) – so even the most blinkered dinosaur could see that convoy was the only way to apply a tourniquet to the gushing artery of lost tonnage. At the same time, the first *milchkuw*, *U459*, appeared on the scene to extend the endurance of the boats in the theatre. The battle continued with the U-boats retaining the upper hand through May and June. By the end of July, 681 ships of 3.55 million tonnes had been sunk with the loss of only 11 U-boats; however, in August, the pendulum finally swung against the U-boats when three of their number were sunk and two more seriously damaged. Thus they were finally driven from the east coast 'happy hunting ground', but not before this brilliant strategic move had reduced carrying capacity for the forthcoming Allied reinforcement of both Europe and North Africa, and had seriously worried General Marshall, the US Army Chief of Staff.

The first strokes of the 'writing on the wall' were beginning to appear. The United States' huge industrial capacity soon made up the U-boat–induced deficiencies in tonnage, and, in addition to forcing the U-boat to leave western Atlantic waters, Allied ASW forces were beginning to get the upper hand in the eastern Atlantic, sinking 32 boats in the equivalent period, ominously eight by aircraft in a single month. The downward spiral of inexperience leading to losses, and further inexperience leading to further losses, was beginning to show; despite the fact that German submarine numbers had passed the magic 300, the balance was beginning to tip against them. The Allies now had 400 escorts in the Atlantic, and Coastal Command had increased their strength to 500 aircraft, many of which were fitted with the Leigh Light, a powerful searchlight that was switched on at the last

Above: Sharing the confined space of a U-boat, while extremely uncomfortable, nevertheless generated a great team spirit. These brothers-in-arms paid a heavy price, for, of the 40,900 men who served in U-boats during World War II, 25,870 lost their lives (63 per cent).

THE WALTHER ENGINE

The Walther Engine, using Ingolin (highly concentrated hydrogen peroxide), offered an enormous increase in submerged mobility, thus making a true 'submarine', rather than a 'submersible', possible. Ingolin is a liquid, which is not only the most compact way to carry oxygen (which it gives up when passed over a catalyst), but is also a fuel, as this process involves the generation of heat. The oxygen, when released from the Ingolin, is burnt with a sulphur-free fuel; more water is injected generating more steam, which is then passed through turbines to drive the submarine. The exhaust leaves no track. Ingolin was dangerous to handle and about 10 times more explosive than fuel oil.

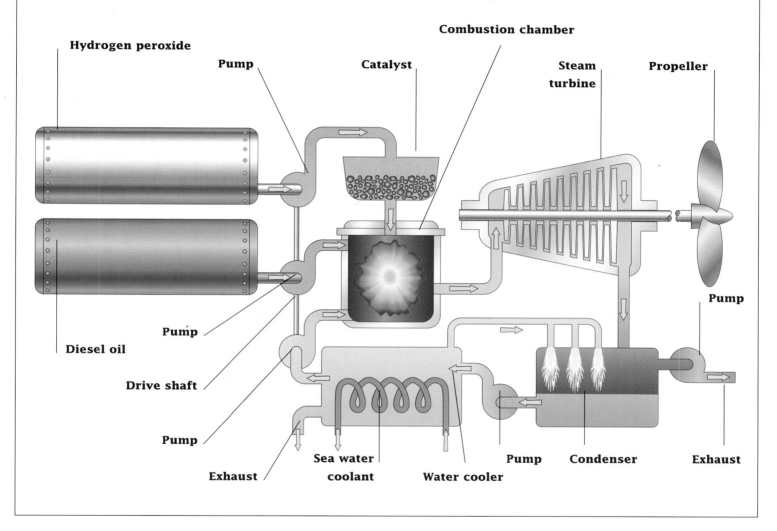

minute to catch a surfaced U-boat. Where the longer-range U-boats were still enjoying considerable success, however, was in the Cape Horn area and out in the Indian Ocean where there were still many independents, and so on paper the battle was finely poised for 1943, with an exchange rate of 10:1.

By May 1943, longer-range shore-based Allied aircraft and those carried by escort carriers finally bridged the air-gap and began to make their presence felt. This was reinforced by the use of bigger convoys, thereby economizing on the number of escorts required. In April, convoy HX233 lost only one ship to a pack of 20 U-boats, and convoy ONS5, although losing 12 ships, retaliated by sinking seven U-boats. It was May that saw the pendulum finally swing.

Left: A German hydrographer compiling coastal traffic information for U-boats at sea. The U-boat campaign cost the Allies 2828 ships totalling 14.7 million tonnes worldwide, the vast majority of it in the Atlantic.

Above: One of the five Japanese Type-A midget submarines that attempted to infiltrate Pearl Harbor is beached. Four were sunk and one ran aground during this disaster for the submarine force, of which so much was expected at the beginning of the war in the Pacific.

Sixty U-boats in four packs sank only 26 merchant ships for the loss of 27 of their number; during the entire month, the convoy exchange rate fell to 0.5:1. Elsewhere, most notably in the Bay of Biscay, U-boats were also suffering, and, for the first time, the loss of 41 submarines in a single month exceeded the replacement rate. As a result, Dönitz ordered the withdrawal of his boats from the North Atlantic and the battle against commerce and the convoys had been lost; 250 of the 650 boats that had been thrown into the battle had been sunk.

On paper, it would appear that the battle against the U-boat was easily won by the Allies. However, Churchill's statement that the 'only thing that worried him was the U-boat' belies this. By alienating the United States, with her huge industrial capacity, early in the conflict – this time through the sinking of *Athenia* – Germany repeated her mistake of World War I. By failing to build enough submarines during the critical year of 1942, she missed a vital opportunity to

buy sufficient time for her later submarine improvements (the electric homing torpedo, the Schnorkel, the Walther Engine submarine, the Type-XXI and Type-XXIII submarines, anechoic (anti-asdic) coating) to play a significant part in the war. By using the wolf-pack system with its excessive communications, Germany played into the hands of superior British use of intelligence. But she was also up against a highly capable enemy, who was both technically and tactically superior. The value of the convoy was quickly recognized as a means not only of protecting vital commerce, but also as a honey-pot for submarines where asdic (overrated, but it still sank 100 U-boats) and radar could be used in the counteroffensive. The Allies also appreciated that there was not a bottomless pit of expertise within the U-boat ranks (remember the figures for World War I!), and the convoy was their selected battle-ground to weaken their enemy to an effective degree.

THE BATTLE OF THE PACIFIC

The Japanese conducted the first submarine action seen in the Pacific, and much was expected of them. Three *B1* scouts preceded the Carrier Group on its way to attack Pearl Harbor in December 1941; a mixture of 30 *B1*s, *A1*s, and *C1*s (with three rear admirals in attendance!) were positioned well ahead of the group to attack any ships escaping from the raid; and five type-A were to enter the Pearl Harbor horseshoe to add to the confusion of the air raids. The expeditionary raid of the midgets turned into a fiasco, with four being sunk and one running aground, her captain S/Lt Kazuo Sakamaki becoming the first Japanese prisoner of war. The remaining squadrons sank a number of merchant ships over the coming days, but all in all it was a hugely disappointing foray for the Japanese submarine community. A submarine (*I-58*) played a minor part in the sinking of *Repulse* and the *Prince of Wales* off the Malay coast when she reported the ships' presence to the land-based aircraft commander in Saigon, a minor compensation for the huge submarine effort that had been committed.

The first interactions with the enemy by US submarines as the Japanese invasion force approached Luzon revealed two unexpected but horrifying prospects to the Submarine High Command. The first was that many of the commanding officers were simply not up to the task of operating a submarine in wartime (40 out of 135 COs were to be relieved early); the second was that there was a major problem with the Mk XIV torpedo – a number of COs reported it hitting targets without exploding.

Captain Edward L. Beach, US Navy, a wartime CO, described the misbehaviour of submarine torpedoes as 'scandalous' and insisted that 'the early years of the war saw many failed torpedo shots, and a controversy erupted over what had caused them. The argument was finally sorted out in 1943; the torpedoes had been carelessly designed and built, and insufficiently tested. We were aiming them well, but no amount of good aim

A MIDGET SUCCESS

The first success for a Japanese midget submarine was against the British battleship *Ramilles* in Diego Suarez harbour on the north-eastern tip of Madagascar. She was there to protect the British supply route for the Middle East via the Cape of Good Hope. Having been spotted by the reconnaissance aircraft of *A1* Headquarters submarine *I-10*, on 29 May 1942, the same night she became the target for two midgets launched from *I-16* and *I-20*. *I-16*'s craft was lost, but *I-20* pressed home her attack successfully, damaging the battleship and sinking a 7112-tonne escorting tanker. On completion of the raid, the battery exhausted, the midget submarine was beached and later surrounded. Rather than be taken prisoner, the crew of two shot themselves.

could get a hit with a torpedo that did not run as touted.' The reason for this he explained was that 'the problem lay in the much-vaunted magnetic exploders, which at times would not detonate, but on other occasions would go off early, giving away the presence of the submarine and often subjecting it to a gratuitous depth-charging [they also ran 30m (10ft) deeper than set]. The submarine force was paying dearly for the total absence of any peacetime firings with the magnetic exploder and for the inadequacy of exercise firings with the Mk XIV torpedo. Making matters worse, the Bureau of Ordnance tried to defend its work. They asked if the submariners were sure they were aiming the torpedoes correctly, whether torpedoes had been maintained and made ready properly. It was a bad example of staff-line relationships.' according to Vice Admiral James F. Calvert)

Above: HMNLS *KXVI* was one of a handful of US and Dutch submarines which tried, unsuccessfully, to stem the tide of the Japanese invasion in Far East waters in its initial stages. The Dutch were outstandingly capable and courageous submariners.

The combination of faults meant that the 44 US boats, and a few Dutch submarines, made no impression whatsoever on the huge Japanese invasion force; indeed, only 10 enemy ships of 43,690 tonnes were sunk for the loss of four Dutch *K*-class, with *KXVI* (Lt. Cdr. L.J. Jarman RNN) being the first Allied submarine to be sunk by a Japanese depth-charge. In return, the Japanese had shown themselves to lack a proper strategy for defending their merchant shipping and to be short of escorts, but this message was lost on the Chief of Naval Operations, Admiral Ernest King. This brilliant officer ('more feared than loved') obstinately stuck to the principle of using submarines only against major military units and entirely missed the opportunity to foreshorten the war by striking at Japan's weakest point – her reliance on supply lines.

US SUBMARINES FULFIL POTENTIAL

Over the next 18 months, there were to be major battles between the two opposing fleets dominated by aircraft carriers at Midway, Coral Sea and Guadalcanal, with a minimal contribution from the submarine service. When they did get into an advantageous position, more often than not their torpedoes let them down. In August 1942, however, a capability was added to US submarines that would fully unlock their potential in due course, and that was the centimetric SJ radar, first trialled in USS *Haddock*, but it was going to be another year before all the problems with the torpedo were to be finally resolved. It was not until September 1943 that they got into their stride – and then they ran with a vengeance. Armed with intelligence information derived from cryptanalysis to get them into the right general area, the submarines' radar could pick up large ships out to 27,432m (30,000yds); on a plan position indicator (PPI), rather than the older A-scope, the commanding officer could see the relative picture of contacts within range with absolute clarity. This allowed a plot of target movements to be evaluated; thus, provided they remained clear of air patrols, submarines could remain on the surface even in daylight and choose their optimum approach course, usually getting ahead of their targets and lying in wait. By the time they were ready to attack, they had a clear idea of target parameters in terms of course and speed, the zig-zag plan in force, and even the disposition of the escorts. For a submarine commanding officer this is close to heaven! The Japanese response to rising losses was, at long last, to convoy, but their effort, with too few escorts – which were further hampered by having no radar – was too little, too

Below: The demise of a Japanese escort, having been torpedoed by a US submarine, possibly following a 'down the throat' shot. This tactic called for great nerve and confidence. The graticules in the periscope were used by the commanding officer to estimate target height and length.

late, as the Americans were able to respond by introducing their version of wolf-pack tactics. Unlike those of the German U-boats that used mass numbers, only three US submarines would participate, with the senior commanding officer (or later a specially appointed senior officer) in tactical command and coordinating the effort. Standard tactics called for two of the group standing off on the flanks, while one ran into attack. The attacker would then drop back to reload while the next conducted an attack, and so on. No confusion, no profusion of communications.

It was in a singleton, however, that the US submarine service was to find its first hero: Lt. Cdr. Dudley W. 'Mush' Morton, of USS *Wahoo*, operating from Midway Island in the north mid-Pacific Ocean. Morton epitomized the new breed of submarine commanding officer. He was cool under pressure, brilliantly aggressive, and revered by his crew whom he trained to perfection. During his first patrol, he conducted the first successful 'down the throat' shot. Rather than lowering his periscope and going deep when threatened by an escort, he would leave it raised, enticing the hunter to charge it in readiness for a depth-charge attack. At the last moment (at about 914m (1000yds) range), he would fire a salvo of torpedoes in anticipation that, when they were seen by the enemy lookouts, the ship would alter course to evade them. Such was the spread that no matter which way this

Above: On war patrol in the Western Pacific, USS *Batfish* slices through the water at high speed on her way to intercept a target possibly detected on her SJ (surface search) radar. Once the target was sighted, it was up to the commanding officer to work his submarine into a firing position, ideally about 915m (1000 yards) on the beam.

I-400

Japan did not use its submarines wisely during World War II. Japanese naval strategy was drawn towards grand and decisive engagements – such as Pearl Harbor – and the covert nature of submarine warfare did not seem to serve this goal. Perhaps the best evidence of the Japanese planners' failure to understand the role of the submarine can be found in the *STO*-class, the largest submarines to be built during the war, of which submarine *I-400* was the first. They were aircraft-carrying submarines, drawn up as part of a futile plan to launch air raids on the Panama Canal. The practicalities of such a vessel surfacing, opening huge watertight doors, launching aircraft, and submerging again – let alone recovering the aircraft later – hardly bear thinking about, but it was accomplished successfully in training.

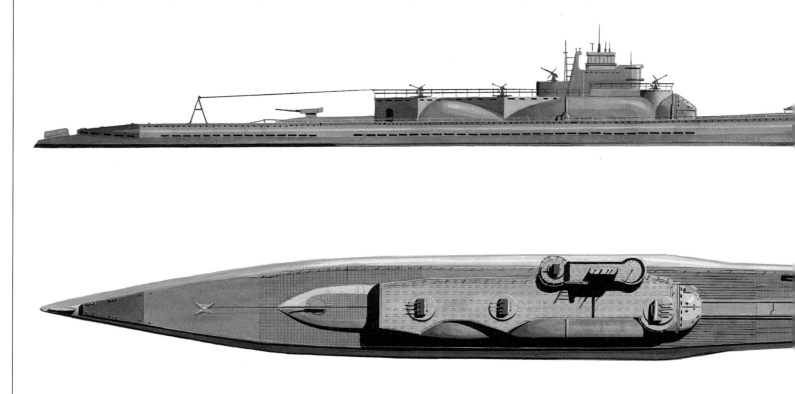

evasion took place, a hit would be assured. This evolution took immense nerve. During his second patrol in the shallows of the Darien peninsula between China and Japan, Morton established an all-time record for a US submarine by sinking nine ships; for this he received the Medal of Honour. *Wahoo* was lost on her fifth patrol, bombed to destruction by a Japanese naval plane in the shallow waters of the south Sea of Japan.

During the second half of 1942, submarines on both sides found themselves drawn into the struggles for the Solomon Islands. The Americans established a blockade of the main Japanese base at Truk, from where the Solomons campaign was supported. Here they sank 23 supply ships, contributing substantially to the US victory in the area. It was in this period, around Guadalcanal, that the Japanese achieved their most important successes of the war. On 15 October, *I-19* sank the aircraft carrier *Wasp* and damaged the battleship *North Carolina*. *Saratoga*, recently repaired, was again torpedoed and damaged, this time by *I-26*, who later sank the cruiser *Juneau*. *I-76* damaged the cruiser *Chester*. Before they could follow up on their successes,

SPECIFICATIONS

Country: Japan
Launch date: 1944
Crew: 144
Displacement: 3530 tonnes/6560 tonnes
Dimensions: 122m x 11.9m x 7m
(400ft 3in x 39ft 4in x 23ft)
Armament: Eight 533mm (21in) TTs;
one 140mm (5.5in) gun; ten 25mm AA
guns; three aircraft
Powerplant: Twin screws, diesel-electric
motors, plus electric motors
Surface range: 68,561km (37,000nm)
at 14 knots
Performance: 18.7 knots/6.5 knots

however, they were drawn off as supply vessels (by reducing to only torpedoes and one gun, they could carry 71 tonnes of stores) to keep their garrisons alive. From November 1942 to February 1943, up to 20 submarines were so employed, and during that time they lost 10 of their number, sunk mainly by surface ships that would detect them initially on radar and relocate them on sonar.

In 1943, American submarines severely curtailed the Japanese war effort; in 1944, they decimated it and wrought wholesale destruction on her merchant fleet. In 1943,

the sinking rate was between 50,800 tonnes and 203,210 tonnes per month, while in 1944 this rose to more than 203,210 tonnes per month, every month. Most significantly they helped to reduce Japan's tanker capacity from 711,235 tonnes to less than 203,210 tonnes in a very short space of time. In the meantime, the main strength of the Japanese submarines were drawn into operations wherever the Americans attacked, and there was a marked increase in their losses, with 23 being sunk. Quite simply, they were too big and 'unhandy', and were no match for radar and sonar; their

Above: USS *Tang*, under the command of Commander Richard O'Kane, was the all-time 'ace' of the US Submarine Service. Deprived of getting into its stride early in the conflict because of torpedo problems, this outstanding force accounted for 57 per cent of enemy shipping losses in the Pacific and paid the highest human price.

Right: Amid the symbols of victory (the broomstick for a clean sweep and flags for ships sunk), two exultant crew members of a US submarine stand on its ice-caked deck in the US naval base at Dutch Harbor in Alaska.

By the end of the war, US submarines had accounted for 57 per cent of Japanese shipping losses with 5.08 million tonnes sunk (including 127 warships, 25 of them submarines), at a loss to themselves of 52 submarines out of 288. Their all-time 'ace' was Commander Richard O'Kane of USS *Tang*, whose tally was 24 ships of 94,899 tonnes.

A DESPERATE LAST RESORT

The Japanese made strenuous efforts to enhance her submarines' capability during 1943 and 1944, and began to fit radar; it was, however, greatly inferior to that of the Americans. In 1943, too, the Japanese began to develop the human 'suicide' torpedo. Known as 'Kaitens' and launched from mother submarines, they were fast and powerful torpedoes steered by a man inside them using a periscope. They were first used against stationary targets, but later were used against ships under way. Despite the numbers fired, they achieved extremely poor results and many of their mother submarines were lost as well. The deployment of such weapons was a sure sign of a failed naval strategy. Right at the end of the war, they were to enjoy one final success when *I-58* sank the unescorted cruiser *Indiana*.

only success was the sinking of the auxiliary aircraft carrier *Liscombe Bay* during the Gilbert Island operations.

During 1944, American wolf-packs (e.g. 'Blair's Blasters' and 'Donk's Devils') sank 603 ships of 2.74 million tonnes, and sealed the fate of the Japanese merchant service. They also played an important role in the final major confrontations between the two navies. When, in June, the Japanese sortied to oppose the Saipan landings – a future forward airbase for the USAF and the start of the Battle of the Philippine Islands – US submarines not only alerted the American carriers to the south, but also sank two of the Japanese flat-tops before they came into action. They were to bag another five aircraft carriers, five light cruisers, and 30 destroyers during the year, contributing significantly to the forthcoming outright victory. By now there was very little of the Japanese Navy left afloat, and by 1945 their war was virtually over. They continued their contribution in other ways, most notably in air-sea rescue duties, during which they picked up 380 downed aviators.

The Japanese deployed 190 submarines during the war and lost 129. They sank 184 merchantmen totalling 914,445 tonnes, plus two aircraft carriers, two cruisers, 10 destroyers, and some smaller vessels including submarines. This total represents about 7112 tonnes per submarine lost, and 5080 tonnes per submarine deployed.

The British rebuilt their submarine presence in the Far East from 1943 onwards,

A DREADFUL IRONY

One of the most ghastly aftermaths of a sinking of a ship occurred when *I-26*, who had previously damaged the carrier *Saratoga*, sank the cruiser USS *Juneau* in November 1942 during the Guadalcanal campaign. *Juneau* blew up and sank almost immediately, but 200 men took to the water. Only 10 survived following a constant feeding frenzy by sharks.

TENCH

USS *Tench* was the lead boat in the *Tench* class, the ultimate evolution of the US wartime fleet submarine. About 30 of the class were built before the war ended. Despite their excellent basic engineering it was not until late 1943 that the US submarine fleet became truly effective due to poor torpedo design, which frequently led to the weapons misfiring or failing to explode. Once remedied the US attack submarines became so successful that follow-on orders were cancelled because the existing force had virtually run out of Japanese targets. During her final war patrol in 1945, *Tench* was attacked by two Japanese bombers but escaped, and survived the war unscathed. The *Tench* and her sister-ships went on to form the backbone of the US submarine fleet until the early 1960s.

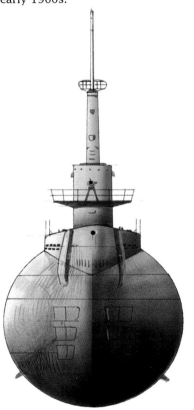

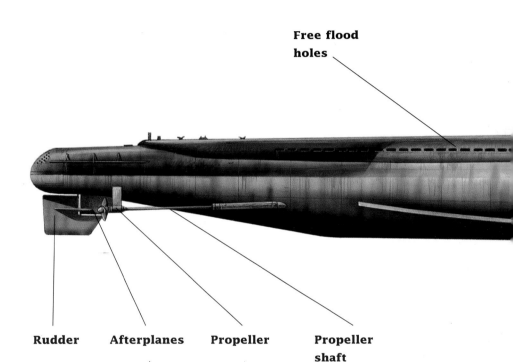

Free flood holes

Rudder   **Afterplanes**   **Propeller**   **Propeller shaft**

SPECIFICATIONS

Country: USA
Launch date: 7 July 1944
Crew: 80
Displacement: 1570 tonnes/2415 tonnes
Dimensions: 94.9m x 8.3m x 4.7m (311ft 8in x 27ft 3in x 15ft 5in)
Armament: 10 533mm (21in) TTs; one 76mm (3in) main gun; two 12.6mm AA machine guns
Powerplant: twin screw diesel/electric motors, plus electric motors
Surface range: 20,372km (11,000nm) at 10 knots
Performance: 20.2 knots/8.7 knots

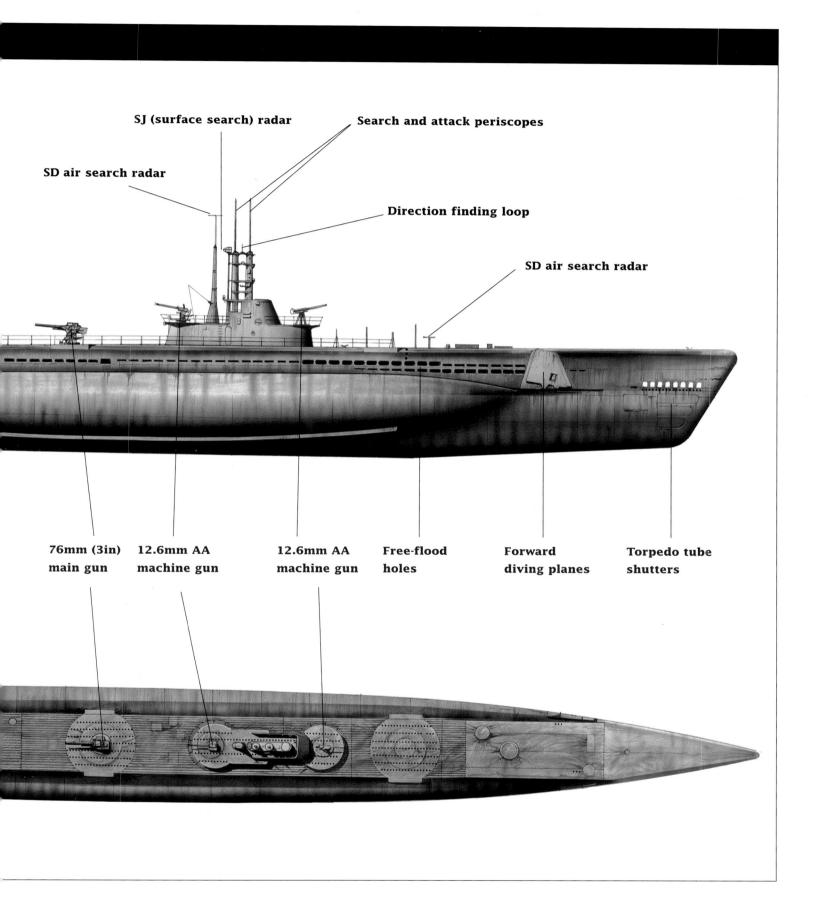

SJ (surface search) radar

SD air search radar

Search and attack periscopes

Direction finding loop

SD air search radar

76mm (3in) main gun

12.6mm AA machine gun

12.6mm AA machine gun

Free-flood holes

Forward diving planes

Torpedo tube shutters

when units could be spared from the Mediterranean. In the main, they were less equipped to operate in the tropics than their US counterparts and were restricted to the shallow waters of the Malacca Strait, where the pickings were much slimmer. In June 1945, however, there was a small compensation for all the toil when *Trenchant* sank the cruiser *Ashigara* in the Banka Straits, and an 'XE' craft, in a daring raid on Singapore, further damaged the cruiser *Takao.* During this last operation, two Victoria Crosses were won and drew to a fitting close the British submarine effort, which had been sustained since 1939.

The American submarine campaign was probably the most important factor in the defeat of Japan and demonstrated that a force, which never constituted more than three per cent of the US Navy, could conduct a *guerre de course* that could beat a nation dependent on the sea.

THE BATTLE OF THE MEDITERRANEAN

During World War II, both sides needed to control the Mediterranean in order to achieve their long-term objectives: the Axis to sustain the Afrika Corps, whose purpose was to control North Africa and capture the Suez Canal before joining up with the supposedly successful Germany Army sweeping all before it in Russia; the Allies to provide a launch pad from which to attack the 'soft underbelly of Europe' and liberate the continent. The protection of Allied trade routes through the Mediterranean was not an issue in the early stages because Britain realized that she could not 'command the sea' as she lacked air superiority and had therefore routed all inbound merchant traffic around the Cape of Good Hope. Thus the situation that saw the Allies controlling the ends, and the Axis controlling the middle, of the Mediterranean made the successful operation of submarine forces of both sides crucial to the battle.

The Italians had 121 submarines at the outbreak of war, of which 30 were 'ocean-goers' and the remainder 'sea-goers'. They were generally reliable, but were inferior in performance to German U-boats; nor were the crews trained in night surface attack.

RUBIS

SPECIFICATIONS

Country: France	Dimensions: 65.9m x 7.1m	Powerplant: Twin-screw,
Launch date: 30 September	x 4.3m (216ft 1in x 23ft 3in	diesel-electric motors
1931	x 14ft 6in)	Surface range: 12,971km
Crew: 42	Armament: Three 550mm	(7000nm) at 7.5 knots
Displacement: 773	(21.7in) TTs; two 400mm	Performance: 12 knots/9
tonnes/940 tonnes	(15.7in) TTs; one 76mm	knots
	(3in) gun; 32 mines	

The Free-French minelayer *Rubis* was an outstanding performer during World War II under her two Commanding Officers, Capitaine de Corvette Goerges Cabanier DSO and Lieutenant de Vaisseau Henri Rousselot DSO DSC*** (the most decorated Allied Officer).

ADUA

Adua was lost in September 1941 off Algeria, while attacking the British Gibraltar fleet. She was one of 66 Italian submarines sunk during the war for the meagre return of sinking just three British cruisers and damaging three others; half of these results were achieved against the 'Pedestal' convoy in August 1942.

SPECIFICATIONS

Country: Italy
Launch date: 13 September 1936
Crew: 45
Displacement: 690 tonnes/ 861 tonnes
Dimensions: 60m x 6.5m x 4m (197ft 6in x 21ft x 13ft)

Armament: Six 533mm (21in) TTs; one 100mm (3.9in) gun
Powerplant: Twin-screw diesel engines, electric motors
Surface range: 4076km (2200nm) at 10 knots
Performance: 14 knots/7.5 knots

They were ineffective in the Atlantic and were to enjoy little success in their *nostre mare*, which was the cause of the diversion of German U-boats into the theatre.

The British submarine campaign also got off to an inauspicious start when war with Italy was declared in June 1940. Ten of the older 'overseas' British submarines had been moved from the Far East to Alexandria when pre-war relationships began to be strained, but, apart from the sighting of the Italian battlefleet by *Phoenix* that led to the Battle of Calabria, they achieved little else, and the Italians were able to supply their armies in North Africa and Greece without impediment. The Italians had laid more than 12,000 mines around their main bases in the first month of the war, and these claimed three submarine casualties. Even though Italian escorts were yet to be fitted with asdic, relying on listening hydrophones only, they still managed to sink another five. In these early months, British submarines therefore paid a heavy price for leaking external fuel tanks and a lack of

realistic training. In addition, the 46 French submarines operational in the western Mediterranean immediately withdrew from the conflict. Only one submarine joined the Free French forces.

Matters improved for the Allies at the end of 1940 when four *T*-class were recalled from the Far East, and another four new arrivals joined them in Alexandria. In addition, 10 new *U*-class were sent out from the United Kingdom and were based on Malta, and became the famous 'Fighting Tenth'. Although of moderate performance and armament, they were to prove highly suitable for the Mediterranean. A third flotilla of *T*-boats was established at Gibraltar. All of these submarines were manned crews who were well trained, experienced and of high morale. The serious battle was about to be joined.

Between February and May 1941, 25 Axis heavy surface- and air-escorted convoys transported the Afrika Corps, consisting of 82,000 men and 508,025 tonnes of stores, to Libya. Because the Luftwaffe controlled the air space in the central Mediterranean, only its enemies' submarines were able to curtail this movement, and they managed to sink five per cent of the force; this was sufficient to worry General Rommel. British submarines also engaged in some activities that were to become more familiar as time went on: they sank a heavy unit of the Italian Fleet and two of their U-boats; they were used as beacons during the ill-fated British invasion of Crete; *Truant* led the bombardment of Tripoli; and *Rorqual* laid her minefields.

BRITISH STRANGLEHOLD ON THE AFRIKA KORPS

Thinking that the job was done, and more concerned with Russia than North Africa, the Luftwaffe withdrew most of their aircraft. This allowed the British to re-establish an air striking force in Malta and for a squadron of cruisers and destroyers to return to the central Mediterranean; British submarine numbers increased, with the sturdy *S*-class joining in. The attack on the Axis communication lines to North Africa now began in earnest. In addition to attacking ships, aircraft provided a great deal of reconnaissance which, although of no immediate tactical use to submarines, nevertheless built up a good overall strategic picture against which patrols could be planned. Just as in the Atlantic, intelligence through breaking Italian cyphers was also to play a significant part in the ultimate defeat of the Axis in this theatre. Ominously for Rommel, the name Wanklyn in *Upholder* was beginning to appear regularly on the score sheet, his efforts culminating in a brilliant attack on the Italian troopships *Neptunia* and *Oceania*. It had been recognized that the Italians were in the habit of running two fast troop convoys each month when there was no moon on a fairly standard route. In August 1941, three submarines were deployed in plenty of time to take advantage of this force of habit, and *Upholder* took full advantage. For this action, Wanklyn was awarded the VC.

During the remainder of 1941, the Afrika Korps was to be consistently denied the supplies required to sustain operations, and the Allies were able to reinforce Egypt from around the Cape and through the Suez Canal.

U-CLASS

The British *U*-class submarine was tiny, but it packed a mighty punch in the confined waters of the Mediterranean. A flotilla of 10 boats was sent out to Malta during 1941. Although of moderate performance and armament, they were manned by crews of high morale, who were trained and experienced in home waters. They became known as the 'Fighting Tenth'.

SPECIFICATIONS

Country: Great Britain
Launch date: 1937–1943
Crew: 31
Displacement: 554 tonnes/752 tonnes
Dimensions: 54.9m x 4.8m x 3.8m (180ft x 16ft x 12ft 9in)
Armament: Four 533mm (21in) TTs; one 76mm (3in) gun
Powerplant: Twin-screw, diesel-electric motors
Surface range: 7041km (3800nm) at 10 knots
Performance: 11.2 knots/10 knots

Submarines accounted for 44 per cent of Axis losses, while aircraft dealt with 34 per cent, surface ships 12 per cent, and the remainder were lost to the mine and other causes. British submarines also engaged the Italian fleet and, following the British retreat from Crete, found themselves also evacuating soldiers in some numbers. The loss of Crete also made supplying Malta more difficult, and so the 'magic carpet' run of supply submarines became established, with aviation fuel, ammunition, food, and passengers among their loads. Landing small clandestine parties to blow up railway lines in Sicily

and the Italian peninsula, and the insertion of agents, also became part of the repertoire. All this showed the submarine to be a versatile warship, and Commander in Chief Mediterranean asked for as many as possible to be provided.

In August, Hitler, now extremely worried about Rommel's position, overruled the objections of Admiral Raeder, his Naval Commander in Chief, and moved U-boats into the Mediterranean. The intention was to operate 20 U-boats in these confined waters and between September and October, 10 passed through the Gibraltar Strait. They had

Below: Following the success of the Italians in December 1941 when six brave men almost changed the balance of power in the Mediterranean by severely damaging the battleships HMS *Valiant* and *Queen Elizabeth*, Churchill insisted that the Royal Navy be similarly equipped. This British Mk1 chariot with its two crew are negotiating their way through a harbour net.

During the remainder of 1941, the Afrika Korps was to be consistently denied the supplies required to sustain their operations, and the Allies were able to reinforce Egypt from around the Cape and through the Suez Canal.

immediate success when they sank the carrier *Ark Royal*, the battleship *Barham*, and the cruiser *Galatea*. The Italians added to these British disasters when the Italian submarine Scire carried three human torpedoes to Alexandria Harbour where they penetrated the harbour, seriously damaged the battleships *Valiant* and *Queen Elizabeth*, and put them out of action for a considerable period. All of this amounted to a serious defeat for the British and almost persuaded the Germans to make the Mediterranean the focus of their U-boat effort.

THE U-BOATS FIGHT BACK

The end of 1941 saw the Allies in trouble, and it was to worsen in early 1942. U-boats, whose strength had risen to 23, continued to pick off Allied shipping; the Italians fitted the German asdic to their escorts, and the Second Air Force returned to Sicily. Malta became the focus of a massive air bombardment with 6096 tonnes of bombs being dropped in April, and, apart from the effect on the civilian populations and air activity, Allied submarines were now finding it impossible to use their base on Manoel Island. The Axis was able to resupply the Afrika Corps, and Rommel advanced to El Alamein. The British evacuated Alexandria, and, on her way to Haifa, the submarine depot ship *Medway* was sunk by *U372*. Nine submarines were lost, including *Upholder* on her 25th patrol, and the battle was becoming a very bloody affair.

Then, in May 1942, the German High Command repeated its earlier mistake and withdrew the Luftwaffe. It took the Allies and Malta a little while to recover, with the famous 'Operation Pedestal' convoy in August (during which the Italian U-boat arm enjoyed its greatest success) playing a major part. In addition, aircraft were once again being delivered to Malta, and so the fight-back resumed. Rommel was once again starved of supplies, and the 8th Army drove him westwards. In November, the Allies landed in North Africa with the help of submarines

acting as navigation beacons, and HMS *Seraph* (disguised as USS *Seraph*) was famously responsible for bringing General Giraud out of France. This exploit followed an earlier trip when she had landed General Mark Clark (General Eisenhower's deputy) prior to the landings for 'Operation Torch'.

As a counter to the North Africa landings, the Axis had seized Tunisia, and the Italian Navy did a magnificent job in the face of overwhelming odds to keep this garrison supplied for five months. Desperately short of fuel and escorts, they ran more than 100 convoys and 500 separate trips by individual small craft, including submarines, in a valiant attempt to maintain this foothold. It fell in May 1943.

In between these defining events, British submarines were maintaining pressure elsewhere in the Mediterranean and paying a heavy price. A chariot raid was conducted against Palermo in December 1942 with some success, but at the loss of *P311*; soon afterwards 'Tubby' Linton in *Thunderbolt* failed to return from patrol. Like the loss of Wanklyn earlier, Linton's demise was hard to bear. He had been in command of a submarine since the beginning of the war and was due to return to the United Kingdom after his fateful patrol. He had accounted for roughly 101,605 tonnes of enemy shipping, which included 26 enemy supply ships. He was posthumously awarded the VC. The third VC winner in large submarines was Tony Miers in *Torbay*. He won his award for the extraordinary feat of remaining in the heavily defended anchorage of Corfu for 17 hours and sinking two important supply ships.

Italy collapsed in September 1943, and Allied invasions of Sicily and Crete followed the success in North Africa. The bulk of the work was done, and T-boats were once again transferred to the Far East. Two small flotillas were left behind to operate on the south coast of France and in the Aegean, during which time they sank five U-boats, three destroyers and 53 merchant vessels of 193,049 tonnes for a loss of six submarines. In August 1944, these submarines were also recalled to British waters.

The Mediterranean campaign cost the Royal Navy 45 submarines, approximately half of the total numbers deployed there. A total of 22 were lost to the 54,000 mines laid by the Axis and 19 were sunk by surface ships, but not a single one was lost to aircraft attack at sea, belying the oft-quoted but ill-informed myth of the Mediterranean's transparency. Where aircraft did play a part was reporting torpedo tracks to the surface escorts, which undoubtedly resulted in the establishment of a datum and the subsequent loss of the attacking submarine. Despite their primitive torpedo and lack of gyro-angling capability, British commanding officers' marksmanship was good, with 43 per cent of attacks resulting in at least one hit, roughly the same performance as that achieved by the Americans in the Pacific. Their success was not because the opposition was weak; they were almost always pitted against convoys with air escort and,

for the last 18 months, against escorts fitted with asdic. It was because they stuck with the principle of remaining undetected when at all possible, remaining dived by day and only surfacing under the cover of darkness. Thus, despite their losses, they were able to sustain their influence on the battle for a prolonged period.

This was in sharp contrast to the Italian U-boats who, as they spent much of their time passively waiting for targets to come to them, dissipated their strength in the central Mediterranean and often fell victim to marauding British submarines. They lost 66 of their number (16 to submarines) in exchange for the sinking of three British cruisers and damaging three others.

The Germans ordered 95 U-boats into the Mediterranean, but only 62 made it. Five were lost in the Atlantic before arrival, six were sunk penetrating the Gibraltar Straits, and 22 turned back. Of those that did make it, all were eventually destroyed by the Allies, but not before they had achieved significant military successes, particularly during their

Below: The Polish submarine Orzel. The Poles were wonderful allies to the British, and, although small in numbers, provided great support to the Allied submarine effort in Northern European waters and in the Mediterranean. Three of their captains received the Distinguished Service Order for their exploits.

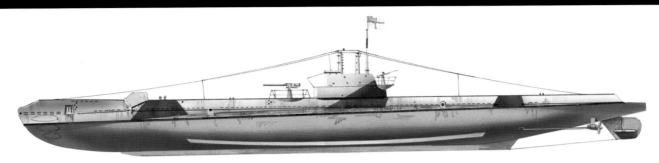

STORM

The British *S*-class was the medium 'standard type' submarine. They were active in every theatre of World War II and won many accolades. They were handy boats and much loved by their crews. HMS *Storm* was the first submarine in British history to be commanded by an officer of the Royal Navy Volunteer Reserve, Lt. Cdr. E.P. Young DSO DSC* RNVR.

SPECIFICATIONS

Country: Great Britain
Launch date: 18 May 1943
Crew: 44
Displacement: 726 tonnes/1006 tonnes
Dimensions: 61.8m x 7.2m x 3.2m (202ft 6in x 23ft 9in x 19ft 6in)

Armament: Six 533mm (21in) TTs; one 76mm (3in) gun
Powerplant: Twin screws, diesel-electric motors
Surface range: 15,750km (8500nm) at 10 knots
Performance: 14.7 knots/9 knots

first year of operations. The sinking of two aircraft carriers before Japan's entry into the war had particularly harsh ramifications for the British Far East Fleet. However, on the commerce front, they managed only to sink 95 merchant ships, and the absence of the players in this considerable side-show was sorely felt in the Atlantic.

THE BATTLE IN NORTHERN WATERS

Despite the full operational strength of both the British and German submarine fleets being deployed during Germany's invasion of Norway, they had little effect on the campaign. The U-boats had a number of opportunities to intervene and make their presence felt against major British warships, but were badly let down by their torpedoes' performance. Their magnetic fuses were severely affected by Earth's magnetism in high latitudes, and their torpedoes' poor depth-keeping, because of air leaking from the air vessels, denied the contact fuses the opportunity to explode against hulls.

British submarines fared little better. They were concentrated in the Skaggerak and off the south coast of Norway, but found that patrolling during almost constant daylight gave them very little time on station, as they had to withdraw a considerable distance in order to surface and recharge their batteries. In the end, they managed to sink only two per cent of German invasion forces. The Home Fleet, because of the presence of German aircraft, did even more poorly and was forced to withdraw altogether. Thus in terms of reputation and stature, Royal Navy submarines found themselves a notch or two higher, particularly as their front-line presence came at a heavy human price. In addition, now under the command of Admiral Sir Max Horton DSO, they had set a tone of determination and readiness for sacrifice that was to prevail throughout the war. Nevertheless, the capture of *Seal* in 1941 in the Kattegat, after receiving damage by mines and aircraft, came as a particular shock.

Two Polish submarines, *Orzel* and *Wilk*, had

immediately joined forces with the Royal Navy. After France fell, many of her submarines that had started as allies returned to French ports; however, seven vessels entered British ports, but the terms of Petain's armistice with the Germans called for them to return. The British did not trust the promise that they would not be used against the Allies, so, in July, following Dunkirk, they boarded all French ships in British ports. In only one case, *Surcouf*, did this transfer occur with bloodshed, and, because of the existence of General de Gaulle's Free French movement, they were subsequently able to serve in French uniform and colours. The French minelayer *Rubis* was to conduct particularly sterling work over the next few years. The Dutch submarines' enjoinder with their British allies was seamless and saw service in every theatre.

EXTREME HARDSHIP IN THE ARCTIC

When Germany invaded Russia in June 1941, two other areas of submarine activity were opened up. In the Baltic, the Russians (highly determined but poorly trained) fought alone with their coastal *M*-class, spending much of their time trying to break out of the anti-surface and minefield blockade imposed by the Germans. In the Arctic, their larger *K*-class and small *Shch*-classes were supported by British submarines of the *S*- and *T*-class. The Russian boats conducted mining operations in the Norwegian fjords and landed special reconnaissance teams, but had little success against surface shipping because of technical problems with their torpedoes and machinery, and deficiencies in operational training. From 1942 onwards, operations to cover North Russian convoys occupied the British Royal Navy submarines a great deal. This theatre presented the worst of operating conditions through extreme discomfort from the cold and regular storms, conditions which, of course, were experienced by both sides. Convoys to Russia were large and heavily defended, so relatively few ships were sunk by U-boats in comparison with the Atlantic. The greatest disaster for the Allies was the scattering of Convoy PQ17 in 1942, which allowed submarines to sink 10, and aircraft

FLUTTO

The Italian *Flutto* was one of 136 submarines employed at one time or another in the Mediterranean. In 1939, the Italians had over twice as many boats as the Germans or British, but overall they proved to be an insignificant factor in the war. They were misemployed in a defensive role, instead of being used offensively against merchant shipping. *Flutto* was sunk off the coast of Sicily on 11 July 1943 by the British motor torpedo boats *640*, *651*, and *670*.

SPECIFICATIONS

Country: Italy
Launch date: November 1942
Crew: 50
Displacement: 973 tonnes/1189 tonnes
Dimensions: 63.2m x 7m x 4.9m
(207ft x 23ft x 16ft)
Armament: Six 533mm (21in) TTs; one 100mm (3.9in) gun
Powerplant: Twin-screw diesel engines, electric motors
Surface range: 10,000km (5400nm) at 8 knots
Performance: 16 knots/7 knots

SURCOUF

The search for a weapon with greater range and flexibility than the torpedo has continued almost since the inception of the submarine. For a long time attention concentrated on the only available alternative, the gun, and it was not until the 1960s that a really effective weapon, the submarine-launched cruise missile, became available. The last, and arguably the epitome of the gun-armed cruiser, was the *Surcouf*. Designed under the 1926 French naval programme, the *Surcouf* was, in her time, the biggest submarine in the world, her enormous dimensions being necessary to carry all the items considered necessary for her role of world-wide commerce raiding. She was forced to leave Brest on 18 June 1940, to avoid capture by the Germans. She lay at Plymouth for some weeks before being seized by the Royal Navy on 3 July; three Britons and one Frenchman were killed and two men wounded during the incident. Thereafter *Surcouf* served with a French crew under British operational control. There was much discussion as to the best use for this 'white elephant'; eventually it was decided to send her to the Pacific, but she was rammed and sunk with all hands on 18 February 1942, while en route from Bermuda to the Panama Canal. Ironically, having been built to sink merchantmen it was by a US merchant ship, the *Thomas Lykes*, that the *Surcouf* was sunk.

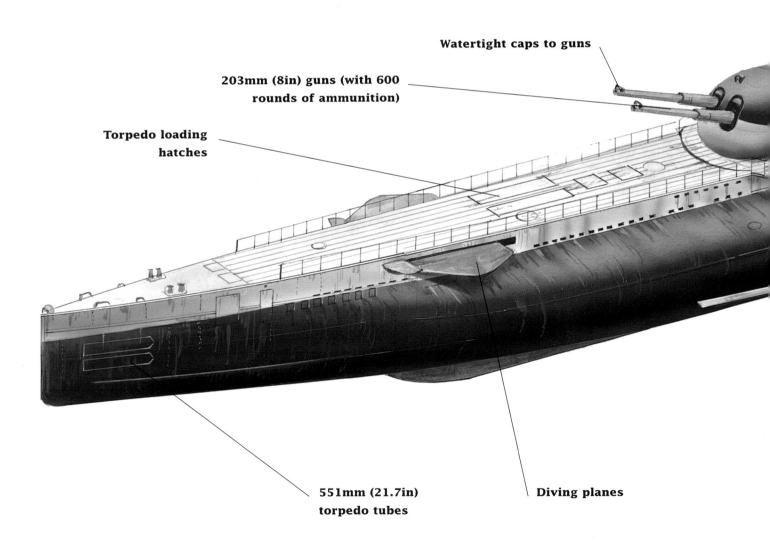

Watertight caps to guns

203mm (8in) guns (with 600 rounds of ammunition)

Torpedo loading hatches

551mm (21.7in) torpedo tubes

Diving planes

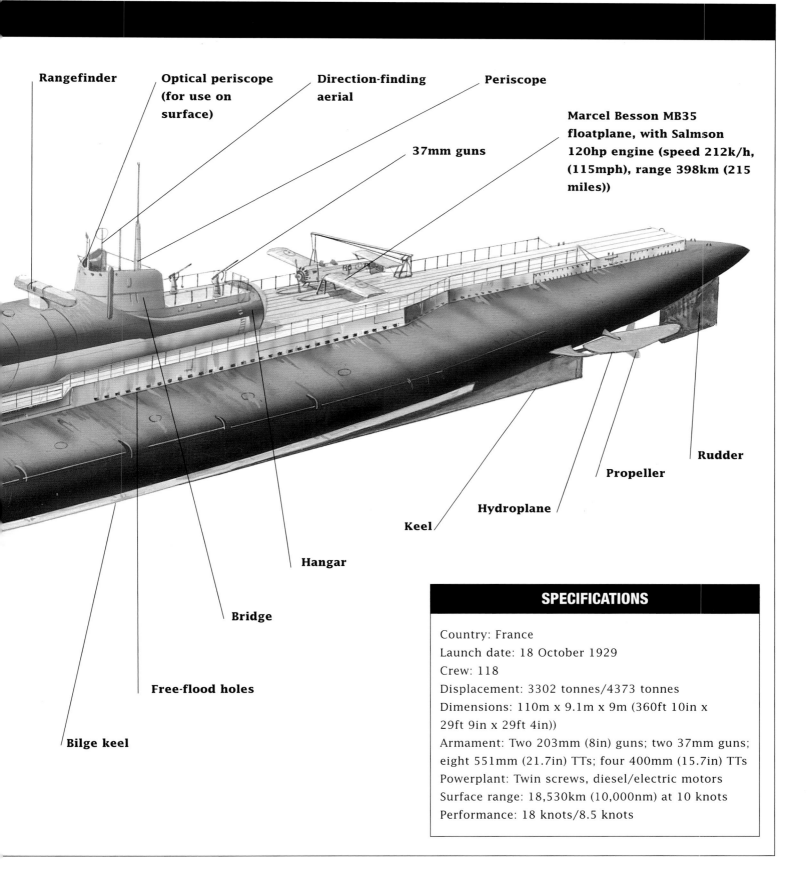

Rangefinder

Optical periscope
(for use on
surface)

Direction-finding
aerial

Periscope

Marcel Besson MB35
floatplane, with Salmson
120hp engine (speed 212k/h,
(115mph), range 398km (215
miles))

37mm guns

Rudder

Propeller

Hydroplane

Keel

Hangar

Bridge

Free-flood holes

Bilge keel

SPECIFICATIONS

Country: France
Launch date: 18 October 1929
Crew: 118
Displacement: 3302 tonnes/4373 tonnes
Dimensions: 110m x 9.1m x 9m (360ft 10in x
29ft 9in x 29ft 4in))
Armament: Two 203mm (8in) guns; two 37mm guns;
eight 551mm (21.7in) TTs; four 400mm (15.7in) TTs
Powerplant: Twin screws, diesel/electric motors
Surface range: 18,530km (10,000nm) at 10 knots
Performance: 18 knots/8.5 knots

Right: The British X-craft was a perfect submarine in miniature, designed to penetrate areas denied larger submarines. They would be towed to within about 110km (70 miles) of their target by a large submarine, the operational crew would change over with the passage crew, and in they would go to plant their side cargoes of four tonnes of high explosive. They carried a diver who would also attach limpet mines if required.

14, of the 36 ships that had left Iceland.

The Allied landings in North Africa in November 1942 took the Germans totally by surprise. They had observed activity in Gibraltar, but had assumed that this was a precursor for another Maltese convoy, so no special disposition was ordered. There were many U-boats operating to the west of Ireland against transatlantic trade, and one group off the Azores that might have provided alertment became involved with an ordinary trade convoy (SL125). As a result, the main assault was under way before U-

boat HQ could muster sufficient strength to make a worthwhile attack. The assembled submarine force did succeed in sinking five per cent of total tonnage involved, but much of it was empty, and in return they lost eight German and six Italian U-boats.

On the British side, despite reinforcements from Allied navies, it is a simple fact that, because of the demands of the Mediterranean theatre, there were insufficient submarines to fulfil the major task of guarding against the breakout of Germany's surface raiders, whether it was from their southern or northern bases and lairs. For example, in early 1942, when intelligence indicated that *Scharnhorst*, *Gneisenau*, and *Prinz Eugen* were about to leave Brest, every training submarine, most veterans of World War I, was sent to the Bay of Biscay to help form a 'ring of steel'. This exercise was to be repeated, again without success, six months later.

In September 1943, the whole of the British operational strength in British waters was used to tow six X-craft 1609km (1000 miles) to Alten Fjord, Norway, to attack what Churchill named the 'beast': *Tirpitz*. Like the *Chariot,* the purpose of the X-craft was to extend submarine capability (stealth and surprise) into restricted areas denied to

RUSSIAN SUBMARINES

Soviet submarine crews were brave and well disciplined; however, because of a huge expansion programme, they were generally inadequately trained. Their submarines, with enclosed bridges and adequate heating, were well equipped for the terrible Arctic conditions. The top submarine shown here is a Series Xbis submarine launched in 1940, and the lower is a Series XIIIbis minelayer.

SERIES Xbis

Country: Soviet Union
Launch date: 1940
Crew: 39
Displacement: 587 tonnes/705 tonnes
Dimensions: 58.7m x 6.2m x 4.2m (192ft 9in x 20ft 4in x 14ft 1in)
Armament: Six 533mm (21in) TTs; two 45mm guns
Powerplant: Twin-screw diesels, plus electric motors
Surface range: 12,038kn (6500nm) at 8 knots
Performance: 13.6 knots/8 knots

SERIES XIIIbis

Country: Soviet Union
Launch date: 1940
Crew: 55
Displacement: 1123 tonnes/1416 tonnes
Dimensions: 83.3m x 7m x 4m (273ft 3in x 23ft x 13ft 5in)
Armament: Eight 533mm (21in) TTs; one 100mm (3.9in) gun; one 45mm gun; two 7.62mm machine guns; 20 mines
Powerplant: Twin-screw diesels, plus electric motors
Surface range: 11,112km (6000nm) at 9 knots
Performance: 18 knots/10 knots

If German U-boat opposition to the 'Torch' landings was barely relevant, then their performance against the Normandy landings was a disaster. A total of 36 submarines was kept at short notice to oppose such a landing, but they were deployed too late to have any impact.

bigger submarines. The X-craft was a perfect submarine in miniature, and armed with two side cargoes that packed a monster punch of 4.06 tonnes of clockwork-timed high explosive. When about 96.5km (60 miles) from their objective, the now exhausted passage crew of three would change over with the operational crew of four, enhanced by a diver. Three of the six craft deployed managed to penetrate Kaafjord, *Tirpitz*'s lair. *X5* was sunk before she reached her objective, but *X6* and *X7* managed to drop their charges underneath the battleship before their crews were either captured or killed. The resultant explosions removed

Tirpitz from the war. The two COs, Plaice and Cameron, were each awarded the VC for this extraordinary demonstration of courage and skill. HMS *X24* was also successfully deployed on two occasions against a U-boat floating dock in Bergen, and two were used for reconnaissance of beaches for the Normandy landings and then to act as navigation beacons for the main assault.

If German U-boat opposition against the 'Torch' landings was barely relevant, their performance against the Normandy landings was a disaster. A total of 36 submarines was kept at short notice to oppose such a landing, but they were

deployed far too late to exert an influence. Such was the Allies' superiority, both in the air and on the sea, that only 12 merchant ships, four landing craft, and five escorts were sunk at a cost of 20 submarines (schnorkel and non-schnorkel fitted). A veritable rout! In addition, the Germans deployed significant numbers of their own version of the mini-submarine (K-craft). The *Neger* ran awash; the *Marder* could run submerged; the *Biber* carried two rather than a single torpedo; the longer-ranged *Seehund* had a two-man crew. They achieved very little. The fact that Dönitz banned trained submariners from going

near these desperate weapons sums up their capability. Indeed, in misguidedly producing 800 of them, the Germans wasted precious resources.

Protection of the North Russian convoys by British submarines, which continued throughout 1944 and 1945, ended on a highly historical note when *Venturer* conducted the first ever submarine-versus-submarine attack when both were dived when she sank *U864*. The commanding officer, Lieutenant J.S. Launders, used a combination of asdic and visual bearings to work out his fire-control solutions. Submarining was never to be the same again.

Above: At the end of the war the British people were given the chance to see with their own eyes the type of boat that had almost brought the country to its knees. Here, *U776*, now manned by a British crew, is seen at Westminster Pier on the River Thames in the heart of London.

123

POST-WAR CONVENTIONAL SUBMARINES

The victorious Allies captured many submarines from their German adversaries and immediately examined their innovative designs in great detail. The United States and Britain also wanted to be better warned of what to expect from submarine opponents in the future. On both sides of the Atlantic, there was determination to retain the lead in submarine development and tactics.

The end of World War II had seen the deployment of the atom bomb, and it was clear that the composition of future fleets was going to change significantly. At the same time as the lesson that the aircraft-carrier had taken over from the battleship as the primary platform for power-projection was being digested, strategists also had to wrestle with the 'what ifs?' of facing an nuclear-capable enemy. That particular concern was still some time in the future,

Left: The Swedish *Gotland*-class, Stirling air independent engine-propelled (AIP) submarine, the first of its kind. The type of AIP adopted runs on liquid oxygen and diesel in a helium environment, and it is reported that the submarine can remain on patrol for some weeks without snorting. It is very well suited to Baltic Sea operations.

however; the more immediate challenge was how to counter, and exploit, the fast-dived submarine, a capability that had been demonstrated by the streamlined German Types XXI/XXIII and the Walther HTP (High Test Peroxide) driven Type XVII. On top of that, the schnorkel-fitted submarine – which could run its engines and recharge its battery without having to surface – had also surprised the Allies, even though it should not

haul of technological material to be examined and exploited. Following the surrender, U-boats of every description either made their own way to the British ports of Llisahally and Harwich (the 'Deadlight Fleet') or were captured in Kiel and Hamburg, and moved directly to the Allies' own dockyards. As well as Britain, the United States, and the Soviet Union, Norway, Canada, and France also benefited from the division of material.

Above: A German Type XVII HTP-propelled boat being lowered into the water. Britain had captured *U1407* intact and ran a series of trials on her. Sufficiently encouraged, the British built two further HTP submarines, *Explorer* and *Excalibur*.

have. Dutch submarines possessed such a capability when they fled to Britain following the German invasion of the Low Countries in 1939; however, at that stage, it was considered to be 'dangerous' and was promptly removed! All the Germans had done was simply dusted off a good idea and improved the mechanics.

To the victors the spoils, and, thanks to the activities of T-Force, there was a plentiful

REAPING THE BENEFIT OF GERMAN TECHNOLOGY

The Royal Navy was determined to be better warned of what might be expected from the submarine in the future, so its guiding policy became to ensure that its anti-submarine warfare (ASW) measures were developed against the most capable opposition. This meant uprating its current stock of submarines. This was a measure that of course suited the submarine service very well, and it thereby escaped the massive ravages of post-war cuts suffered by other elements of the Royal Navy. It also suited the long-range thinkers who saw the submarine as the only platform that might survive an exchange of tactical nuclear weapons between battlefleets.

The British scrapped all their remaining really old hulls and cancelled another 50 that were on the stocks, but they completed 16 of the *A*-class that had been designed for the Pacific and had the characteristics of high-speed submersibles. These boats, which had similar capabilities to the US Navy 'fleet' submarines, were recognized as only stopgaps until new designs, similar to the type-XXI, came off the drawing boards. The captured type-XXI, *U2518*, was put through a series of trials, and, as a result, all British submarines were fitted with schnorkels (snort systems) and some *T*-class were lengthened and given an extra battery section to provide them with enhanced submerged performance. They were known as *T*-conversions. A few S-boats were

Left: HMS *Acheron* from right ahead. This class was destined for the war in the Pacific and hence had a high surface speed. After World War II, they were modernized with a snort system and a relatively sophisticated sonar set under the dome. One of the class, HMS *Affray*, was lost in the English Channel in 1951. Submarine safety, even in peacetime, cannot be guaranteed.

Right: HMS *Sidon*, a veteran of World War II, was fitted with HTP-driven 'Fancy' torpedoes. One of these torpedoes blew up in a tube when the submarine was about to slip from Portland in Dorset. The result of the explosion can be seen here. The Captain, Lieutenant Verry (in the white jumper), was on the bridge at the time and escaped injury.

Below: HMS *Astute* as she was built. There is a marked difference between her configuration and the smooth lines of the German Type XXI ocean-going submarines that were to have such an influence on all future modernizations and builds. The days of the chunky surface raider had gone.

streamlined for experimental purposes, and they became known as the 'slippery Ss'. All types were also provided with telescopic radar masts and a basic passive ESM (electronic countermeasure) outfit. There was one oddball in the *A*-class ranks, the HMS *Alaric,* which was fitted with the prototype submarine-launched anti-helicopter missile (SLAM). It never reached service because ultimately it was concluded that its appearance above the surface would guarantee an accurate attack by the aircraft.

One of the small Walther-boats, *U1407,* was commissioned into the Royal Navy as HMS *Meteorite,* and she was refitted and fully trialled during 1949. Hydrogen peroxide (H_2O_2) – known as Ingolin in the German Navy and named after Dr Walther's son Ingol – is, when at high concentration, a relatively unstable compound that breaks down easily into water (H_2O) and oxygen (O_2) accompanied by a significant generation of heat. To assist the 'breakdown' process, the HTP is passed over a catalyst, and the subsequent products are fed into a combustion chamber and sprayed with fuel (e.g. kerosene). This

mixture generates great heat, producing steam, and the addition of more water results in more steam that powers a turbine, which in turn drives the submarine through the water. Speeds of up to 25 knots were attainable from this technology, despite the small size of the powerplant. Britain ordered two unarmed experimental vehicles, *Explorer* and *Excalibur,* to be built. They were not ready for service until 1958, and, when they did join the ranks, they were immediately dubbed the 'exploder' class. They ended their days as expensive and impractical high-speed targets.

To underline the volatility of HTP as a fuel, experiments with the HTP-driven 'Fancy' torpedo were discontinued when a unit blew up in a torpedo tube of HMS *Sidon* alongside Portland Harbour, in Dorset, England, in 1955. The blast killed many of the crew and sank the submarine.

Although utilizing its own design and construction techniques, British submarine post-war design was based almost entirely on German ideas. Concerns of how to combat the submarine of the future were so

SNORT INDUCTION

During World War II, aircraft ranges were so increased that they were able to cover most of the U-boat operating areas and were thus able to pick off submarines charging their batteries on the surface during transit or patrol. A Dutchman called Schnorkel had, in 1937, devised a means whereby air could be drawn down a tube in a submarine to feed air to the engines while the submarine remained at periscope depth. The Germans revived the idea in 1944 and perfected the system, which in turn was adopted by all submarine nations after the war.

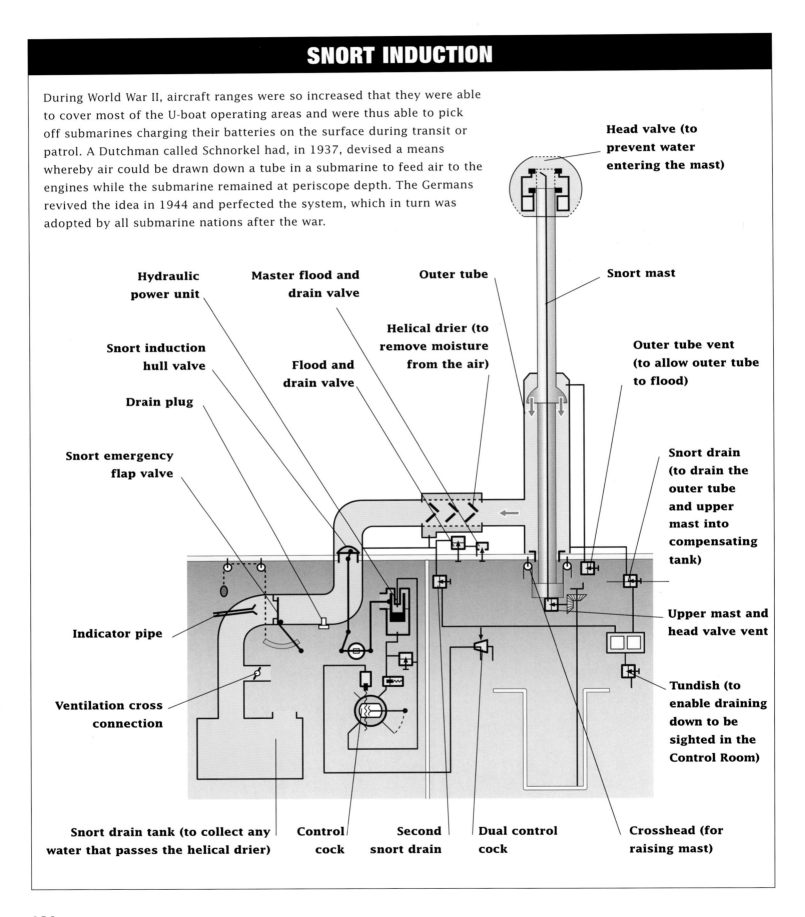

Head valve (to prevent water entering the mast)

Snort mast

Outer tube

Hydraulic power unit

Master flood and drain valve

Helical drier (to remove moisture from the air)

Snort induction hull valve

Flood and drain valve

Outer tube vent (to allow outer tube to flood)

Drain plug

Snort emergency flap valve

Snort drain (to drain the outer tube and upper mast into compensating tank)

Indicator pipe

Upper mast and head valve vent

Ventilation cross connection

Tundish (to enable draining down to be sighted in the Control Room)

Snort drain tank (to collect any water that passes the helical drier)

Control cock

Second snort drain

Dual control cock

Crosshead (for raising mast)

UPHOLDER

SPECIFICATIONS

Country: Great Britain
Launch date: 2 December 1986
Crew: 47
Displacement: 2203 tonnes/
2494 tonnes
Dimensions: 70.3m x 7.6m x 5.5m
(230ft 7in x 25ft x 17ft 7in)

Armament: Six 533mm (21in)
TTs; Sub Harpoon SSMs
Powerplant: single shaft,
diesel-electric motors
Surface range: 14,816km
(8000nm) at 8 knots
Performance: 12 knots/20 knots

HMS *Upholder* was the lead submarine of the last conventionally powered class to serve in the Royal Navy. She was built specifically as a floating sonar station to surveille the Greenland-Iceland-Faroe gaps against Soviet submarines exiting the Norwegian Sea. With the end of the Cold War in 1990, she became superfluous to Royal Navy needs, but happily this capable submarine and her three sisters received a second lease of life with the Royal Canadian Navy.

great that the primary objective of ASW was also adopted for the submarine service in 1948. The U-boat 'bag' for Royal Navy submarines during World War II had been 38, most of them when surfaced, but Jimmy Launders in *Venturer* opened a Pandora's box of potential when he sank *U864* late in World War II. Greatly improved sonar (the American acronym for 'sound and ranging' was now universally adopted) and noise quietening (through sound mounting machinery) became top priorities for the new class, the *Porpoise*-class.

THE CAPABLE AND POPULAR *OBERON*

These submarines, and their successors the *Oberon*-class, were a joy to drive. They were quiet even when snorting, had a nice dash speed of 15 knots underwater (although this did put a monster 'suck' on your battery), were well armed, and had an array of sonar that covered all the frequencies. During the course of their distinguished 30-year career, they were continuously upgraded and were eventually fitted with towed arrays for really long initial low-frequency detection that supplemented the

medium (type 2007) and high frequency (type 187c/2054 and 719) sets already fitted. They also had a sonar intercept set (type 197). For above-water work, they were equipped with two periscopes, a radar set (rarely used except for navigation), and good ESM. Most were eventually equipped with satellite communications. In the 1980s, they were armed with Tigerfish wire-guided torpedoes, and a number were capable of firing the Royal Navy Sub-Harpoon (RNSH) anti-ship missile.

All this potential, and a crew of 65, was entrusted to a lieutenant who might be as

Above: HMS *Porpoise* (1957) was the first British post-war design. She and her sisters of the *Oberon* class (1961–67) were the best diesel-engine submarines of their era. Heavily influenced by the Type XXI, they were fast, quiet, heavily armed, and festooned with sensors. They were eventually fitted with towed-array (low-frequency) sonar and armed with RN Sub-Harpoon missiles.

Right: A US *Balao*-class submarine sitting in quiet reflection after World War II. The remaining members of this class became subject to a number of trials. Three were used to test the effects of an atom bomb explosion against the hull at Bikini in 1946, while two were fitted for troop carrying, two for radar picket duties, and one as an oiler.

STIRLING ENGINE

The Stirling Engine is an air independent propulsion (AIP) closed-cycle diesel, designed for slow speed patrolling which minimizes use of the battery. Liquid oxygen (LOX) provides the combustible air for the engine, while exhaust products are pumped over the side and dissolve in the water.

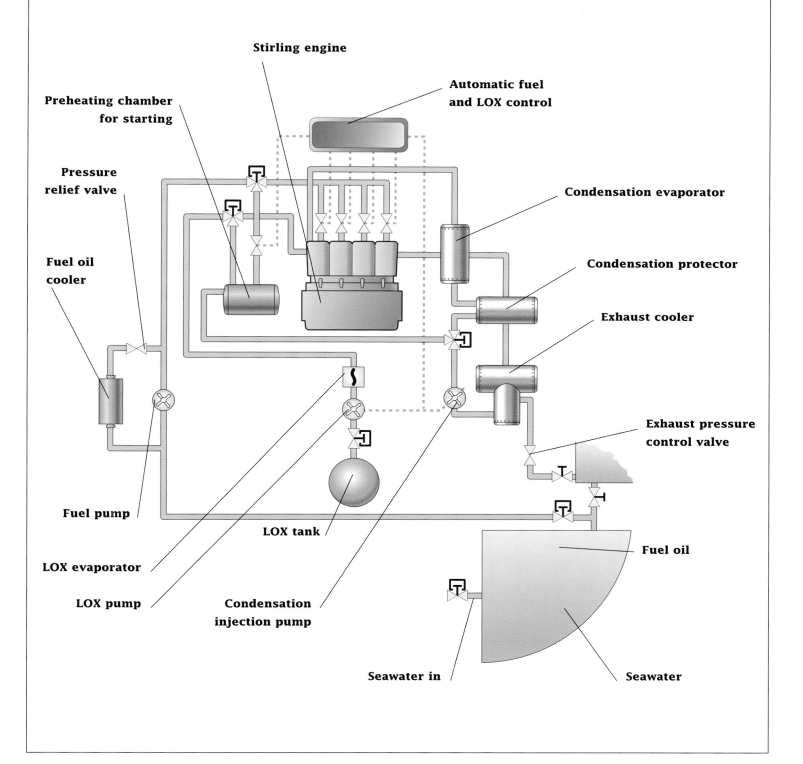

Stirling engine

Automatic fuel and LOX control

Preheating chamber for starting

Condensation evaporator

Pressure relief valve

Condensation protector

Fuel oil cooler

Exhaust cooler

Exhaust pressure control valve

Fuel pump

Fuel oil

LOX tank

LOX evaporator

LOX pump

Condensation injection pump

Seawater in

Seawater

young as 28. He was, of course, thoroughly tested by 'Teacher' during six months of the Submarine Commanding Officers Qualifying Course, colloquially known as the 'perisher'. This name was a corruption of 'periscope course', but its resonance also indicated its failure rate, which was in the region of one-third of students. As well as an agile mathematical mind that had to be able to handle the 1159 times table (and some of us had to rely heavily on rhythm!) which converted the angle subtended by target height into range, and thence into time between looks at a threatening escort (of which there might be five, as well as the target), the two other absolute requirements for success were 'periscope eye' (accuracy of target estimations) and 'spatial awareness' (where to look after an alteration of course having made allowance for own movement and all the other ships in the engagement). In short, you had to have a real hunger for the job that you were about to do, and Teacher saw to it that there was no such thing as compromise! This experienced commanding officer would take you apart initially and then slowly put you back together again with the purpose of revealing personal limits while instilling the confidence required to accept the greatest responsibility that a young man could possibly be offered: a multi-million, front-line platform the crew of which placed their lives in your hands and unquestionably trusted your skill and judgement. The

moment that my teacher, Commander Terry Woods, said 'Congratulations, *Olympus*' was one that I will never forget.

In addition to her agility and good listening capability, *Olympus* could gather intelligence (including bottom looks) against relatively benign (slow, stopped, or anchored) targets; could lay mines; could conduct 'delouse' operations; could insert special forces (who usually ate you out of house and home!); could provide ASW training for friendly forces; could conduct weapon trials; could show the flag; and, above all else, provided young commanding officers with great experience! The *Oberon*s were without doubt the most capable conventional submarines of their era, and Australia, Canada, Brazil, and Chile bought them.

Like all conventional submarines, however, *Olympus* had her limitations. Covert transit speed was about six knots, thus speed of

Left: The US Navy has always indulged in this practice of exercising an emergency surface in a dramatic fashion. The USS *Pickerel* of the *Tench*-class came out at an angle of 48 degrees. The majority of this class were converted under the 'Guppy' (Greater Underwater Propulsive Power) programme, which gave higher speeds as a result of streamlining and increased battery power.

TANG

The post-war US *Tang*-class had a short hull and was designed for high underwater speeds. In addition to conventional employment, a number of the class was converted to carry the Regulus cruise missile (*Grayback* and *Growler*) and troop transports. The influence of the Type XXI can be seen yet again.

SPECIFICATIONS

Country: USA
Launch date: 19 June 1951
Crew: 83
Displacement: 1585 tonnes/
2296 tonnes
Dimensions: 82m x 8.3m x 5.2m
(269ft 2in x 27ft 2in x 17ft)

Armament: Eight 533mm (21in) TTs
Powerplant: Twin shafts, diesel-electric motors
Surface range: 18,530km (10,000nm)
at 10 knots
Performance: 15.5 knots/18.3 knots

ALBACORE

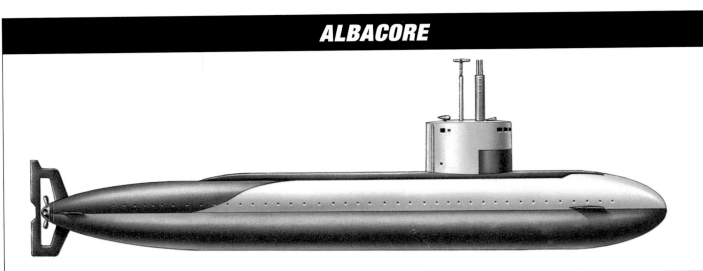

USS *Albacore* had a radical new hull form. Her purpose was hydrodynamic research, and she proved that a short, fat, streamlined form with a single screw was the most effective shape for very high underwater speeds. This was the shape adopted for the nuclear submarines that succeeded USS *Nautilus*.

SPECIFICATIONS

Country: USA
Launch date: 1 August 1953
Crew: 52
Displacement: 1524 tonnes/ 1880 tonnes
Dimensions: 62.2m x 8.4m x 5.6m (204ft x 8ft5in x 15ft 7in)

Armament: None
Powerplant: Single-screw, two diesels, one electric motor
Surface range: Not released
Performance: 25 knots/33 knots

deployment and speed of closure of a contact were invariably painfully slow. Often translation of initial detection into localization and attack simply could not be achieved because of 'limiting lines of submerged approach', so the only way to 'convert' was in concert with a third party, more often than not an marine patrol aircraft (MPA), latterly the RAF *Nimrod*. This

Right: USS *Grayback*, with her Regulus nuclear-tipped cruise missile, immensely enhanced the submarine as a warship. The best that a submarine could achieve before her arrival was to sink ships; now it could attack land targets several hundred miles away, with relative covertness and complete surprise.

was fine, provided that we were operating in an area where we enjoyed air-superiority, that we could communicate without wasting hours thumbing through code-books, and that we both knew where we were to establish an accurate relative picture. This problem would often be resolved by the aircraft conducting an 'on-top' to lock plots. Additionally, endurance was limited, not least the stamina of the CO, through whom all things were authorized and whose major concern was always the condition of his battery. Whatever method of power generation is employed (closed-cycle engines, fuel cell technology) a conventional submarine will always be faced with the problem of replenishing 'amps' at some stage, particularly if the commanding officer is forced to use speed in order to achieve his aim; every submarine on patrol has an aim, and it is rarely that of simply drilling holes in the water! That implies that he must snort at some stage, and, at that moment of exposing a mast, the submarine instantly becomes vulnerable to detection.

The Royal Navy built a successor to the *Oberon*s, and that was the *Upholder*-class. These four highly capable, hi-tech, stealthy submarines had one planned role in life: acting as a mobile SOSUS station in the Iceland-Faeroe-Greenland gaps. Their sensor suite, tactical data handling system, communications kit, and weapon outfit were tailored to make a round trip of about 3200km (2000 miles), spend a month or so on patrol, and then return to base. When the Cold War ended in the early 1990s, it was soon realized that the British Royal Navy submarine service would have to make a sacrifice as part of the 'peace dividend'. Running two streams (nuclear and non-nuclear) of personnel who required training and expected (rightly) a proper career path is highly expensive, so, in order to retain its 'blue' as well as 'brown' water capability, the Royal Navy opted for an all-nuclear submarine service. When HMS *Unicorn* went into mothballs in 1995, she took with her almost a century of wonderful heritage. It gives all British submariners great pleasure to see these excellent submarines given a new lease of life with the Royal Canadian Navy.

'GUPPY' CONVERSIONS OF US WAR-TIME SUBMARINES

At the end of World War II, the Americans scrapped more than 70 of their more elderly submarines and cancelled another 92 of those building, leaving just under 200 'fleet' type in service. They ran trials with their German captures, notably *U2351*, a Type XXI. In the same way as the British, but independently, they produced what was known as the 'Guppy' (greater underwater propulsive power), which had a high underwater speed. They subsequently built the *Tang*-class, but did not enter into the realms of experimenting with HTP, as they had other plans afoot in order to achieve very high-submerged speeds. In addition to their 'Guppy' programme, the US Navy experimented with advance radar-pickets, and store and personnel carriers; while these proved to be fruitless 'rabbit-holes' into which to pour money, however, a much more fruitful experiment was begun.

The US post-war strategy was based on the aircraft carrier whose aircraft were A-bomb capable with the intention of destroying enemy bases and harbours. The purpose of all other units was to support the carrier in this primary mission. The arrival of the SLCM (air-breathing, turbine-driven submarine-launched cruise missile) in the shape of Regulus missile-armed conversion heralded a new dawn for the submarine. The missile was based on the V1 cruise missile, notorious for its use by the Germans against London, but with a nuclear warhead, giving it a strategic role. It was designed to attack shore targets inland and was intended to complement the manned bomber. A guidance system enabled a degree of mid-course guidance, thereby delivering its payload with a high degree of accuracy. Submarines were ideal vehicles for its deployment because they could provide such control from 555km

Above: A dressed-overall Soviet *Tango*-class submarine (in the foreground) is moored astern of a *Whiskey*-class attack submarine, armed with two SSN-3 anti-ship missiles. This submarine was an early response to the growing power and influence of the US Battle Groups and their powerful air wings.

FOXTROT

The *Foxtrot*-class was a splendid class of 62 diesel-driven submarines. They were highly successful and reliable and were deployed worldwide, bearing the main brunt of Soviet foreign deployments. They were most numerous in the Mediterranean in the 1960s and 1970s. Eight of the class were transferred to the Indian Navy in the early 1970s, and further units were subsequently exported to Libya and Cuba. All Russian *Foxtrot*s were withdrawn by the late 1980s.

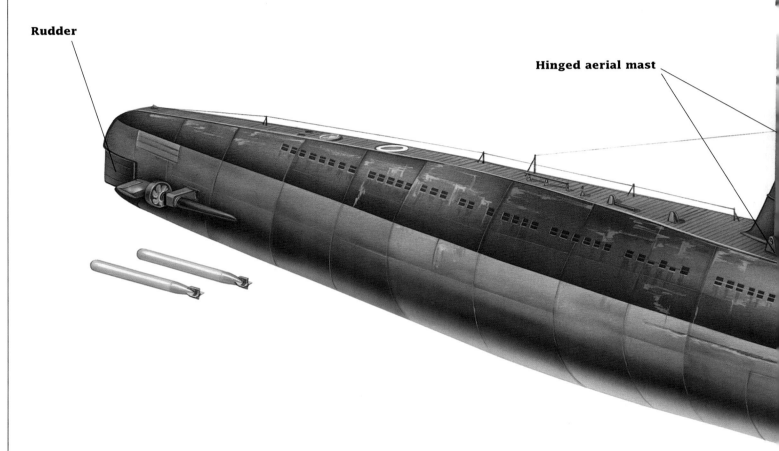

Communications aerial

Rudder

Hinged aerial mast

SPECIFICATIONS

Country: Russia
Launch date: 1959 (first unit)
Crew: 80
Displacement: 1950 tonnes/
2500 tonnes
Dimensions: 91.5m x 8m x 6.1m
(300ft 2in x 26ft 3in x 20ft)

Armament: Ten 533mm (21in) TTs
Powerplant: Three shafts, three
diesel engines, plus three electric
motors
Surface range: 10,190km (5500nm)
at 8 knots
Performance: 18 knots/16 knots

Armament
**1 533mm (21in) heavyweight
anti-ship torpedoes, with
alternative conventional or
nuclear warheads
2 Acoustic-homing anti-
submarine torpedoes
3 Mines (two of which can be
carried instead of each torpedo)**

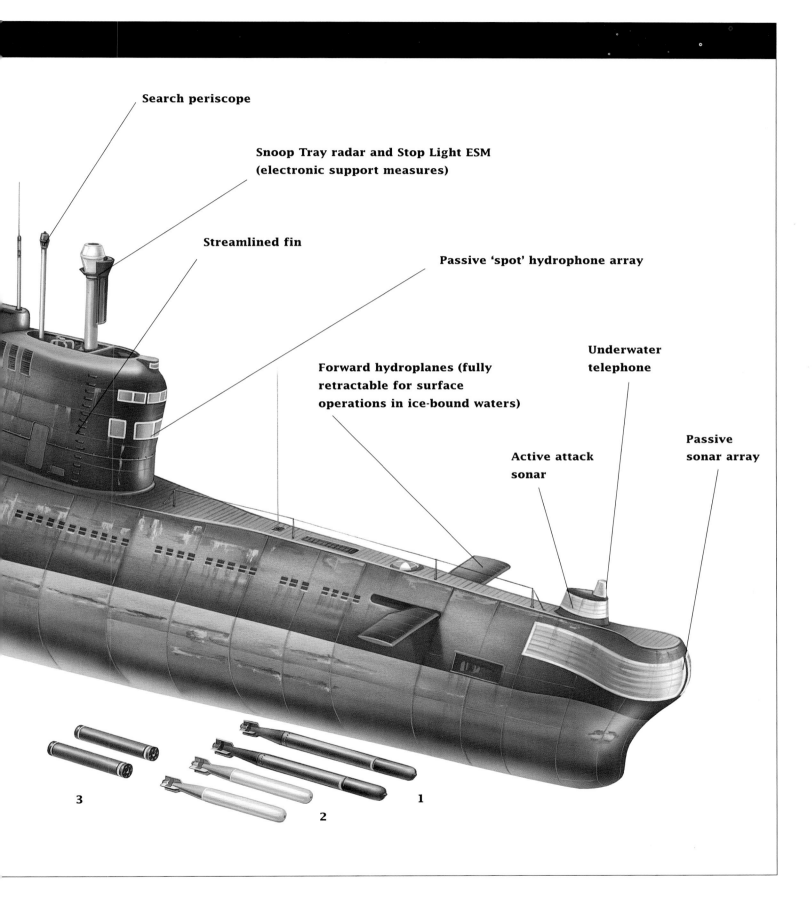

Search periscope

Snoop Tray radar and Stop Light ESM
(electronic support measures)

Streamlined fin

Passive 'spot' hydrophone array

Underwater
telephone

Forward hydroplanes (fully
retractable for surface
operations in ice-bound waters)

Passive
sonar array

Active attack
sonar

3

2

1

In the 1950s, experiments began on a new shape for a submarine hull. USS *Albacore*'s shape could best be described as 'tear-drop', and because of its hydrodynamic qualities, *Albacore* delivered a stunning 33 knots. A new era was about to dawn.

Above: The *Kilo* class is the Russian export submarine, and is a candidate for AIP (air independent propulsion). Although fairly basic by Western standards, it is an extremely safe submarine with a 32 per cent reserve of bouyancy and is heavily compartmented. India, Romania, Poland, Iran and China have all bought them.

(300nm) from an enemy coast, using the remaining 370km (200nm) of range to reach its land-based target. Its deployment was crude by modern standards. It was housed in a hangar, and the firing submarine had to surface to fire it. Two large conventional boats, *Grayback* and *Growler,* and one nuclear, *Halibut,* were built to operate it. The importance of the submarine as a warship was once again greatly enhanced, building on the tradition of shore bombardment introduced by HMS M1.

In the 1950s, with the US nuclear-power programme advancing apace, experiments began on a 'new' shape for a submarine hull. Looking remarkably like the *Holland*-class of 1900, USS *Albacore*'s shape could best be described as 'teardrop', and, because of its hydrodynamic qualities, *Albacore* delivered a stunning 33 knots! A new era was about to dawn in US submarine circles.

POST-WAR SOVIET DESIGNS

The Soviet Union's spoils included a lot of rocketry, but not much on propulsion, although they did pick up 12 partly built Type XXIs from the Danzig building yard. The overall submarine philosophy centred on the Russian concept of 'all-arms' warfare, with submarines being used in the vanguard of operations to warn of any advancing maritime threats to the 'motherland' based on concentric defence zones.

Their first two post-war types built in the mid-1950s, the *Whiskey* and the *Zulu,* were derivatives of their World War II *S*-class (coastal) and *K*-class (overseas) designs. It is rumoured that a number of the latter class were Walther-engine driven, which was built from first principles after finding a wooden mock-up in a drawing office! The coastal *Quebec*-class, also built in the 1950s, was of particular interest because, to begin with, it used a 'closed cycle' diesel propulsion system. The *Romeo*- and *Foxtrot*-classes were built during the early 1960s were replacements for the *W*- and *Z*-class vessels, and followed the traditional Soviet methodology of design, which was evolution rather than revolution. With the *Foxtrot*-class, however, they now had a submarine that was capable of operating in the deepfield, which they did on a regular basis. The 'West of Ireland' *Whiskey* and *Foxtrot*, interlopers in Western exercises, were regular visitors and often became inadvertent players!

A SUCCESSFUL EXPORT

In 1954, the Federal Republic of Germany was once again permitted to build submarines. The revived U-boat arm was commanded by Germany's World War II ace (now) Admiral Otto Kretschmer. With the help of another 'ace', Kapitan zur See Topp, he arranged in 1956 for two scuttled Type XXIII boats to be raised and brought back into service. They became the *Hai* and *Hecht*. At the same time, a Type XXI was also raised and used as a trials vessel, named *William Bauer*. The first U-boats of the new generation were the Type 201, tiny submarines but revolutionary in that they had eight torpedo tubes arranged concentrically around the bow. They were all-electric and had to return to harbour each night for battery charging. Since those early days, the 200-series built by HDW has gradually got bigger, and its submarines have enjoyed phenomenal popularity all over the world: 10 x 206 went to the German Navy; 14 x 207 went to Norway (*Kobben*-class); 8 x 209 went to Greece (*Glavkos*-class); 2 x 209 went to Argentina (*Salta*-class); 2 x 209 went to Colombia (*Pijao*-class); 3 x 209 went to Turkey (*Atilay*-class); 3 x 209 went to Venezuela (*Sabalo*-class); 2 x 209 went to Ecuador (*Shyri*-class); 3 x 209 went to Indonesia (*Cakra*-class); 6 x 209 went to Peru (*Casma*-class); 2 x 209 went to Chile (*Chipana*-class); 2 x 209 went to India; 2 x TR-1700 went to Argentina.

The next generation is the Type 212 and Type 214. The Italians are buying the former, the primary capabilities of which are its impressive sonar suite, stealth characteristics and propulsion system, which is a combination of air independent propulsion using fuel cell technology (combining hydrogen and oxygen to create electricity) for silent slow cruising. The Type 214 has been ordered by Greece and North Korea, and will have even more impressive qualities of stealth, including the capability of diving beyond 400m (1312ft) and remaining submerged for periods of more than two weeks.

Above: When Germany re-entered the submarine construction industry, the Germans very quickly demonstrated that they had retained their brilliance in submarine design last demonstrated during the two world wars.

TANGO

The *Tango*-class attack submarine was the diesel-electric counterpart to the nuclear-powered *Victor*-class boats, and was designed to conduct anti-submarine warfare. Introduced in the early 1970s, she was the world's largest conventional submarine of her time, and was noted for her quietness. Great emphasis was also placed on endurance, to enable the *Tango* to undertake lengthy patrols in defence of the Soviet 'bastion' areas. The *Tango* has an essentially cylindrical hull form, which is maintained throughout the length of the boats. This improved hull form provided a substantially increased internal volume, used to accommodate the low-frequency bow sonar, the SS-N-15 anti-submarine missile, and its fire-control systems. Well armed and anechoically coated, she would have been a difficult target for ASW forces in shallow water.

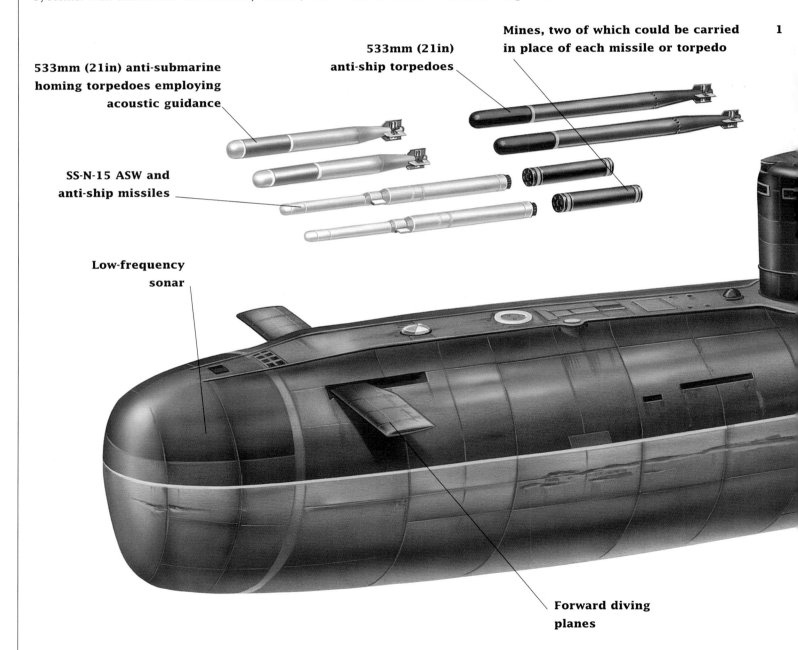

533mm (21in) anti-submarine homing torpedoes employing acoustic guidance

SS-N-15 ASW and anti-ship missiles

533mm (21in) anti-ship torpedoes

Mines, two of which could be carried in place of each missile or torpedo

Low-frequency sonar

Forward diving planes

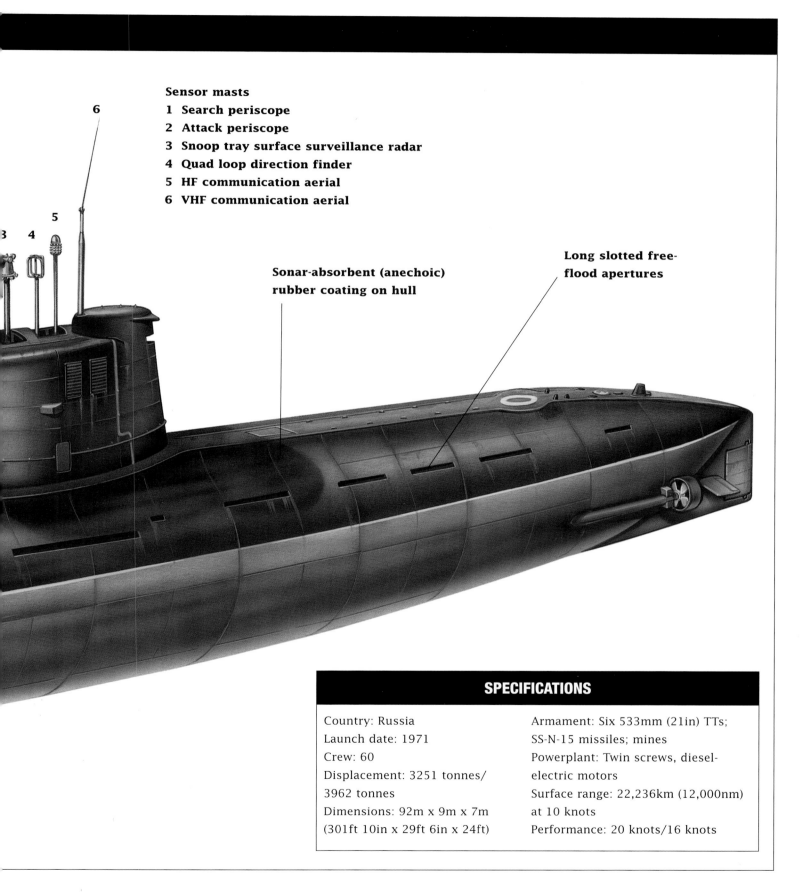

Sensor masts
1 Search periscope
2 Attack periscope
3 Snoop tray surface surveillance radar
4 Quad loop direction finder
5 HF communication aerial
6 VHF communication aerial

Sonar-absorbent (anechoic)
rubber coating on hull

Long slotted free-
flood apertures

SPECIFICATIONS

Country: Russia
Launch date: 1971
Crew: 60
Displacement: 3251 tonnes/
3962 tonnes
Dimensions: 92m x 9m x 7m
(301ft 10in x 29ft 6in x 24ft)

Armament: Six 533mm (21in) TTs;
SS-N-15 missiles; mines
Powerplant: Twin screws, diesel-
electric motors
Surface range: 22,236km (12,000nm)
at 10 knots
Performance: 20 knots/16 knots

Above: French *Daphne*-class submarines conducting a sail past of surface forces. *Minerve* was lost in the Western Mediterranean in 1968. These *Daphne*-class submarines were a successful export class in the 1960s, being bought by South Africa, Pakistan, Portugal and Spain.

Right: The Japanese *Oshio*, one of the first Japanese-built post-war submarines, sails from Kure Naval Base, Western Japan, in the late 1960s. She was bigger and better able to cope with the heavy weather off the Japanese coasts than her predecessor, *Hayashio*, built in 1962.

They compensated for poor fire-control accuracy with the big-bang of nuclear-tipped torpedoes.

Soviet interest in the SLBM (rocket-driven submarine-launched ballistic missile) had its origins in the German Laffarentz project, at the heart of which were V2 (ballistic (free-fall) rather than cruise (guided)) missile silos designed to be towed behind Type XXI submarines to attack the United States. The *Zulu V* submarine (a conversion of the basic *Zulu* hull) appeared in the mid-1950s, and it was armed with two SS-N-4 vertically launched SLBMs that had a range of 650km (350nm). The missile was a three-stage, inertially guided, liquid-fuel missile that delivered a single 800KT nuclear warhead. The six vessels of this class were followed by 23 units of the *Golf*-class, armed with three SS-N-4 missiles. The next development was the SS-N-5 (Sark) missile that not only had twice the range of its predecessor, but also had the major advantage of being capable of underwater launch. A number of the *Golf*-class were retrofitted with Sarks and were designated *Golf II*s.

SOVIET MISSILE TECHNOLOGY

The Soviets' focus on the inertially guided SLBM meant that they were slow to see the potential of the SLCM; however, once it was recognized, its development was pursued with great vigour. The first two SLCM missiles (Scrubber and Styx) were tactical anti-ship variants fitted to destroyers and fast patrol craft, respectively, while the third variant, SS-N-3 (Shaddock), was designed as a strategic missile with a similar capability to the US Regulus missile, except that it had no mid-course guidance capability. It first appeared at sea mounted in a single cylindrical container on the afterdeck of a converted *Whiskey*-class in the late 1950s and was soon followed by five units fitted with a pair of missiles on a submarine designated the *Whiskey Twin Cylinder*-class. This class was succeeded in turn by the *Whiskey Long Bin* in 1962. They carried four Shaddocks in a long, low streamlined fin, from tubes angled at 100 degrees. Given the relatively short range of the *Whiskeys*, it is fairly certain that their missiles were intended for Japanese or European targets.

VASTERGOTLAND

The *Vastergotland*-class of Type A17 attack submarines preceded the *Gotland*-class. These single-hulled submarines were completed in the late 1980s and are unusual because of their 'X' configuration rudder and after-plane design. The boats are optimized for operations on the Baltic, especially in shallow coastal waters. Torpedo load comprises 12 FFV Type 613 wire-guided weapons, effective to a range of 20km (10.8nm) at a speed of 45 knots, and six FFV Type 431/450, also wire-guided, which are effective to a similar range. In addition to their swim-out discharge torpedoes, they can also carry up to 48 mines in an external girdle. Plans to equip these boats with four SSM vertical launch tubes in the sail were abandoned because they were not considered cost effective in the Baltic environment, where any naval engagements would be fought at fairly close range.

Propeller

X-form rudder and after-planes

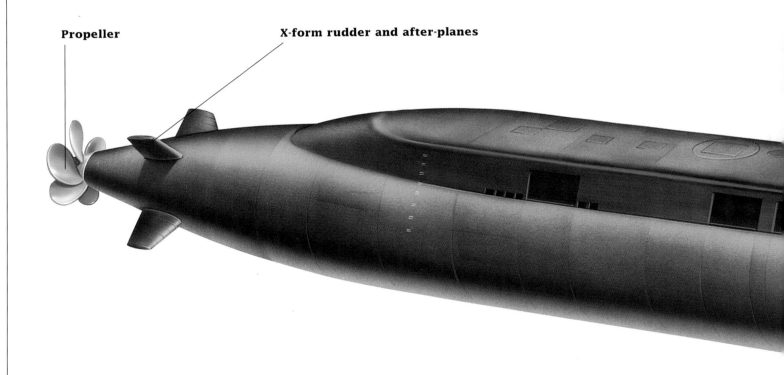

SPECIFICATIONS

Country: Sweden
Launch date: 17 September 1986
Crew: 28
Displacement: 1087 tonnes/
1161 tonnes
Dimensions: 48.5m x 6.1m x 5.6m
(159ft 1in x 20ft x 18ft 5in)

Armament: Six 533mm (21in) TTs;
three 400mm (15.7in) TTs; mines
Powerplant: single shaft, diesel-
electric motors
Surface range: Not known
Performance: 11 knots/20 knots

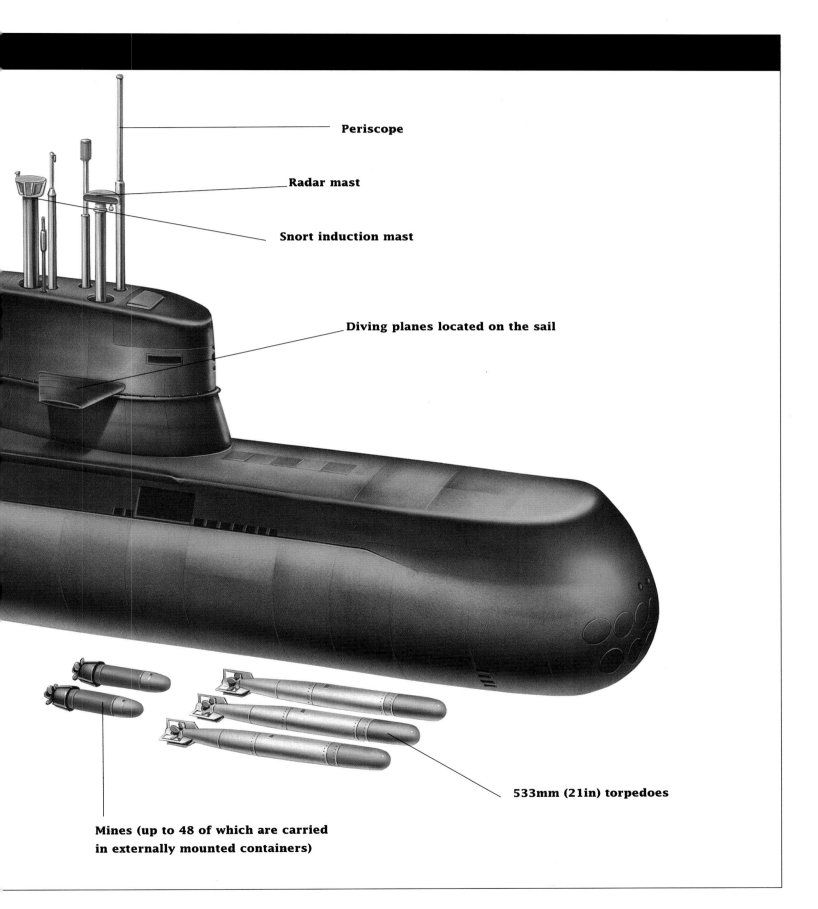

Periscope

Radar mast

Snort induction mast

Diving planes located on the sail

533mm (21in) torpedoes

Mines (up to 48 of which are carried
in externally mounted containers)

the urgency of providing platforms to counter the US Striking Fleet that a conventionally powered interim was developed to complement the Echo II nuclear SSGN. It was the *Juliett*, and a completely new design, being much bigger in the beam than the *Foxtrot*-class. It carried four anti-ship Shaddocks in two nests and the Front Door/Front Piece guidance radars in the front of the fin. Sixteen units were built during the 1960s.

With the advent of the massive 7408km (4000nm) range of the SS-N-8 SLBM, Soviet SSBNs (their firers) would no longer have to transit the open ocean in order to reach their land-based targets. Instead, they could sit in heavily defended areas in the Barents and Okhost seas, enjoying defence-in-depth proffered by surface ships and submarine 'minders'. These areas were known as 'bastions' and had the further great advantage of being fairly close to home, thereby allowing cheaper and easier-to-build conventional submarines to play a bastion-defence role. In 1972, the *Tango*-class appeared. At 3962 tonnes submerged, she is a big submarine, providing room for an array of sensors and weaponry equivalent to that of the *Victor II* nuclear-powered submarine. Eighteen were built until the design was succeeded in 1982 by the *Kilo*-class.

Whereas the *Tango*-class was built for a specific purpose, the *Kilo*-class (which is still being built) is the successor to the *W*-, *R*-, and *F*-classes, to be employed in the roles of long-range surveillance, special forces missions, and anti-shipping strike in enemy-dominated waters, particularly those characterized by much shallow water (e.g. the Baltic, Black and Japanese seas). A short stubby submarine, she employs an *Albacore*- shaped hull, rather than the traditional Soviet 'cigar' shape, and has only a single shaft. The *Kilo* is a relatively unsophisticated machine and designed to be a 'workhorse', one that is eminently suitable for the export market.

Above: The German-designed Type 212 is due at sea in 2003 and will be propelled by a battery/fuel cell combination. Fuel cells convert chemical energy directly into electrical energy, using the same principle as a battery, except that the cell is continuously fed with hydrogen as fuel. Fuel cells are reliable and silent, with no moving parts.

The SS-N-3A did possess a mid-course guidance capability, and it was specifically designed to be fired at US Navy aircraft carriers. Guidance corrections were issued to the missile by the firing platform, which in turn was viewing the radar picture – generated by a third party – of the intended target. Because Soviet industrial capacity was incapable of producing the vast numbers of nuclear-powered submarines demanded by Defence Minister Nikolai Krushchev and his Naval Commander in Chief Admiral Sergei Gorshkov, such was

Left: The Japanese *Yushio*-class SSK is a powerful all-rounder. Equipped with towed array sonar, Sub-Harpoon missiles, dual-purpose torpedoes and stowage for 20 further weapons, it represented the epitome of non-nuclear submarine development in the 1980s.

OTHER SUBMARINE OPERATORS

France received a selection of submarines as war spoils after World War II, including a Type XXIII, a Type XXI (*Roland Morillot*), two Type VIICs (*Mille* and *Lanbie*) and two Type IXs (*Blaison* and *Bouen*). As with most post-war developments, there was little love lost between France and her allies, and she pursued her own submarine strategy. The first of her modern designs was the *Narval*- and *Daphne*-classes that proved popular with overseas customers. The last of her conventional classes is the *Agosta*-class, four of which were completed in the 1970s. One of these 1788-tonne submarines has been decommissioned, but the other three have been modernized. They carry both torpedoes and the Exocet sea-to-surface (SSM) missile.

Sweden has emerged as a major international builder in recent years, largely through her development of the Stirling engine, an air independent system designed to produce electricity created by burning liquid oxygen (LOX) and diesel together in a pressurized combustion system. The exhaust products are dissolved by sea water and leave no wake. The engine will operate as long as the LOX lasts; thereafter the submarine can revert to the more familiar diesel-electric variety. The first experiment was conducted in Nacken in the late 1980s and proved a success. The Australian *Collins*-class is a Kockum's design.

There are 16 submarines in the Japanese Self Defence Force (JSDF) order of Battle, the largest of which, the *Yushio*-class, weighs 4064 tonnes.

China operates a large number of conventional submarines of the Russian *Whiskey*- and *Romeo*-types, although she is now concentrating on building up her nuclear-propelled hulls.

To those countries listed as operators of submarines should be added Denmark, Italy, The Netherlands, Spain, Portugal, Cuba, Iran, North Korea, Libya, Pakistan, Poland, South Africa, Taiwan, Yugoslavia, and shortly Singapore and Malaysia. The lessons of history have not been lost on them.

NUCLEAR SUBMARINES

—

'The nuclear powerplant was revolutionary enough in itself, but when married to the weapons system of the submarine it opened an entirely new era in undersea warfare. Nucelar power cut the submarine completely free from the surface, ending the need for the air-breathing advertisement of the schnorkel.'
(Richard Humble, 1981)

Following World War II, the Soviet Union, by creating a buffer zone of satellite nations around itself and the ruthless imposition of communist regimes on oppressed peoples, prompted Winston Churchill to make his famous 'Iron Curtain' speech of 1948. The great states-man was echoing a deep fear of expansionism from the East, and the enormous conventional military might ranged against the West created great concern. The only option open to the West was to remain ahead in the military technological battle, a policy that inevitably created an arms and space race, but it was one that had to be won. In the process, it also created an economic battle, as it forced both sides to expend huge resources to wage it, and, as history has shown, it took the West 45 years to win it.

Left: In December 1998 Russia ordered certain military units to a higher state of readiness following US and British air strikes against Iraq. Here an *Oscar II* SSGN is seen leaving its base of Kamchatka.

HOW A NUCLEAR REACTOR WORKS

The heat created from a nuclear reactor comes from the splitting of atoms, a process known as *fission*. When the atom of the element U-235 is bombarded by neutrons (smaller parts of an atom), it may absorb one of these neutrons, become unstable, and split. In the process the atom produces additional neutrons (an average of 2.5 each fission) that go on to split more U-235 atoms, which creates more neutrons, and so on. The result is a chain reaction. Once this chain reaction is creating a sufficient flux of neutrons to keep the process going, criticality is reached. In order to prevent an over-abundance of neutrons, control rods made of a neutron-absorbing 'dull' metal (e.g. hafnium, cadnium, boron) are positioned between the fuel rods. Their removal, which exposes fuel plates to each other, controls the neutron flux.

The neutrons that are released from a split atom are usually going too fast to be absorbed consistently by other atoms; in order to achieve guaranteed interactions, the neutrons are slowed through a moderator, either water, gas, or liquid metal.

Heat is created by the fission fragments (the by-products of a split atom in addition to the neutrons, and which may number 200 or more) colliding with one another and in the process giving up some of their kinetic energy (motion) to thermal energy (friction).

In most reactors in nuclear-powered submarines, water is used as the moderator and 'coolant'. The coolant – which flows around rods containing fuel elements – is the means of removing the heat generated by the fission process. Because it contains radioactive impurities, this coolant is contained in its own circuit (known as the primary circuit), which interacts within a steam-generator with another circuit of water (known as the secondary circuit) which boils off as steam. This steam drives the main engine and turbo-generators. The primary circuit is pressurized, thereby raising the boiling temperature of the water within it to several hundred degrees centigrade. Keeping the primary water as a homogenous mass avoids 'cavitation' (bubbles) damaging the fuel rods.

A pressurized water-cooled reactor (PWR) has an elegant simplicity in its operation. The more steam that is taken off in the steam generator by the secondary system (e.g. opening the throttle of the main-engine), the cooler the primary circuit water re-entering the reactor. The cooler the water, the greater its moderating effect, which in turn slows more neutrons and enhances the neutron flux. The higher the neutron flux, the greater the number of interactions, the hotter the water leaving the reactor to service the demand for more steam. The reverse is also true; less demand equals a higher residual temperature, which reduces the neutron flux.

To stop the process, the control rods are inserted between the fuel plates, and this is known as 'scramming' the reactor.

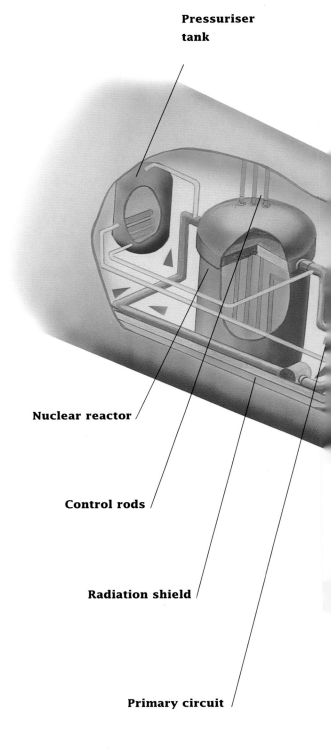

Pressuriser tank

Nuclear reactor

Control rods

Radiation shield

Primary circuit

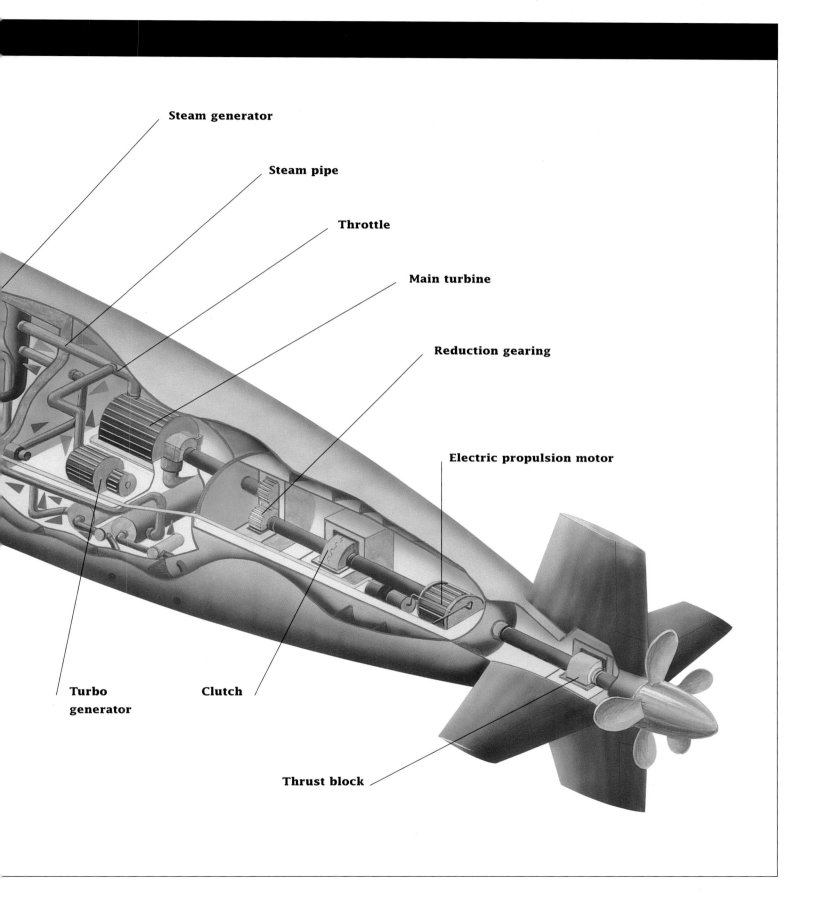

Steam generator

Steam pipe

Throttle

Main turbine

Reduction gearing

Electric propulsion motor

Turbo
generator

Clutch

Thrust block

Right: US sailors wave their caps from an accompanying tug as USS *Nautilus*, the world's first nuclear-powered submarine, moves up New York Harbour against the Manhattan skyline. Armed Forces Week in May 1956 witnessed the first public display of this revolutionary submarine.

Below: In 1958, USS *Nautilus* navigated under the North Pole; in 1959, USS *Skate* surfaced there. These achievements opened up submarine warfare possibilities for the waters beneath the ice canopy. *Skate* circumnavigated the globe in 50 minutes – when she drove in a circle two miles in radius around the Pole!

NAUTILUS: A COMPLETE SUCCESS

The Americans began their atomic energy project in 1948, and, under the guidance of an extraordinary naval officer, Captain (later Admiral) Hyman G. Rickover, in 1955 they commissioned their first nuclear sub-marine, USS *Nautilus*; she was a complete success. She was a large boat of 3231 tonnes with a speed in excess of 20 knots and carried 20 torpedoes. At first, her sister ship *Seawolf* was powered by a liquid-sodium cooled reactor, but this proved unsatisfactory, so she was retro-fitted with a PWR. This first-generation class consisted of six submarines, and they were soon setting records that caused a revolution in maritime warfare doctrine and tactical thinking throughout the world. *Seawolf* remained submerged for 60 days in 1958 and cruised 25,261km (15,700 miles). In the same year, *Nautilus* made the first submerged crossing of the Arctic Ocean when she transited dived from

SKATE

Laid down in July 1955, USS *Skate* was the world's first production-model nuclear submarine. She made the first completely submerged crossing of the Atlantic Ocean. To maximize her underwater endurance and avoid having to come to periscope to take a navigation 'fix' regularly, USS *Skate* was fitted with SINS (ships inertial navigation system), which gave a constant accurate readout of geographical position.

SPECIFICATIONS

Country: USA
Launch date: 16 May 1967
Crew: 95
Displacement: 2611 tonnes/ 2907 tonnes
Dimensions: 81.5m x 7.6m x 6.4m (267ft 8in x 25ft x 21ft)

Armament: Six 533mm (21in) TTs
Powerplant: Two shafts, one nuclear PWR, turbines
Range: Unlimited
Performance: 20 knots/25 knots

Hawaii to Portland, England. In March 1979, *Skate* surfaced at the North Pole. In addition to demonstrating the marvels of nuclear power, these submarines also introduced a revolution in navigation by using SINS (ships inertial navigation system), a device that uses electronic and engineering precision through gyros that sense movement in every direction (up, down, forwards and sideways) and applies the resultant motion to a known starting position. Gone were the days of visual and astro-navigation! Another record was set in May 1960 when *Triton*, the only US submarine to have a dual reactor, completed the first submerged navigation of the world. She followed Ferdinand Magellan's route and covered more than 65,969km (41,000 miles) in 84 days.

Building on the success of the *Albacore* hull, the next class was the *Skipjack*-class, which emerged in 1959. *Skipjack* was tear-

drop in shape and reached a beam of 9.4m (31ft) compared with the usual conventional beam of 4.8km (16ft), and her greatly improved hydrodynamic shape allowed her to reach a speed in excess of 30 knots and for a sustained period. In her first interaction with a large gathering of surface ships during an exercise, 'hostilities' ceased when *Skipjack* 'sank' every large carrier involved in the war game!

Another major advance was achieved through *Tullibee*, an experimental submarine whose 'nose' housed a spherical ball that contained a combined active/passive sonar suite optimized for the detection of other submarines. The anti-submarine submarine, first developed by the British in World War I through their *R*-class, had finally come of age. When this capability was added to *Skipjack*'s proven anti-surface success, yet another era in submarine warfare had dawned with blinding clarity.

NAUTILUS

Nautilus was the world's first nuclear-powered submarine. The one insurmountable problem with diesel-electric submarines is that they must periodically approach the surface to run their diesel engines and recharge their batteries, and to replenish life-support systems. Even when just the head of schnorkel is exposed, there is great danger of detection. It had been appreciated from early on in the US nuclear weapons programme that a controlled nuclear reaction could produce enough heat to generate the steam to power conventional steam turbines. Accordingly, in 1949, the US Cheif of Naval Operations issued a formal requirement for a nuclear-powered submarine, and the result was the USS *Nautilus*. *Nautilus* was by far the largest submarine to have been built at that time, and, despite her revolutionary powerplant, was otherwise conventional. She was designed with a conventional hull form, based on Type XXI and 'Guppy' technology, rather than an *Albacore* hull, presumably to avoid risking too many revolutionary advances in one project.

Sustained high speed and unlimited endurance with respect to fuel is all very well; however, if it was necessary to come to the surface to refresh the air inside a nuclear-powered submarine on a regular basis, then much of USS *Nautilus*'s potential would have been wasted. Those problems were solved by the fitting of carbon-dioxide 'scrubbers' and an electrolyzer. In this latter machine, distilled water was subjected to a high electrical current that split it into its component parts of hydrogen and oxygen. The oxygen was retained, and the hydrogen (unhealthy stuff in a submarine) was pumped over the side.

During her service, the *Nautilus* made numerous historic voyages; she made the first submarine polar transit, starting in Hawaii and finishing in Portland, England, after passing under the North Pole on 3 August, 1958. She was used as a research craft and was preserved as a museum exhibit at Groton, Connecticut, USA, in 1982.

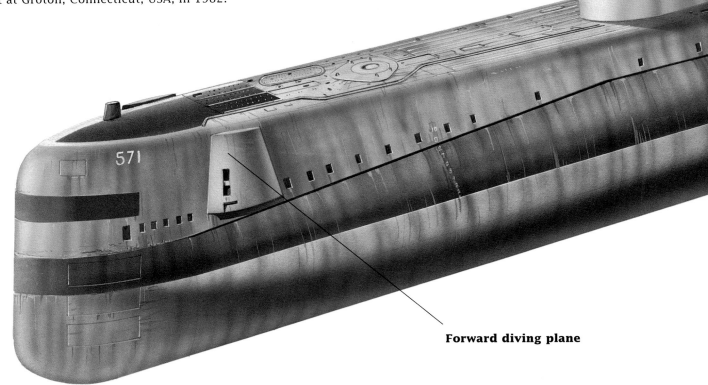

Forward diving plane

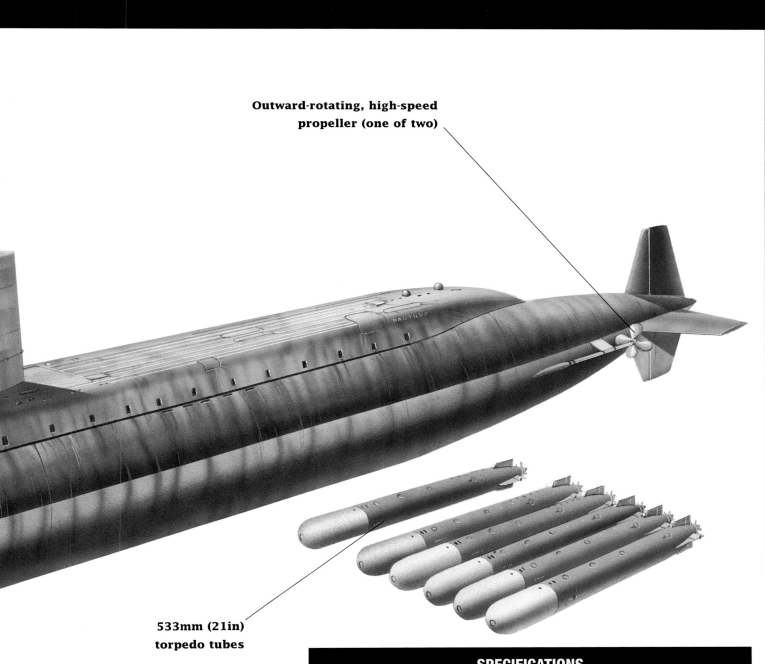

Outward-rotating, high-speed propeller (one of two)

533mm (21in) torpedo tubes

SPECIFICATIONS

Country: USA
Launch date: 21 January 1954
Crew: 105
Displacement: 4157 tonnes/
4204 tonnes
Dimensions: 97m x 8.4m x 6.6m
(323ft 7in x 27ft 8in x 21ft 9in)

Armament: Six 533mm (21in) TTs
Powerplant: Twin screws, one S2W
reactor, steam turbines
Range: Unlimited
Performance: 20 knots/23 knots

Right: The decision by the United States to introduce the Polaris strategic weapon system was encouraged by the stunning successes of the Soviet space rocket programme in the late 1950s, which not only humiliated America, but in a bound surpassed the latter's air supremacy. By 1962, the United States had fully tested its new naval deterrent, which was now undetectable and capable of deployment anywhere in the world's oceans. USS *Henry Clay* is seen conducting a surface test firing (the list to port is deliberate).

Right: The decision by the
United States to introduce
the Polaris strategic weapon
system was encouraged by the
stunning successes of the
Soviet space rocket programme
in the late 1950s, which not
only humiliated America, but
in a bound surpassed the
latter's air supremacy. By
1962, the United States had
fully tested its new naval
deterrent, which was now
undetectable and capable of
deployment anywhere in the
world's oceans. USS *Henry
Clay* is seen conducting a
surface test firing (the list to
port is deliberate).

TRITON

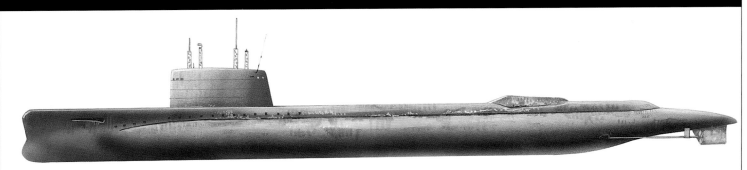

USS *Triton* was designed and built for use as a radar picket submarine to operate in conjunction with surface carrier task forces, submerging only when in danger of enemy attack. At the time, she was the longest submarine ever built. In 1960, *Triton* circumnavigated the globe entirely underwater, except for once instance when her sail structure broke surface to allow a sick submariner to be taken off near the Falkland Islands.

SPECIFICATIONS

Country: USA
Launch date: 19 August 1958
Crew: 172
Displacement: 6035 tonnes/
7905 tonnes
Dimensions: 136.3m x 11.3m x
7.3m (447ft 6in x 37ft x 24ft)

Armament: Six 533mm (21in) TTs
Powerplant: Two shafts, one nuclear
PWR, turbines
Range: Unlimited
Performance: 27 knots/20 knots

A DETERRENT STRATEGY

Hardly had the trials of *Nautilus* finished than the United States conceived another role for submarines that was far more important than anything that had gone before. When Soviet Russia exploded a nuclear weapon in 1953, the world's strategic situation changed. The West's absolute power was undermined, and the prospect of mutual extermination became a real possibility. The only way to counter the threat of a 'first-strike' pre-emptive attack was to threaten with an unacceptable retaliatory attack: in short, create a deterrent. This deterrent had to survive the first strike, and the submarine was recognized as an excellent delivery system for the second-strike weapon, as, unlike land-based missile silos, it was mobile, thereby making its delivery point uncertain for the enemy, extraordinarily difficult to find, and able to be kept continuously on station, and its missile could be smaller (and therefore cheaper) because of its proximity to the potential target. The result was the Polaris system, and it provided the third 'leg' of the United States' triad of strategic weaponry invested in ground-, air- and sea-launched weapons.

Polaris was demonstrated for the first time from USS *George Washington* in July 1960. The SSBN was created by cutting the hull of the SSN (USS *Scorpion*) in half and inserting a new section complete with 16 launch tubes, fire control, and navigation systems. The second boat, USS *Patrick Henry*, also followed in 1960; the force was gradually built up to a strength of 41 and became known as the '41 for Freedom'. In 1963, USS *Sam Houston* became the first SSBN to be assigned to conduct a patrol in the Mediterranean, underlining any potential enemy's problem in knowing where to look for them. The Polaris A2 missile, with a range of 2414km (1500 miles), was replaced by the 4022km (2500-mile) range A3 missile in 1964, and it was in that year that USS *Halibut* completed the last Regulus patrol.

THE BENEFITS OF NUCLEAR POWER TO A SUBMARINE

The reactor does not need oxygen, so the nuclear-powered submarine is a true submarine because it can operate entirely independently of the surface – a conventional submarine, because it has to use a mast to recharge its batteries, is actually a submersible. In addition, the reactor provides a virtually everlasting source of power that:

- generates high speed. This transforms the submarine from being a weapon of position (that is relying on its target coming within the submarine's limited engagement range) into an aggressive hunter, capable of overtaking any potential target which it can pursue relentlessly.

- supports a large hotel (domestic) load through steam-driven turbo-generators. This gives nuclear-powered submarines true independence through their ability to run air-purification machinery. Such machinery tends to be 'amp-hungry', and only the power generated by a reactor is sufficient to do the job. The regeneration of oxygen by the electrolysis of water (splitting it into oxygen and hydrogen), and the control of carbon dioxide through scrubbers, means that there is no requirement to visit the surface in order to sustain life.

- allows for bigger hulls to be built that can incorporate a large weapon suite and sensor outfit. To achieve effective coverage of the whole noise frequency spectrum when conducting a search for a target requires a variety of sonar sets, some of which have very wide apertures. The diameter of the hull of an SSN (submarine submerged nuclear) is in the order of 9.8m (32ft), in order to contain the necessary mechanical and electrical machinery to support the reactor, which is roughly twice that of an SSK (submarine submerged killer (non-nuclear)). The bigger size allows for a larger armoury of weapons.

- provides an endurance limited only by the amount of food that can be carried and the morale of the crew. Most SSNs and SSBNs (submarine submerged ballistic nuclear) have fridge and freezer space to support a patrol of 90 days. With the addition of false decks of canned food, this endurance can be increased to 120 days. It is generally accepted that beyond three months continuously dived, crew morale begins to suffer (mainly because they will have seen all the movies!). The longest continuous patrol conducted by a Royal Navy submarine lasted 108 days, and that was by the Port crew of HMS *Resolution* (Cdr D.M. Tall OBE RN) in 1991.

In short, the marriage of the traditional submarine qualities of stealth and surprise with high speed of deployment and long endurance was an immense step, as great a step as of that taken from the use of TNT to nuclear explosives.

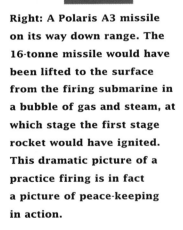

Right: A Polaris A3 missile
on its way down range. The
16-tonne missile would have
been lifted to the surface
from the firing submarine in
a bubble of gas and steam, at
which stage the first stage
rocket would have ignited.
This dramatic picture of a
practice firing is in fact
a picture of peace-keeping
in action.

EARLY SOVIET NUCLEAR SUBMARINES

It was Kruschev that brought a high degree
of urgency to the development of Soviet
nuclear-powered submarine technology in
order to maintain a balance with US
military capability. For such a major enter-
prise, it would be usual, as was the case in
the USN, to build at least one prototype;
however, such was the concern felt at being
about four years behind the power curve
that the Soviets embarked immediately on
a full-series production of the *November-*
class SSN, with the first being commissioned
in 1958. The Soviets were slow to appreciate the benefits of a single-hull submarine,
and persisted with a double-hull
construction (good for transporting lots of
diesel fuel, but unnecessary for nuclear
power). This resulted in a long and heavy
submarine (110m (360ft) and 5385 tonnes)
which, despite being a tear-drop shape,
required two reactors to provide a speed in
the order of 30 knots. Because of the haste
in its introduction and its lack of testing,

this class – and its sisters the *Hotel* and *Echo* – was to suffer from a variety of mechanical failures and reactor accidents over the next 20 years.

Whereas the Americans and British were focussing on anti-submarine warfare (ASW) as the primary role for their submarines, the *November* was built with anti-surface warfare (ASUW) in mind. It packed a big punch, with eight bow tubes capable of firing nuclear-tipped 500-mm (20-in) torpedoes, and four stern tubes filled with retaliatory 400-mm (16-in) anti-submarine torpedoes. They were intended to operate independently against the US Aircraft Carrier force, ahead of the defensive barrier of SSKs.

The conventional *Golf*'s nuclear-powered equivalent was the *Hotel*, of which 16 were built in the late 1950s and early 1960s. They carried four SS-N-4 ballistic missiles. As the submarine had to surface to launch its missiles, its shape reverted to the traditional 'cylinder' to provide it with greater stability.

In the 1950s, the US Navy embarked on a programme of building 'super aircraft carriers' weighing in excess of 60,963 tonnes and superbly equipped to deal with a short-range air threat. Their purpose was to carry a large aircraft wing of A3 Skywarriors – which had a strike radius in the order of 1931km (1200 miles) – to a position from which a launch could be conducted against the heart of 'Mother Russia'. This immediately opened up vast tracts of ocean from which to launch such a strike, so the traditional Soviet barrier concept of torpedo-armed submarine defence had to be reconsidered. The answer lay in the stand-off cruise missile that could be fired by submarines and aircraft alike, assisted in long-range targeting by a third-party surveillance aircraft. The missile adopted was the inertially guided 463km (250nm) SS-N-3A (Shaddock), fitted to the *Juliett*-class conventional submarine. The nuclear equivalent was the *Echo-II*, which carried eight of the missiles in four twin elevating pods. Mid-course guidance for the missile was provided by the Front-Door radar that occupied the whole of the front

Above: USS *Halibut* conducted the last firing of the Regulus cruise missile in 1964. The introduction of Polaris in 1960 demonstrated how far and how quickly the United States had advanced in technology in a very short space of time.

of the fin, and the complete procedure for firing and guiding the missiles to their target meant that the submarine had to remain on the surface for almost 45 minutes.

To deploy these long-range missiles against US task groups, the Soviets relied on their integrated 'combined arms' network of aircraft and submarines for success.

Long-range surveillance and targeting information emanated from the huge Bear-D aircraft fitted with Big Bulge radar. From this aircraft's information, shore HQ would home in a number of assets – *EII*s with their high speed being the most useful – in order to launch a massive coordinated strike. Because the Shaddock missile was subsonic, the *EII* extremely noisy, and the Bear-D highly vulnerable to interception by Carrier-borne Combat Air Patrol (CAP) aircraft whose first priority would be to 'hack the shad', it is unlikely that this combination would have succeeded.

AMERICA'S NUCLEAR PARTNER

It was Earl Mountbatten, the First Sea Lord between 1955 and 1959, who realized that, unless Britain joined the nuclear club, her already diminished maritime power would totally wither on the vine. The first British SSN, HMS *Dreadnought*, was authorized in 1955, but it soon became apparent that the

Above: The *November* SSN was the Soviet Union's first nuclear-propelled submarine and went to sea in 1958, less than four years after USS *Nautilus*. Reliability problems plagued this and other early classes, and would cause several major casualties. Nevertheless, it was a fast and well-armed submarine; these capabilities surprised Western analysts and intensified the arms race.

Right: A Royal Air Force Nimrod Maritime Patrol Aircraft (MPA) overflies a Soviet *Echo-II* SSGN. These submarines carried eight SSN-3 'Shaddock' anti-ship missiles which were designed to counter US aircraft carriers.

country's nuclear industry would take a considerable time to produce a reactor suitable to be taken to sea. Mountbatten's excellent personal relationship with Admiral Rickover meant that, in 1959, the Royal Navy was able to purchase a complete American propulsion plant, and *Dreadnought* was commissioned in 1963. Having Britain as a partner capable of confronting the growing Soviet expansionist aspirations was important to the United States, particularly given Britain's strategic geographical position. Submarines deployed from the UK could reach forward areas several days earlier than those sailing from US east-coast bases.

Dreadnought was a successful submarine, and Britain soon followed her with the first all-British design, HMS *Valiant*. SSNs of this class were to follow at roughly 18-month intervals.

Admiral of the Fleet Earl Mountbatten also got wind that the USN had established a 'Special Projects Office' which was investigating a solid-fuel rocket motor for its deterrent missile. At that time, Britain had placed its deterrent faith in the new US underground 'Blue Streak' intercontinental

missiles, but quickly realized that an attack on their silos might destroy the whole country. She then opted for the developmental 'Skybolt' air-launched deterrent missile that could be carried by their existing fleet of V-bombers, but this project ran into trouble on the grounds of cost and was cancelled by President John Kennedy in mid-1962.

RESOLUTION AND POLARIS

Thanks to Mountbatten's foresight and the co-operation of his former colleague and friend, Admiral Arleigh Burke, the Royal Navy had had a representative in the 'Special Projects' office for almost two years, so the Chief of the Defence Staff was able to offer Mr Harold Macmillan a swift answer to his deterrent dilemma. On 22 December 1962, the United States passed Polaris-missile technology to Britain at the Treaty of Nassau, and the *Resolution*-class submarine was born. The warheads for the missile would be British-built and British-controlled, making it a truly independent nuclear deterrent. In 1968, HMS *Resolution* fired Britain's first test missile within five

Above: Britain's first nuclear-powered submarine, HMS *Dreadnought*, commissioned in 1963. She was in fact half-American in that her reactor was provided by Britain's ally. There was a point onboard called 'Checkpoint Charlie' beyond which only specially selected members of the ship's company could proceed. This situation eased when the first all-British design, HMS *Valiant*, appeared.

RESOLUTION

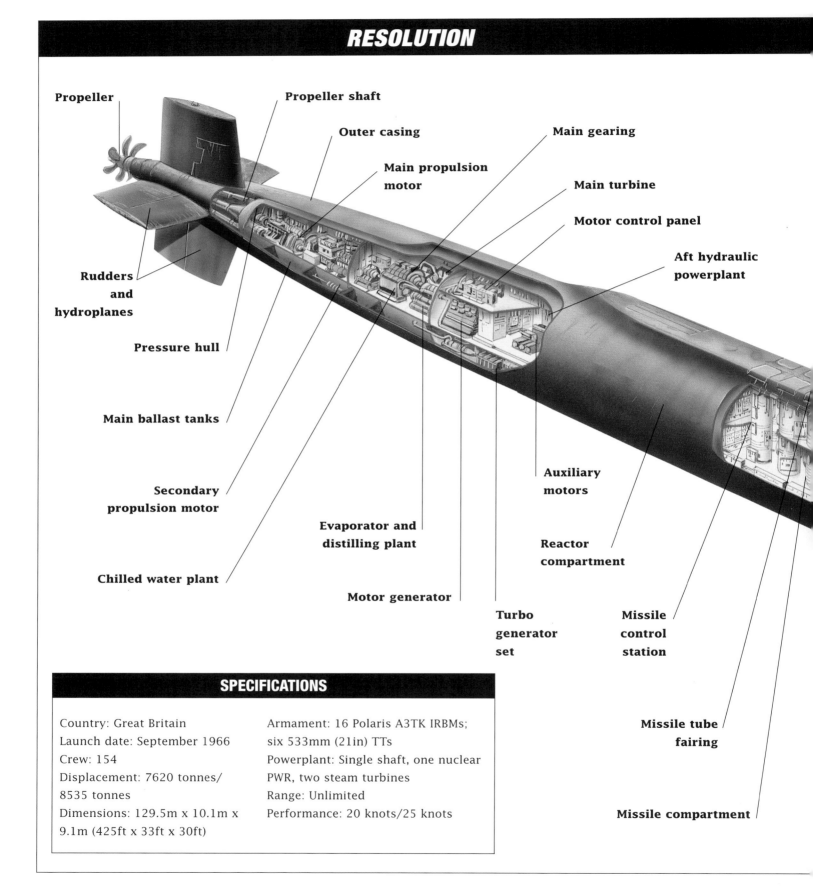

Propeller

Propeller shaft

Outer casing

Main gearing

Main propulsion motor

Main turbine

Motor control panel

Aft hydraulic powerplant

Rudders and hydroplanes

Pressure hull

Main ballast tanks

Secondary propulsion motor

Evaporator and distilling plant

Auxiliary motors

Reactor compartment

Chilled water plant

Motor generator

Turbo generator set

Missile control station

Missile tube fairing

Missile compartment

SPECIFICATIONS

Country: Great Britain
Launch date: September 1966
Crew: 154
Displacement: 7620 tonnes/
8535 tonnes
Dimensions: 129.5m x 10.1m x
9.1m (425ft x 33ft x 30ft)

Armament: 16 Polaris A3TK IRBMs;
six 533mm (21in) TTs
Powerplant: Single shaft, one nuclear
PWR, two steam turbines
Range: Unlimited
Performance: 20 knots/25 knots

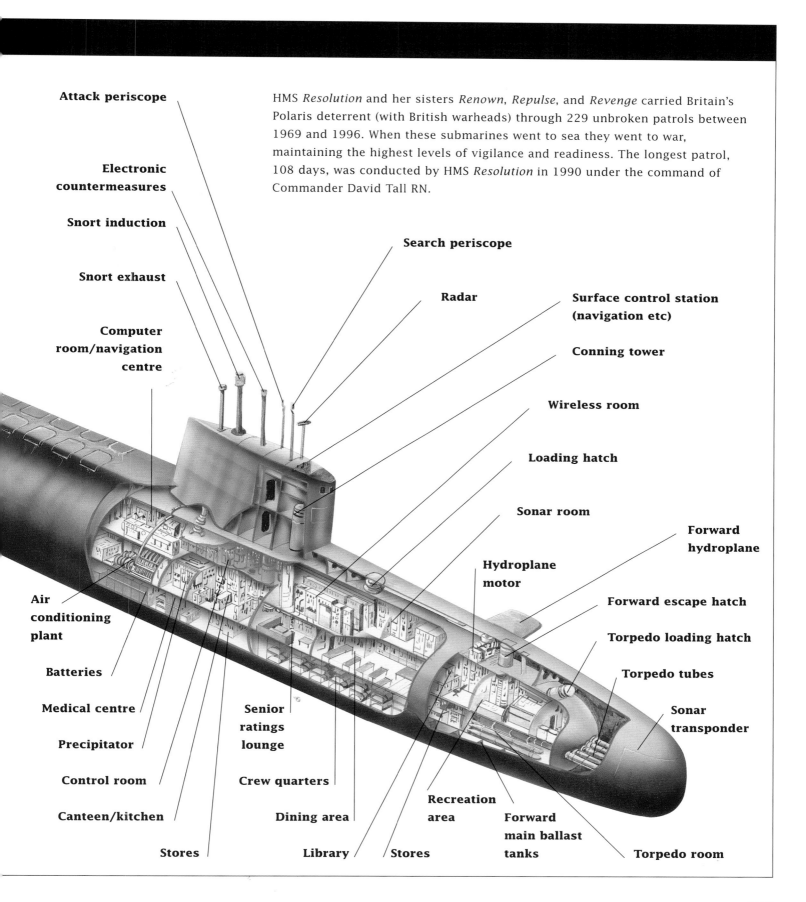

HMS *Resolution* and her sisters *Renown*, *Repulse*, and *Revenge* carried Britain's Polaris deterrent (with British warheads) through 229 unbroken patrols between 1969 and 1996. When these submarines went to sea they went to war, maintaining the highest levels of vigilance and readiness. The longest patrol, 108 days, was conducted by HMS *Resolution* in 1990 under the command of Commander David Tall RN.

Attack periscope

Electronic countermeasures

Snort induction

Snort exhaust

Computer room/navigation centre

Search periscope

Radar

Surface control station (navigation etc)

Conning tower

Wireless room

Loading hatch

Sonar room

Forward hydroplane

Hydroplane motor

Forward escape hatch

Torpedo loading hatch

Torpedo tubes

Sonar transponder

Air conditioning plant

Batteries

Medical centre

Precipitator

Control room

Canteen/kitchen

Senior ratings lounge

Crew quarters

Dining area

Library

Stores

Stores

Recreation area

Forward main ballast tanks

Torpedo room

VALIANT

Valiant, Britain's second nuclear submarine, was slightly larger than *Dreadnought*, but of basically the same design. Work on her was held up because of the priority given to the Polaris submarines of the *Resolution* class, and she was not commissioned until 18 July 1966. She was followed by a sister ship, HMS *Warspite*, and three *Churchill*-class boats.

SPECIFICATIONS

Country: Great Britain
Launch date: 3 December 1963
Crew: 116
Displacement: 4470 tonnes/
4979 tonnes

Dimensions: 86.9m x 10.1m x 8.2m
(285ft x 33ft 3in x 27ft)
Armament: Six 533mm (21in) TTs
Powerplant: One nuclear PWR
Range: Unlimited
Performance: 20 knots/29 knots

Right: HMS *Repulse*, armed with Polaris missiles, Britian's nuclear deterrent at the end of the twentieth century. *Repulse* was built by Vickers-Armstrong in Barrow and was launched on 4 November 1966. She was the last boat of this historic class to be paid off.

milliseconds of the time planned five years earlier! When she sailed for patrol early in the next year, the British newspaper the *Daily Telegraph* said: 'By diving into the waters of a troubled world, HMS *Resolution* takes with her the best insurance policy the nation ever had.' This single SSBN carried with her the threat of destruction of about a quarter of the larger cities of the USSR.

When *Resolution* went on patrol, she was effectively at war; it was essential that she and her three sisters maintained three aims with no compromise: to remain undetected (by friend and foe alike); to maintain communications (listening to shore HQ); and to be constantly ready to fire at short notice.

The essence of deterrence is that the response of a second-strike against aggression must be guaranteed and its results unacceptable to the aggressor. This implies that the means of its delivery must be constantly available and it must be able to overwhelm any defences established against it. Anything less might encourage

POLARIS

During the late 1970s, in response to growing concerns about the capabilities of the Soviet anti-ballistic missile systems around Moscow, Great Britain developed the 'Chevaline' system to enhance the capability of its Polaris A3 missile. The Penetration Aid Pack (PAC) carried chaff to blind and confuse Soviet ABM radars, in addition to the warheads.

1 Nose cap
2 Mounting plate
3 Nose fairing jettison rocket
4 Firing unit
5 Ignition inverter
6 Equipment section access door
7 Interlocks
8 Guidance electronics assembly
9 Snubber

10 Flight control electronics package
11 Flight control gyro package
12 Main umbilical
13 Hydraulics battery pacakge
14 Hydraulics power distribution package
15 Aft umbilical
16 Hydraulic actuator package cover
17 Hydraulic actuator
18 Interstage access door

19 Guidance cooling system
20 Guidance gimbal assembly
21 Base structure and thermal barrier
22 Electronics power distribution package
23 Electronics battery package

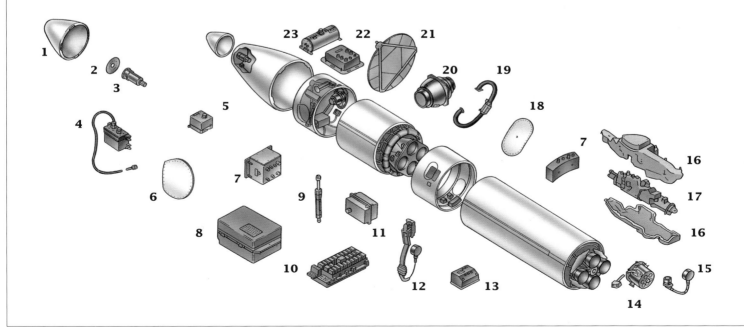

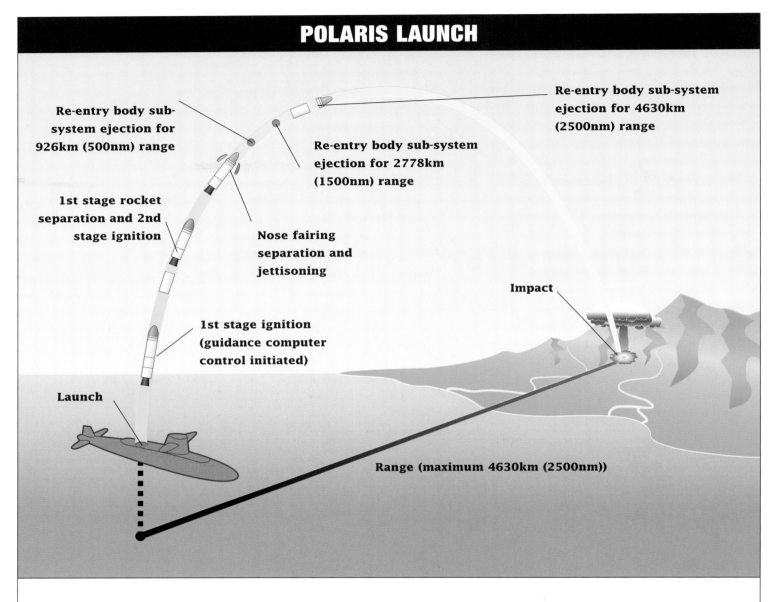

POLARIS LAUNCH

Re-entry body sub-system ejection for 926km (500nm) range

Re-entry body sub-system ejection for 2778km (1500nm) range

Re-entry body sub-system ejection for 4630km (2500nm) range

1st stage rocket separation and 2nd stage ignition

Nose fairing separation and jettisoning

Impact

1st stage ignition (guidance computer control initiated)

Launch

Range (maximum 4630km (2500nm))

The Polaris missile is a ballistic system, in that its payload is ejected at a pre-determined point to continue its journey to its target. At the heart of the system lies accurate navigation on the part of the SSBN through its two SINS systems. They told the missile where it was, and the target tape loaded onboard the submarine told the missile where it had to go.

Opposite: In 1960, USS *Scorpion* was the first US nuclear submarine to pay a port visit to the United Kingdom. Sadly, this submarine sank in 1968, probably as a result of a torpedo accident onboard. She was neither the first nor the last submarine to suffer such a fate.

an irresponsible regime to chance its arm in an attempt to come out on top in a nuclear exchange. Britain adopted the policy to have one SSBN constantly on patrol, and although Vice Admiral Sir Rufus Mackenzie DSO DSC – the first Chief of Polaris Executive (CPE) – argued strongly for five submarines in order to provide the required cover, limited finance and a grudging political will meant that he had to make do with four. Given the refit

and maintenance cycles demanded by these highly complex submarines, keeping one constantly on patrol posed a tremendous challenge to operators at sea and their shore supporters. To get the maximum availability from the hulls, a two-crew system of manning was adopted.

To maintain the deterrent required great skill and expertise in every area of maritime warfare both afloat and ashore, and it also

required great political determination in the face of a vociferous opposition to the very concept of nuclear weapons. The Soviet Union realized that, if she was able to undermine confidence in the deterrent by detecting a British SSBN, she might be able to remove one player from the scene; she went to considerable lengths to achieve that aim. She never succeeded, and the fact that the *Resolution*-class conducted 229 unbroken patrols over the next 28 years, when HMS *Repulse* was paid off, was a great achievement for the Royal Navy and the British Defence industry alike.

NEW SONAR AND WEAPONS

In 1961, the Americans introduced the SSN-594 *Permit*-class. The first submarine of this

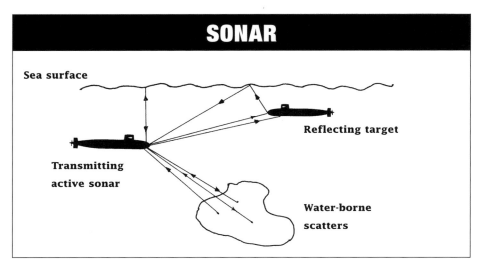

TOWED ARRAY

Sea surface

Tow ship

Tow cable

Towed passive array

'Noisy' target

Sea bottom

SONAR

Sea surface

Reflecting target

Transmitting active sonar

Water-borne scatters

class of 14, USS *Thresher*, was lost during sea trials; however, her sisters were nevertheless highly capable SSNs. The emphasis was now to enhance reactor design and introduce new sonars and improved weaponry.

There is an adage in submarining that says that, in order to enhance your own survival, you should 'engage your enemy from further away'. At the end of World War II, the hesitant first steps in developing weapons capable of chasing a submarine once it had left periscope depth were taken. This took the shape of autonomous acoustic homing torpedoes, but these relied on a very accurate fire-control solution and on being placed very close to the evading target. The next refinement was to introduce wire-guidance, the ability for a submarine to pass course and depth corrections to its weapons in the water. They were steered down the bearing of the target and did not require a pin-point accurate solution against which to be fired. All the CO had to determine was that the target was within the range of the torpedoes' guidance wire. Once the weapons had been steered to the proximity of the target, their own homing equipment took over to complete the attack.

Two major steps forward were made in the 1960s. The first was the introduction of low-frequency detection towed-array sonar specifically tuned to detect turning machinery (e.g. turbo-generators, main coolant pumps). The second was the siting of an advanced active/passive sonar that was wrapped around the bow. This increased initial detection ranges significantly and, with much improved target-motion analysis (TMA) techniques, provided the opportunity to deliver a long-range weapon. The vehicle chosen was SUBROC, an ASW rocket fired from a dived submarine to a range of about 56km (35 miles). The payload was a small nuclear bomb that had an effective 'killing range' of 3.7–7.4km (2–4nm).

In addition to improving on-board sensors, the United States put enormous investment into the seabed surveillance

system known as SOSUS. The arrays, strategically placed around the world's oceans to monitor Soviet submarine movements, fed their information to shore-based analysis centres, where a collation of clues, often combined with other all-source intelligence, provided a picture of 'who was in and who was out'. This information was passed to selected submarines at sea, who then reacted to the information received to fulfil their mission.

In 1966, an enlarged and improved *Permit* design appeared in the shape of the *Sturgeon*-class. With raft and flexible-mounted machinery, the 37 of the class that were built were significantly quieter than their predecessors, and they became the workhorses of the US SSNs during the Cold War. Dominance over an expanding and increasingly capable Soviet Navy was essential if the West was to preserve maritime superiority, and 'knowing your enemy' was an essential part of that superiority. Hence finding out what the opposition was capable of, where they went, and what they did when they got

there became routine missions that were undertaken by US/UK SSNs in every ocean of the world.

In 1971, the United States uprated its free-falling, three-warhead Polaris A3 missile into a 10-warhead MIRV (multiple, independently targetable re-entry vehicle) Poseidon C3 missile. In essence a single Poseidon, although delivered at the same range of Polaris, it could engage more than one target and was introduced to overcome the perceived increase in capability of Soviet anti-missile-missile defences ranged around Moscow. Thirty-one of the USN SSBNs (FBMs in US parlance) were converted.

The 1980s saw the adoption by NATO of the 'Forward Maritime Strategy', a military thrust by Aircraft Carrier Battle Groups into ocean areas accessible to the Soviet Union in order to prevent an invasion of Norway. Such a thrust, although essential, would involve long transits with the possibility of at least being shadowed by Soviet submarines, and, as the destination was approached and tension rose, there was a real possibility of attack from a variety of

Above: SSN-676, USS *Billfish* (*Sturgeon*-class) breaking through the ice at the North Pole. Periodic demonstrations of suddenly popping up at the top of the world were a regular reminder to the Soviets that these waters, used by them as under-ice bastions, were not being neglected by the West.

STURGEON-CLASS ANTENNAS AND MASTS

In addition to the array of masts shown here that provided a significant electronic surveillance capability, the *Sturgeon*-class was also fitted with impressive underwater 'ears' through her BQQ-5 sonar outfit. This was a digital multi-beam system employing both hull-mounted and towed-array acoustic hydrophones. The key to the excellence of this system lay in its powerful processing equipment which could identify the quietest target against the traditional cacophony of underwater noises experienced by all submariners.

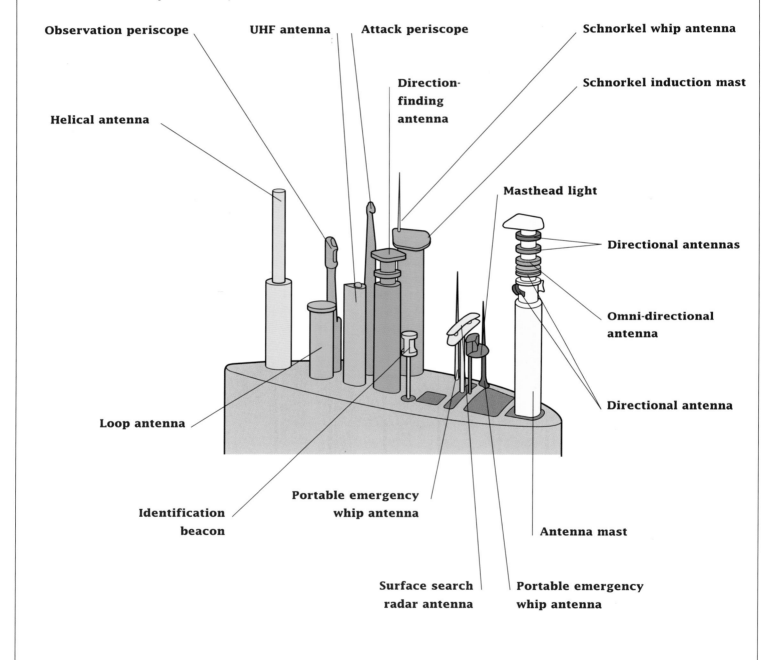

Observation periscope

UHF antenna

Attack periscope

Schnorkel whip antenna

Direction-finding antenna

Schnorkel induction mast

Helical antenna

Masthead light

Directional antennas

Omni-directional antenna

Directional antenna

Loop antenna

Portable emergency whip antenna

Antenna mast

Identification beacon

Surface search radar antenna

Portable emergency whip antenna

Left: A submarine launched Sub-Harpoon missile is seen early in its flight, soon after the nose of its capsule has been blown clear. This high subsonic anti-ship missile is operated by several navies in a number of variants. The Block 1C in service with the Royal Navy has programmable waypoints and selected terminal trajectories that enhance its lethality.

platforms, most notably from the air and beneath the surface. As the best way of catching a submarine had become another submarine, it is obvious that SSNs had a huge part to play in ensuring the safe passage of the High Value Units (HVUs). They were needed in numbers. Some swept ahead in the transit route planned to be taken by the task groups before falling in behind them to take up defensive seaward barriers once the relative safety of the fjords had been reached; one or two others might guard the 'bananas' astern of the carrier; others SSNs conducted precursor

operations within the carrier havens before they arrived; yet others carried out area operations, seeking out the big missile carriers (*Oscar* in particular) that could threaten the task force from several hundred miles range. This strategy was maintained and exercised regularly until 1989, when the first signs of the break-up of the Warsaw Pact appeared.

Another activity that was regularly undertaken and demonstrated was Arctic warfare, as it was assessed that the Soviets maintained SSBN bastions under the ice. In May 1986, three US submarines, USS fectef f

Archerfish, Hawkbill, and Ray, surfaced together at the North Pole.

In addition to the capability of supporting the battle groups in area (independent) or support (designated) operations, other capabilities were developed. The 130km (70nm) range anti-surface Sub-Harpoon missile was added to the weapon inventory in the early 1970s, and, in the early 1980s, the Tomahawk Cruise Missile entered service. This extraordinarily versatile cruise missile, which is still in service, comes in a number of variants and can provide the following: a wide area search and attack profile against enemy surface ships at a considerable range, using inertial navigation

SUBMARINE SENSOR AND WEAPON SYSTEMS

This 'explosion' of sensors and weapon fits of a typical SSN underlines the spectrum of capability embodied in the platform. The fact that this array of sensors and weapons can be deployed covertly into an area, and out again, with neither opposition knowledge nor political embarrassment gives the SSN an unparalleled capability. When in area they can conduct intelligence, surveillance, and reconnaissance missions to provide timely intelligence to policy makers.

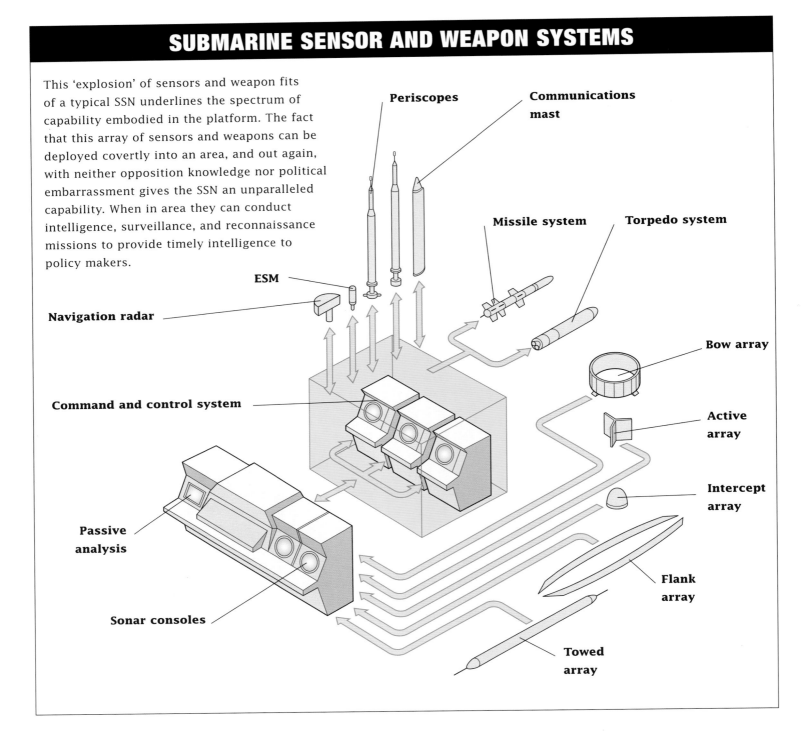

and missile radar guidance; precision strike against land targets at ranges of approximately 1609km (1000 miles), using Digital Scene Matching Area Correlation (DSMAC); and a nuclear attack option, using Terrain Contour Matching (TERCOM).

The USS *Los Angeles*, the lead ship of the *688*-class, was commissioned in 1976. Sixty-two of this class were built, with the last, the USS *Cheyenne*, being completed in 1996. This large SSN was built with the primary mission of escorting the fast CVNs (nuclear-powered aircraft carrier) into their strike areas at very high speed. It was fitted with the BQQ-5 sonar, a digital multi-beam system employing both hull-mounted and towed acoustic hydrophone arrays. Class capability was gradually improved over the two decades of building, with the later units having their under-ice capability significantly enhanced through the strengthening of their sails ('fins' in UK parlance) and the moving of their forward hydroplanes to the bow.

The USS *Providence* was the first to have 12 vertical launch tubes installed under the forward casing to carry TLAM. In 1991, during Operation Desert Storm, USS *Louisville*, operating in the Red Sea, fired the first Tomahawk from a submarine in a combat scenario. In addition to the cruise missile, the standard torpedo, the Mk 48, was uprated by the 'Adcap' programme to be able to take on the most capable Soviet submarine.

In 1981, the *Ohio*-class SSBN – with a reactor refuelling period extended to 20 years and armed with the Trident C4 missile – entered service, and the United States' strategic capability took a quantum leap. This large submarine (19,305 tonnes) carries 24 missiles. The C4 was a three-stage ballistic missile powered by solid fuel motors guided by a self-contained inertial guidance system to a maximum range of 7000km (4350 miles). The accuracy of the post-boost vehicle (PBV) containing eight 100-knot MIRVs was enhanced by stellar

navigation (taking a star-sight). A further development to this missile is the Trident D5, which is currently in service. It weighs 59,000kg (almost 60 tons!), was introduced in the 1990s, and has an awesome capability. Its payload is 8–12 re-entry vehicles, with a range capability of 12,000km (7458 miles).

As the strategic situation in the world changed, US submarines took on additional roles. In 1989, USS *Memphis* was withdrawn from active service to become a research platform to test advanced submarine technologies such as optronic non-hull penetrating masts, unmanned underwater

Above: A Tomahawk cruise missile starts its flight, having been fired from a submarine. Onboard, the missile sits in a stainless steel capsule in the tube that provides protection during the underwater launch. On firing, the boost motor drives the missile through the water to the surface; it is jettisoned once the missile is in the air. The turbofan cruise motor then provides power for passage to the target.

LOS ANGELES

The *Los Angeles*-class submarine provides the backbone of the US Navy's SSN force. Big, fast, and heavily armed, the last 23 submarines of the class, designated 'improved *688*s', are quieter and incorporate advanced combat systems. In addition to their surveillance role, typically, two of their numbers are assigned to US Carrier Battle Groups to provide force protection.

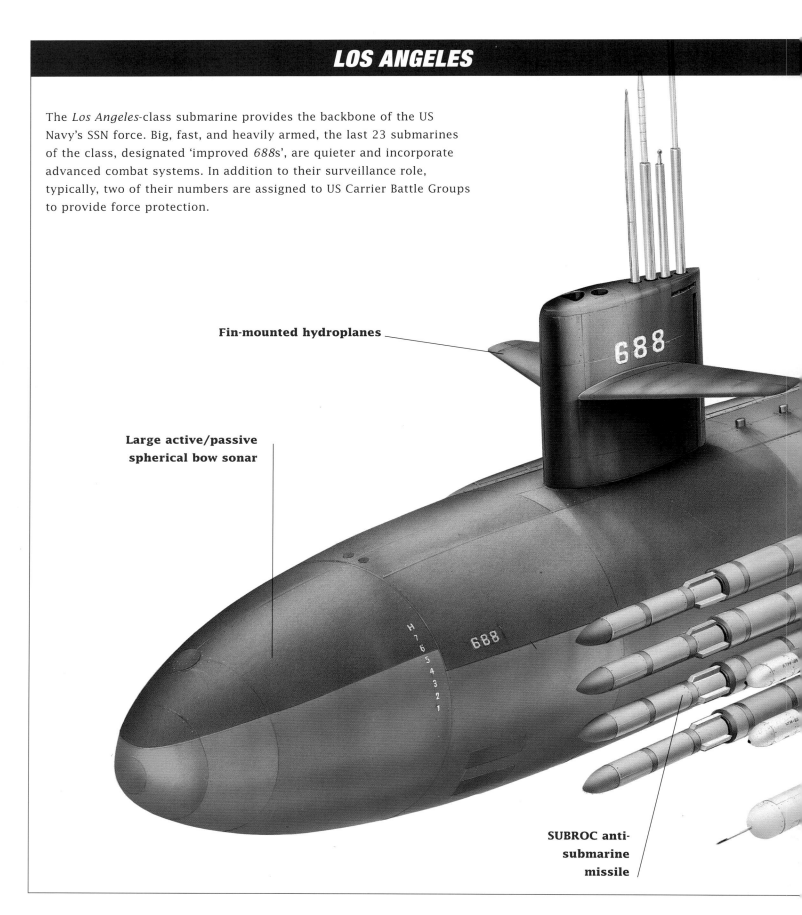

Fin-mounted hydroplanes

Large active/passive spherical bow sonar

SUBROC anti-submarine missile

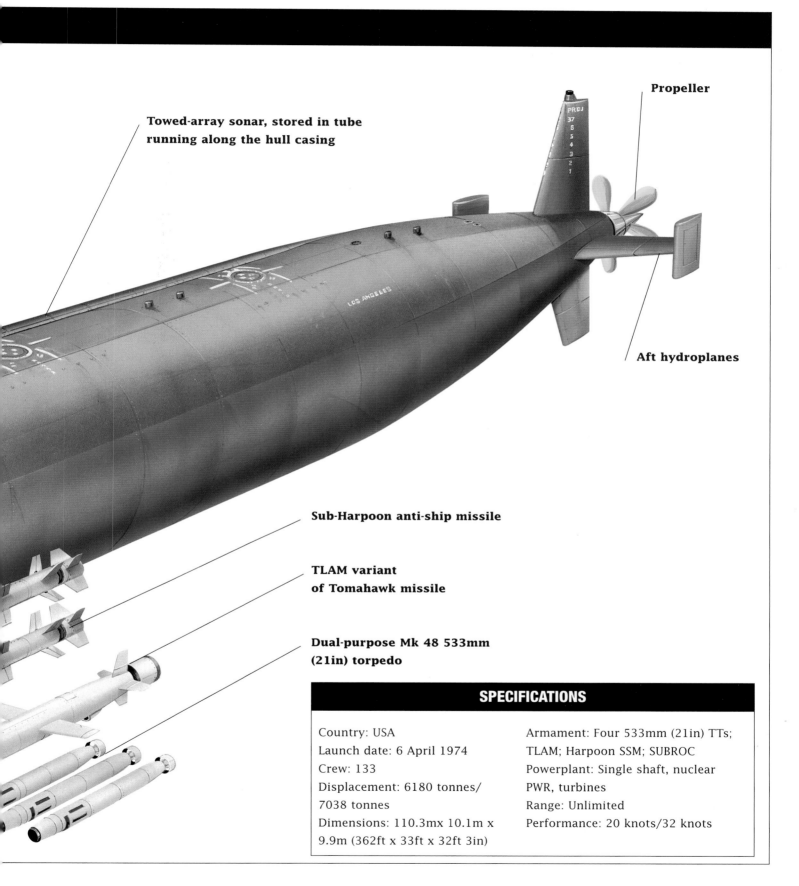

Towed-array sonar, stored in tube running along the hull casing

Propeller

Aft hydroplanes

Sub-Harpoon anti-ship missile

TLAM variant of Tomahawk missile

Dual-purpose Mk 48 533mm (21in) torpedo

SPECIFICATIONS

Country: USA
Launch date: 6 April 1974
Crew: 133
Displacement: 6180 tonnes/ 7038 tonnes
Dimensions: 110.3m x 10.1m x 9.9m (362ft x 33ft x 32ft 3in)

Armament: Four 533mm (21in) TTs; TLAM; Harpoon SSM; SUBROC
Powerplant: Single shaft, nuclear PWR, turbines
Range: Unlimited
Performance: 20 knots/32 knots

Opposite: The difference in size between the Trident 1 (C4) ballistic missile (on the right), and its successor, the Trident II (D5) missile (on the left), is striking. The former had a range of 7400km (3995nm); the latter's range was 12,000km (6479nm). To improve the aerodynamic performance of these massive rockets, an aerospike emerges after the missile clears the water.

vehicles (UUVs), and larger diameter torpedoes. In 1993, two SSBNs, *Kamehameha* and *James K. Polk*, were converted into swimmer delivery vehicle (SDV) carriers.

In 1996, USS *Cheyenne*, the last of the *688*-class was commissioned, and later that year USS *Seawolf* (SSN-21) underwent sea trials. The programme was cancelled after USS *Connecticut* was commissioned in 1998, to be replaced by the SSN-774 (USS *Virginia*) programme. She was laid down in September 1998 and is classed as an 'affordable' SSN. She is designed to dominate the coastal region while maintaining open-ocean supremacy. The class will include Tomahawk missile capability; advanced sonar systems for anti-submarine and mine warfare; a reconfigurable torpedo room for special missions; advanced SEAL delivery system (ASDS) and nine-man lock-out trunk to launch unmanned underwater or aerial vehicles for mine reconnaissance, intelligence gathering and other missions; enhanced stealth; and enhanced electronic support measures (ESM). The *Virginia* is expected to be completed in 2004.

COLD WAR ARMS RACE

Accurate navigation is at the heart of SSBN operations to achieve an accurate strike. Soviet submarines were at a disadvantage in that they were not equipped with SINS. It was therefore necessary for them to patrol close (less than 1609km (1000 miles)) to the east and west coasts of the United States. This allowed for little time on-station and it was also (correctly) assessed that these areas were monitored by SOSUS and patrolled by US SSNs. As a result, the Soviet Navy's nuclear role was downgraded in favour of land-based intercontinental ballistic missiles (ICBMs).

To overcome this inherent navigation weakness, the Soviet Union embarked on a massive ocean survey programme in the 1960s which provided bottom-contour information sufficiently accurate to sustain strategic missile operations. At about the same time, the longer ranged SS-N-6 'Sawfly'

was developed. A combination of these two factors (and the dismissal of Krushchev) saw a shift in policy and the appearance of the *Yankee*-class, remarkably similar in characteristics to western SSBNs, carrying 16 missiles. A major variation in design was that *Yankee* was driven by two reactors, making it a significantly noisy boat and relatively easy to detect. Another drawback to the system was that the 'Sawfly' missile still suffered from 'short legs', meaning that the *Yankees* – of which 34 were built in the late 1960s/early 1970s – still had to patrol in areas close to the West's front doors. They were highly vulnerable; nevertheless, in war they would have to have been dealt with.

In 1967, the Soviets introduced a new class of submarine that was to tax Western navy tactical thinkers a great deal, and that was the *Charlie* SSGN. This submarine, designed to operate against US aircraft carriers, carried eight SS-N-7 'Starbright' missiles, which had a range of 56–65km (30–35nm), and – unlike the SS-N-3 fitted to the *Echo II*- and *Juliett*-classes – could be fired from deep and required no mid-course guidance, as its J-band radar was expected quickly to acquire a target. The SS-N-7, with its 'pop-up' (little warning) capability, greatly extended the 'limiting lines of submerged approach' (the range astern beyond which a submarine was no longer a threat) and forced a US Task Group to seek even more ASW assets to defend itself. The US response in the 1970s was the jet-propelled S3 Viking surveillance aircraft and the development of the very high-speed *Los Angeles*-class SSN. In the late 1970s, an upgraded version of the submarine appeared (designated *Charlie-II*) which carried the SS-N-9 'Siren' missile which had a maximum range of 111km (60nm). This increase in capability was in turn triggered by the introduction of the S3 Viking aircraft – a classic example of an arms race!

The year 1968 saw the introduction of the *Victor*-class SSN. This was the first true Soviet anti-submarine submarine, and she

OHIO

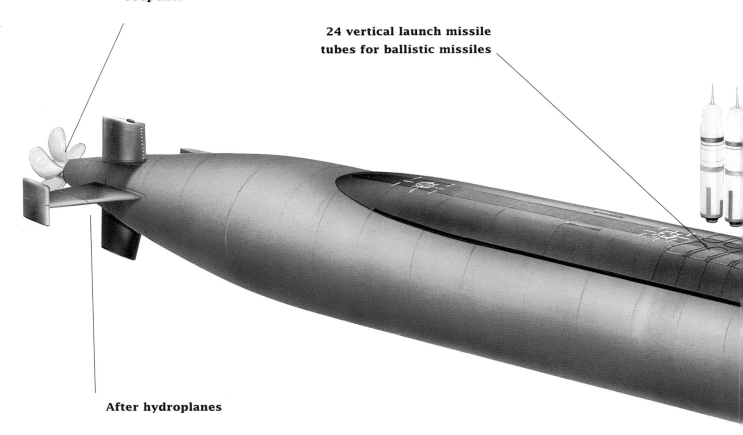

Propeller

**24 vertical launch missile
tubes for ballistic missiles**

After hydroplanes

SPECIFICATIONS

Country: USA
Launch date: 7 April 1979
Crew: 155
Displacement: 16,360 tonnes/
19,050 tonnes
Dimensions: 170.7m x 12.8m x
11m (560ft x 42ft x 36ft 5in)

Armament: 24 Trident II D-5
missiles; four 533mm (21in) TTs
Powerplant: Single shaft, nuclear
PWR, turbines
Range: Unlimited
Performance: 24 knots/28 knots

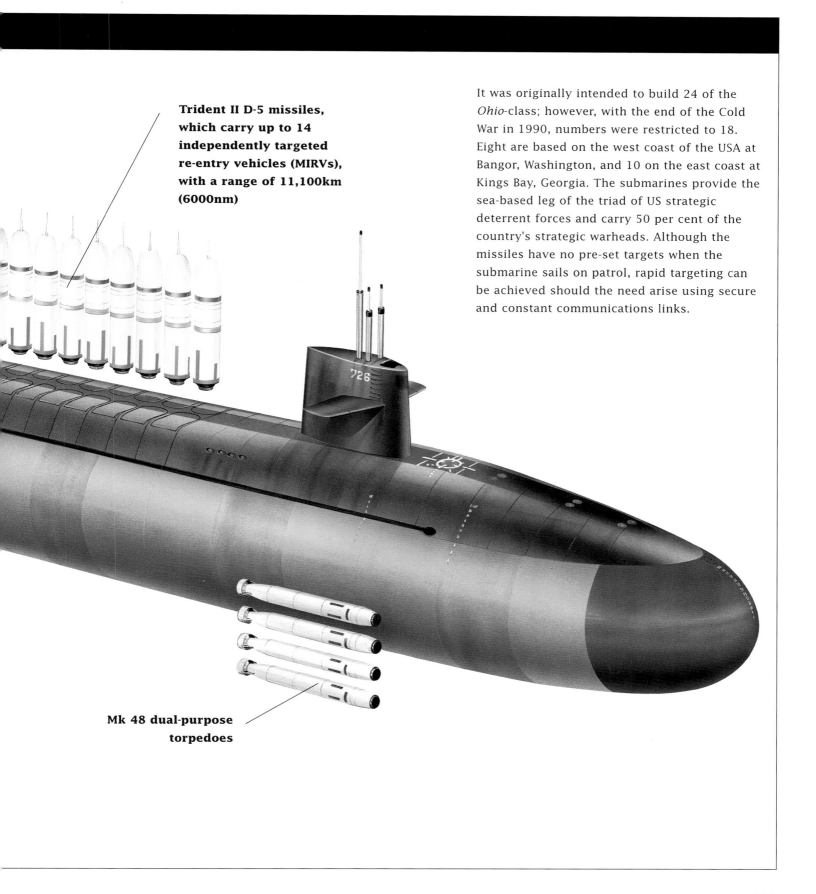

Trident II D-5 missiles, which carry up to 14 independently targeted re-entry vehicles (MIRVs), with a range of 11,100km (6000nm)

Mk 48 dual-purpose torpedoes

It was originally intended to build 24 of the *Ohio*-class; however, with the end of the Cold War in 1990, numbers were restricted to 18. Eight are based on the west coast of the USA at Bangor, Washington, and 10 on the east coast at Kings Bay, Georgia. The submarines provide the sea-based leg of the triad of US strategic deterrent forces and carry 50 per cent of the country's strategic warheads. Although the missiles have no pre-set targets when the submarine sails on patrol, rapid targeting can be achieved should the need arise using secure and constant communications links.

Above: The flight-deck (after casing) of an *Ohio*-class SSBN, under which are housed 24 Trident II missiles. As with any SSBN, this extent of casing causes great difficulty at periscope depth in very rough weather because of a suction effect. The adage 'Happiness is six hundred feet in a force ten' is particularly true for these leviathans of the deep.

designed to reduce the sonar pulse reflectivity of U-boats – and they had a creep-speed propulsion system that was designed to be used when operating in areas thought to contain Western SSBNs.

In the 1970s, the hull was lengthened to accommodate the SS-N-15 'Starfish' nuclear-tipped ASW missile that was very similar in concept to the US SUBROC. Seven of these units were built and designated as the *Victor-II*–class. In keeping with the Soviet 'all-arms' philosophy, they were designed to be operated with the *Moskva*-class, helicopter-equipped, anti-submarine ship, and the long-range Bear-F maritime patrol aircraft. The role of this combined force was to hunt down Western SSBNs that might be operating in the North Atlantic and Mediterranean Sea, and the submarine was provided with a commensurate communications suite.

In the early 1980s, the hull evolved yet again into the *Victor-III*–class and grew to 6096 tonnes. The 23 units' most striking feature was the massive pod on top of the rudder stack that contained a deployable towed array. To support the sought-for improved detection capability provided by this sonar, a new family of weaponry was housed in an enlarged bow section. A longer range torpedo was housed in the 65mm (2.5in) tubes (designated SET65) and this was propelled by an advanced closed-cycle thermal propulsion system, giving it a range of 50km (27nm) at 50 knots and 30 knots for getting to 93km (50nm). It could home on wake (the disturbance in the water created by the passage of another ship or submarine) and was undoubtedly backed up by a sensor capable of measuring such disturbances. This family of sensors are known as 'non-acoustics'. The larger tube also allowed the *Victor-III* to carry the SS-N-16 'Stallion' anti-submarine missile that had a payload of a homing torpedo rather than a nuclear bomb.

In the late 1980s, it was becoming apparent to all naval thinkers that the deployment of a nuclear weapon at sea was unlikely unless

bore all the hallmarks of western ASW influence. Undoubtedly designed for long high-speed transits (she had two reactors), her primary role was to seek out Western SSBNs in both the Atlantic and Pacific oceans. She was fitted with 2001-ski, a chin-strap low frequency active-passive sonar based on the British-SSN fitted sonar set, the designs for which had been passed by the spies Houghton and Gee in the 1950s. This notorious pair worked at the Admiralty Research Laboratory at Portland, England. The *Victor*s were also anechoically coated – readers will recall the German experiment with 'Alberich' at the end of World War II, a rubber overcoat that was

there had been a similar exchange ashore, thus the reversion to a conventional payload and the need for greater accuracy in fire-control. The *Victor-III*, in the right hands, was similar in capability to the US SSN-637 and, being significantly quieter than her predecessors, had the respect of her Western SSN counterparts. Maintaining the tactical advantage over them called for a good deal of care because, until the introduction of the Spearfish torpedo in the RN and Mk 48 Adcap torpedo in the US Navy, they probably held the edge in a 'dog-fight' (more than 1828m (2000yds)) scenario with their big fire-and-forget torpedoes and copious, quickly deployed, torpedo countermeasure suite. It is stressed that such a scenario was never likely to be encountered by a Western SSBN; it would have been long gone.

EXPERIMENTAL HULLS

While the *Victor* hull represented Soviet ASW tactical thinking, two experimental hulls appeared in the 1970s that were intended to advance anti-surface capability against the Western carrier groups. The first was the *Alfa*. This cigar- rather than teardrop-shaped submarine had the extraordinary capabilities of achieving a dived speed of about 42 knots and an operating depth of 914m (3000ft). It achieved the former by using lead-bismuth as reactor coolant, a highly efficient heat-transfer method, and building the hull of titanium rather than steel. The submarine was intended to dash out and intercept the approaching task group, deliver its weapon, and withdraw at high speed; therefore, it required neither a large armoury nor a sophisticated sonar suite. Its appearance caused some consternation amongst Western analysts and gave further impetus to improved weaponry, as there was nothing in the contemporary torpedo armament that could touch it. Apart from an occasional uncomfortable interaction for Western SSNs, however, experience was soon to reveal that the *Alfa* was beset by technological problems inherent in its

reactor design and operation at depth. The latter in particular demonstrated that, while titanium did indeed improve the weight/strength ratio enormously and allowed forays to previously unheard-of depths, it had nowhere near the elasticity of steel over extended operations and was subject to cracking. The six that entered service never realized their hoped-for potential.

The second hull that attracted considerable attention in the 1970s was the *Papa*. This big SSGN armed with the SS-N-9 anti-ship missile had a significantly higher

Below: In order to house the large BQQ-5 sonar array, the bow of the US *Ohio*-class is necessarily bulbous. When the Tomahawk missile was introduced, the weapon stowage compartment of these submarines began to get extremely crowded! To relieve congestion, vertical launch tubes for the missile were fitted into the boats' casing.

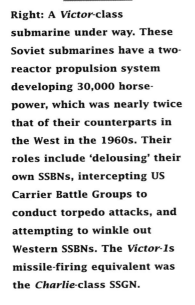

In 1968, a US Navy Chief Warrant Officer called John Anthony Walker handed the Soviets untold riches in the shape of cipher settings for the US Navy's most sophisticated communications machines.

speed than its predecessor the *Charlie-II* and, once again, could have revolutionized the ASW defence of the task group. As it happens, it would appear that *Papa* was beset with mechanical problems and the design never reached series production.

One class that did reach high levels of production was the 14,732-tonne *Oscar*-class, the replacement for the *Echo-II,* which had the significant advantage over its predecessor of launching its missiles from deep. The great capability of the *Charlie/Papa* concept was the short reaction time given to a target of missile launch, which is lost to the long-range shooter. The compensating factor used by this genre of anti-ship missile firer is weight of attack, and here the *Oscar*-class scores heavily with its 24 SS-N-19 'Shipwreck' missiles that have a range of 463–556km (250–300nm). The turbojet-propelled missiles are supersonic, can be equipped with either nuclear- or conventional warheads, and are housed in tubes situated between the outer hull and the pressure hull, occupying about 4m (13ft) and giving *Oscar* a total diameter of about 18m (59ft). Targeting for the missile is provided via satellite and the onboard 'Punch Bowl' system. The 'Shipwreck' system is also fitted in the nuclear-powered

Kirov-class cruiser, so it is unsurprising that, with this might of weaponry ranged against it and outside its ASW ring, SSNs would be expected to provide the task group with its 'deepfield' protection. 'Getting the archer before he fires his arrows' would have been their aim.

On the strategic front, the successor to the SS-N-6 'Sawfly' missile was the liquid-fuelled SS-N-8 that could deliver its 1MT warhead to the significant range of 8000km (4320nm). It was first deployed in the 12-tube *Delta-I* SSBN, a modified *Yankee*-class with a missile silo added to the after-casing to house the considerably larger missile. The class was also fitted with satellite navigation and a Very Low Frequency (VLF) communications buoy. With the extra missile range, it was no longer necessary for the Soviets to patrol in forward areas, and they adopted the 'bastion concept' for the protection of their strategic missile-firers. The Barents Sea represents the western bastion and the Sea of Okhotsk the eastern. These bastions would be protected in depth, with SSNs patrolling the outer ring and SSKs the inner.

The *Delta II* was developed to carry 16 SS-N-8 missiles, and the *Delta III*, completed between 1975 and 1982, to carry 16 SS-N-18

Right: A *Victor*-class submarine under way. These Soviet submarines have a two-reactor propulsion system developing 30,000 horse-power, which was nearly twice that of their counterparts in the West in the 1960s. Their roles include 'delousing' their own SSBNs, intercepting US Carrier Battle Groups to conduct torpedo attacks, and attempting to winkle out Western SSBNs. The *Victor-1s* missile-firing equivalent was the *Charlie*-class SSGN.

'Stingray' ballistic missiles. These missiles were capable of carrying up to seven MIRVs and represented a major step forward in penetrability. The *Delta IV*s, introduced in 1985, had to be built for the eastern coast SSBN force to carry the large SS-N-23 'Skiff' missile in order to take advantage of the 8300km (4482nm) range offered by its three-stage liquid fuel rockets and 10 MIRV capability.

SPIES AND CIPHERS

In 1968, a US Navy Chief Warrant Officer called John Anthony Walker handed the Soviets untold riches in the shape of cipher settings for the US Navy's most sophisticated communications machines. He and two family members – plus a friend recruited from within the submarine community, Lt. Cdr. Jerry Whitworth – kept the Soviets supplied with crypto material for the next 17 years. The emergence in the 1980s of two submarines that were to take the West by surprise because of their degree of

sophistication was almost certainly due to the information that the Soviets gathered in over the years via the Walker-Whitworth spy-ring. They were the *Typhoon*-class SSBN and the *Akula*-class SSN.

The first *Typhoon* was completed in 1981 and at 26,417 tonnes dived is the biggest submarine ever to be built. It consisted of

Above: The *Alfa*-class of the 1970s and 1980s was a revolutionary example of advanced Soviet submarine technology, and it caused the West to rethink its torpedo technology.

PAPA

The *Papa*-class SSGN was the missile firing stable mate of the *Alfa*. With two reactors capable of producing in the order of 70,000 horsepower and a lightweight titanium hull which provided a significant diving depth, it could have carried the battle well forward to the Carrier Groups' back yard. In the end, only one was built, indicating cost/technical problems.

SPECIFICATIONS

Country: Russia
Launch date: 1970
Crew: 110
Displacement: 6198 tonnes/ 7112 tonnes
Dimensions: 109m x 11.5m x 7.6m (357ft 7in x 37ft 9in x 24ft 11in)

Armament: Six 533mm (21in) TTs; two 406mm (16in) TTs
Powerplant: Two shafts, one nuclear PWR, two turbines
Range: Unlimited
Performance: 20 knots/39 knots

The first *Akula*-class submarine was seen in 1987, and its appearance shook Western experts because of its quietness when operating. It was apparent that many Western noise-reduction techniques had been introduced.

Opposite: This D*elta*-class SSBN is seen flying the Russian naval ensign (based on the cross of St Andrew, Scotland's patron saint), which dates back to its introduction by Tsar Peter the Great. Her presence at sea is a reminder that strategic deterrence is still considered essential to maintain a practical balance of global naval power.

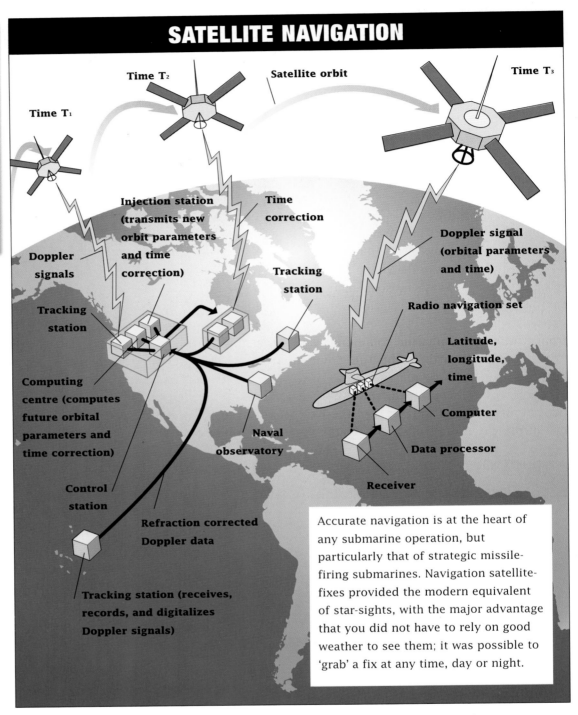

SATELLITE NAVIGATION

Time T₁
Time T₂
Time T₃
Satellite orbit

Doppler signals

Injection station (transmits new orbit parameters and time correction)

Time correction

Tracking station

Doppler signal (orbital parameters and time)

Tracking station

Radio navigation set

Computing centre (computes future orbital parameters and time correction)

Naval observatory

Latitude, longitude, time

Computer

Data processor

Control station

Receiver

Refraction corrected Doppler data

Tracking station (receives, records, and digitalizes Doppler signals)

Accurate navigation is at the heart of any submarine operation, but particularly that of strategic missile-firing submarines. Navigation satellite-fixes provided the modern equivalent of star-sights, with the major advantage that you did not have to rely on good weather to see them; it was possible to 'grab' a fix at any time, day or night.

two complete pressure hulls that housed a complete PWR propulsion system aft and 10 missile tubes forward. These hulls were joined in the middle by a command cylinder that housed the attack centre and communications equipment, and right forward by another cylinder housing the tactical weapon stowage compartment. The two reactor systems provided a high degree of mechanical redundancy, and together they gave this leviathan of the deep a handy 24 knots dived. The submarine was designed around the SS-N-20 'Sturgeon' ballistic missile system; a three-stage solid-fuel missile capable of a range of 8334km (4500nm) and delivering 10 re-entry vehicles.

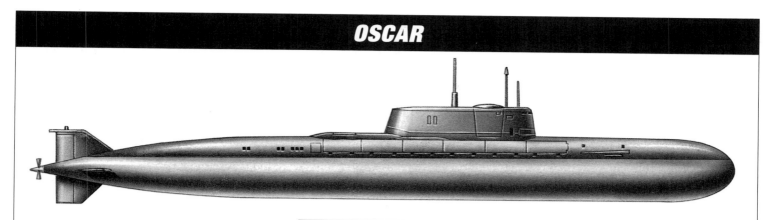

OSCAR

The *Oscar*-class is the largest non-strategic submarine ever built. It was armed with 24 SS-N-19 appropriately named 'Shipwreck' missiles, capable of being fired against battle groups from 480km (300 miles) on third-party targeting from satellite information. These missiles also had a nuclear capability. The only platform with a weapon heavy enough to combat them and long enough 'legs' to reach them were the Western SSNs.

SPECIFICATIONS

Country: Russia
Launch date: April 1980
Crew: 130
Displacement: 11,685 tonnes/ 13,615 tonnes
Dimensions: 143m x 18.2m x 9m (469ft 2in x 59ft 8in x 29ft 6in)

Armament: SS-N-15, SS-N-16, and SS-N-19 SSMs; four 533mm (21in) TTs; four 650mm (25.6in) TTs
Powerplant: Two shafts, two nuclear PWRs, two turbines
Range: Unlimited
Performance: 22 knots/30 knots

The submarine was designed for under-ice operations; it has a long, strong fin with which it can penetrate the ice to fire its missiles and a reinforced rudder to aid this operation. Its retractable forward control planes are sited at the bow. In addition to VLF communications, it is capable of receiving earth-shaking low data-rate Extra Low Frequency (ELF) signals. Operating under ice makes the submarine virtually immune from surface or air surveillance/attack and heightens an opposing submarine's problems by its ability to simply lay 'doggo' on the uneven underside of the ice-pack (a tactic known as ice-picking).

SURPRISING SILENCE

The first *Akula*-class (and its sister *Sierra*-class) was seen in 1987 and shook Western experts because of its quietness when operating. It was apparent that many Western noise-quietening techniques – raft-mounted machinery, flexible couplings, perhaps even a natural circulation reactor – had been

SWIFTSURE

The British *Swiftsure*-class SSN is a highly capable submarine that played a major role during the Cold War. She was fitted with only five torpedo tubes, considered sufficient for her predominantly ASW role. The class has been recently updated with the Tomahawk Land Attack Missile, which must make weapon selection for the torpedo tubes an interesting pastime.

SPECIFICATIONS

Country: Great Britain
Launch date: 7 September 1971
Crew: 116
Displacement: 4471 tonnes/
4979 tonnes
Dimensions: 82.9m x 9.8m x
8.5m (272ft x 32ft 4in x 28ft)

Armament: Five 533mm (21in) TTs;
Tomahawk and Sub-Harpoon SSMs
Powerplant: Single shaft, nuclear
PWR, turbines
Range: Unlimited
Performance: 20 knots/30+ knots

SIERRA

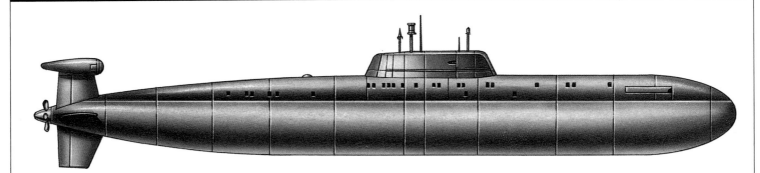

SPECIFICATIONS

Country: Russia
Launch date: July 1986
Crew: 61
Displacement: 7112 tonnes/
8230 tonnes
Dimensions: 107m x 12.5m x
8.8m (351ft x 41ft x 28ft 11in)

Armament: Four 650mm (25.6in) TTs;
four 533mm (21in) TTs; SS-N-15
Starfish and SS-N-21 Samson SSMs
Powerplant: Single shaft, one nuclear
PWR, one turbine
Range: Unlimited
Performance: 10 knots/32 knots

The *Sierra*-class SSN slightly pre-dated the *Akula*-class in 1984. The major difference between them was the fact that the *Sierra* has a titanium hull that gives her a significant depth capability. Soviet experimentation continued with the titanium-hulled *Mike*-class – designed specifically to evaluate 12 new technologies – but the single unit, *Komsomolets*, caught fire and sank in the Northern Norwegian Sea in 1989 with heavy loss of life.

introduced. A larger hull diameter than *Victor-III* indicates a less dense machinery arrangement than its predecessor. Most significant of all was the lack of noise from its propeller, and in this area the Soviets were helped to a great degree by the sale of advanced Japanese milling machinery by a Norwegian company. Industrial espionage and technology 'transfers' were other major feature of Cold War operations! In addition to the standard anti-submarine/anti-surface armament of Type 65 wake-homing torpedoes and 'Starfish' and 'Stallion', *Akula* also carries the SS-N-21 'Sampson' land-attack missile. It is very similar in nature and deployment to the US Tomahawk missile system. A follow-on to the *Akula*-class is planned (the *Sverodvinsk*), but, given Russian financial problems, the two that are building will take some time to be commissioned.

It is ironic that, just as the Soviet submarine force was being equipped with state-of-the-art platforms with an equivalent capability to the West, the Soviet Union should lose the Cold War. However, the sheer cost of arriving in that position and being able to sustain it – having conducted along the way a number of very expensive experiments that had failed – finally proved too much for the Soviet economy. The Cold War was of course, ultimately, an economic war, and the Western democracies won it.

Since the early 1990s, hundreds of vessels, including many submarines, have been deleted from the Russian order-of-battle,

COORDINATED HIGH-INTENSITY STRIKE

HMS *Splendid* fired a number of Tomahawk Land Attack missiles during the Kosovo conflict in 1999. TLAM allows the SSN to influence the land battle by posing a threat in the period prior to hostilities. After hostilities commence, highly accurate and lethal warheads can be used against important targets that might otherwise be relatively invulnerable.

Right: The TLAM-fitted SSN adds significantly to the potency and appropriateness of response to aggression, at a relatively low risk.

and her new building programmes have been halted or slowed. Where there is considerable activity is on the export front, and here there is a continuing significant threat to Western forces as Russia makes available her advanced technologies. These could alter local balances of power in a number of regions.

The *Kilo*-class remains on the market, and there is a much smaller and cheaper version, the *Lada*, that is soon to come off the stocks. The 'Yakhont' anti-ship missile, which is capable of being back-fitted to the *Kilo* export submarine, is an extremely fast (Mach 2 plus) lightweight kerosene ramjet-propelled

ANTI-SUBMARINE AND ANTI-SURFACE UNIT WARFARE

Arguably the most important role of the submarine is the SSN's unrivalled capability to seek out and destroy other submarines that may pose a threat to any friendly force. The Spearfish torpedo can be used against other submarines or surface ships, while Royal Navy Sub-Harpoon missiles are effective against surface ships out to a range in excess of 93km (50nm). These capabilities can be used when the SSN is acting independently or in support of a task group. The SSN is used to great effect when it is deployed in advance of friendly forces in order to reduce the flexibility of an opposition force by denying the use of an area or region. This is known as 'regional sea denial'.

FRENCH NUCLEAR SUBMARINES

France acquired her *Force de Frappe* – now more politically correctly known as her *Force de Dissuasion* – under General de Gaulle. She had originally intended to use Polaris technology, but poor relationships between de Gaulle and the United States caused the offer of the technology to be withdrawn. The French went it alone under the Mer-Sol-Ballistique-Strategique (MSBS) M-2. Five nuclear submarines were built in the 1970s comprising the Sousmarins Nucleaire Lance Engins (SNLE) operating in the Atlantic out of Brest. During the 1980s, she also developed the small *Rubis*-class of SSN.

Above: The French *Saphir* of 2670 tonnes is one of the *Rubis*-class, the world's smallest SSNs. Originally conceived for an anti-surface role their anti-submarine (ASW) capability has recently been enhanced.

weapon. The 'Alpha', a next-generation land attack missile, is capable of being launched from *Kilo* and *Lada* submarines. It has the same accuracy as the Tomahawk, but differs in that it is also supersonic.

NUCLEAR SUBMARINES FOR THE TWENTY-FIRST CENTURY

In 1982, HMS *Conqueror* became the first SSN in history to fire a weapon in anger when she sank the Argentine cruiser *Belgrano* during the Falklands conflict. During this action, she not only underlined the traditional submarine qualities of stealth and surprise, but also reinforced the SSN's strengths of being capable of very long-range deployments and of being able to operate in both 'brown' and 'blue' water, all without the need of support. She and her sister ships *Churchill* and *Courageous* were followed by five *Swiftsure*-class and seven *Trafalgar*-class.

In 1993, HMS *Vanguard* joined the ranks of Britain's strategic submarines. This 16,257-tonne submarine, armed with 16 Trident D5 missiles, has been joined by three sisters and they maintain a constant deterrent patrol. In addition to strategic missiles, they also carry the United Kingdom's sub-strategic deterrent, a role they inherited from the RAF Tornado bomber in 1996.

In January 2001, the keel of HMS *Astute* was laid, and she takes British submarining into its second century of operations. She is the biggest and most powerful attack submarine to be built for the Royal Navy, and, under the Smart Acquisition programme, will be built roughly one-fifth more quickly than earlier boats, with lower running costs and a much smaller ship's company. Although, at 7200 tonnes, *Astute* will be about 30 per cent bigger than the *Trafalgar*-class, the larger hull will be easier to build and maintain. She will carry torpedoes and cruise missiles. HMS *Ambush* starts later in 2001, and HMS *Artful* will follow later.

Opposite: A British *Trafalgar*-class SSN sails out of Portsmouth Harbour, England, saluting HMS *Dolphin* at Fort Blockhouse, the Alma Mater of the Royal Navy Submarine Service. Although no longer an operational submarine base, it is where RN submariners' hearts lie, housing as it does the Memorial Chapel and its neighbour, the Royal Navy Submarine Museum.

SURVEILLANCE AND RECONNAISSANCE

Surveillance is the ability to approach close to opposition forces and monitor their operations and movements while remaining undetected. This surveillance can include underwater photography, sometimes of surface warships who will almost certainly never be aware of the submarine's presence.

Modern submarines can also play a part in inshore and beach reconnaissance. Using modern video technology or digital photography, a submarine, able to approach a coastline in shallow water, can make a significant contribution to the intelligence collection effort prior to any subsequent maritime or land action.

SUB-HARPOON LAUNCH AND TRAJECTORY PROFILE

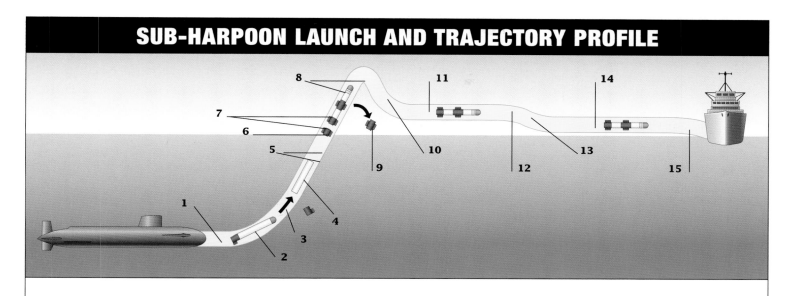

1	Missile clears tube	
2	Pitch manoeuvre: elevators assist buoyancy moment and steer left or right	
3	Buoyant equilibrium glide: elevators neutralize buoyancy moment	
4	Broach sensed: nose jetisonned, tail separated, booster ignited	
5	Harpoon boost phase	
6	End of boost	
7	Sustainer engine ignites	
8	Booster separates and missile-controlled guidance begins	
9	Booster	
10	Normal harpoon pull-out	
11	Low-level cruise begins	
12	Terminal radar seeker activated	
13	Seeker lock-on	
14	Low-level run-in begins	
15	Terminal ballistic manoeuvre initiated	

SUBMARINE ESCAPE AND RESCUE

Anyone who goes to sea in a platform that is packed full of high explosives, driven by steam under high pressure, the air and hydraulic systems of which operate at 4000 and 2500 psi, respectively, and which is being squeezed by relentless outside water pressure is well aware of the dangers. One accident, unless it is truly catastrophic, will not sink a submarine. Three accidents, however, will. The trick is to deal successfully with the first, which is where training comes in.

Getting out of a sunken submarine is fiendishly difficult, and every submariner accepts that there is a risk of sinking involved in his day-to-day life onboard. In addition, he recognizes that the operational capability of a submarine cannot be reduced by fitting a plethora of escape equipment; indeed, during World War II, Royal Navy submarines had metal bars welded over their escape hatches to prevent them

Left: The American deep submergence rescue vessel (DSRV) *Avalon* **(DSRV-2), 'piggy-backed' onto its Mosub (mother submarine), USS** *Billfish*, **in readiness to conduct an exercise.**

Escape is the ability of a submariner to release himself from entrapment. Rescue is the means of an outside body to execute that release.

springing during a depth-charge attack. Thus in war, just as in peace, there is literally no way out in very deep water. However, few submariners suffer from 'coffin-dreams'. In fact, any submariner who views escape as the equivalent of an aircraft parachute is a danger not only to himself, but also, more importantly, is a danger to his fellow crew-members. In everything a submariner does in the course of his duty, he ensures that his submarine is working in tip-top condition; by looking after her, she will look after him.

Peacetime accidents do happen, however, so there is justification for fitting specialist equipment onboard, providing training in it, and developing a shore-side organization that offers support and assistance to a distressed submarine (Dissub).

As the recent tragic Kursk accident revealed, there is often confusion over terms in a layman's mind when it comes to getting people out of a sunken submarine. Escape is the ability of a submariner to release himself

from entrapment. Rescue is the means of an outside body to execute that release.

Escape is possible from 183m (600ft), a depth below which the human body is unable to survive on air. There are many further physiological complexities associated with escape. Rescue is possible from any depth, provided there is sufficient strength to withstand sea pressure in both the Dissub and the rescue vehicle – for every 0.6m (2ft) of depth there is an increase of 0.07kg (1psi) in pressure – and that there is not too great a pressure differential between the two vessels to operate hatches after the mating process.

EARLY ATTITUDES AND ENDEAVOURS

What little thought that had been applied to escape centred on the theory that a sunken submarine, because of its small size, could somehow be grappled and hoisted back to the surface in time to save lives. Two accidents in rapid succession revealed the inadequacies of the theory, because, on both occasions, the

Right: The ill-fated crew of *A1*. HMS *A1* was the first submarine to be lost in the Royal Navy. She was run down by the liner *Berwick Castle* in the Solent in 1904 during an exercise. It is always the responsibility of a dived submarine to remain clear of surface traffic, so no blame can be attached to the merchant ship. It is obvious that the commanding officer, Lieutenant Mansergh, simply did not see, or hear, her coming – unsurprising, given the crudity of early periscopes and the complete absence of listening devices.

THE *BRANDTAUCHER*

The first recorded escape in history was that conducted by William Bauer and his two companions from his sunken *Seadiver* from a depth of 18m (60ft), i.e. 2 atmospheres. Despite the initial violent reactions of his two colleagues – who thought that he was trying to commit suicide when he opened a sea-cock to allow water into the stricken craft – he finally managed to convince them that the only way out was to raise the pressure inside the boat to equal that of the sea outside in order to open the hatch. The equalization eventually occurred, the hatch flew open, and Bauer and his companions 'came to the surface like bubbles in a glass of champagne'. While he was making the preparations to escape, Bauer complained of panting hard, suffering from a splitting headache, and wanting to be sick. He was suffering the classic symptoms of carbon dioxide poisoning, just before which judgement and alertness become blurred, and after which unconsciousness and death will follow. They got out in the nick of time!

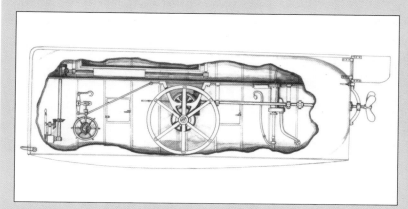

Left: It seems incredible that men actually got out of Bauer's crude submarine. His actions proved not only the principle of pressure equalization, but also how important it was to keep a clear head during an emergency!

Below: Two early examples of self-contained breathing apparatus, which inspired thoughts of a similar device for use during submarine escape. The one on the left was similar to that invented by H.A. Fleuss, which was used by miners during the Seaham Colliery disaster in 1880. The one on the right was adapted to the Siebe-Gorman diving dress and helmet in the 1890s.

weather intervened, interrupting the lifting process and leaving any survivors to their fate. The first victim was HMS *A1*, rammed and sunk in the Solent by the SS *Berwick Castle* in the summer of 1904. Why the French *Farfadet* sank is not entirely clear, but the result was the same. In the latter case, a diver confirmed that men were still alive soon after she sank. This began to set people thinking, and a direct result of the *A1* disaster was that a lower hatch was fitted to the conning tower to improve watertight integrity. Learning from mistakes and introducing material countermeasures was to become a feature of submarining for the next century.

In America young officers experimented by locking-in and locking-out two large dogs from a torpedo tube; the success of the experiment (because the dogs emerged

swimming happily) elicited a declaration that 'Submarines were safe' from the *American Marine Journal*. When Ensign Kenneth Whiting USN himself repeated the experiment in 1909 from USS *Porpoise*, it was met with fury by Mr L.Y. Spear of the Electric Boat Company, who pointed out that the boat was fitted out with a steel trunk around one of the hatches for escape purposes. The process involved the submarine being deliberately flooded to equalize the pressures, and then each man, donning his life-jacket and 'looking his companion steadfastly in the eye', would take a deep breath, duck under the edge of the trunk, and float to the surface. They had fitted a system that is still in use today, with the purpose of the trunk being to maintain an airlock inside the compartment whilst allowing for a column of water to reach from the base of the trunk to the hatch. This airlock could, however, contain a lethal cocktail of carbon dioxide and oxygen, depending on starting levels of each within the whole submarine, so it did not provide the complete answer;

a means of providing breathable air might also be required.

Even before Whiting had completed his escapade, there were others applying scientific thought to the problem of providing breathable air. R.H. (later Sir Robert) Davis of Siebe-Gorman had developed a breathing apparatus for use in coalmine disasters, and he was now attempting to condense it in size so that it could be stored and used in submarines. He was working with the British scientist Fleuss, who had patented his 'closed circuit' oxygen breathing system which, in essence, allowed a man to breathe the same oxygen over and over again by removing the expelled carbon dioxide through a chemical. The small part of oxygen used by the body was replenished from a high-pressure cylinder that formed part of the apparatus. What was not appreciated at the time was that, if pure oxygen is breathed for any length of time under a pressure greater than 3 atmospheres (20m (66ft)), in most human metabolisms, it could induce symptoms similar to an epileptic fit.

Below: The outcome of contemporary thinking in the British *C*-class was the outrageous Hall-Rees equipment, seen here. Apart from the practicalities of stowing the gear, which indicated that they forgot the principle that operational capability should not suffer through an over-abundance of escape equipment, oxygen was generated from a chemical using sodium. In short, you risked either drowning or burning!

Because the Davis device was still too bulky to be passed through a hatch, Fleuss collaborated with Commander R.S. Hall RN and Fleet Surgeon Rees and produced the world's first individual escape equipment. In fact, it was totally unsuitable for submarine work in two ways. First, it required an enclosed diving-helmet to make it effective; secondly, it used sodium peroxide stored in a canister, a chemical that absorbed carbon dioxide while at the same time giving off oxygen, but which, if it got wet, burst into flames. As Captain W.O. Shelford put it in his book *Subsunk*, a submerged wearer had the choice of being burnt alive or drowning!

A parallel design of the Davis oxygen equipment was being pursued by Bernard Draeger in Germany, and his design (the Tauchretter) was adopted by the German Navy in 1912 and, with few amendments, was adopted by the U-boat arm during World War I and World War II.

ESCAPES OF WORLD WAR I

The first recorded escape in World War I was from *UB57*, which came to rest on the seabed in 39m (128ft) of water after striking a mine in the Dover Barrage. The experience of survivors and those who perished alike summed up all the difficulties involved in a 'free-ascent' escape. First there was the process of equalizing the pressure inside the submarine, which had to be achieved through a combination of venting high-pressure air inboard and flooding the compartment through small-bore valves. The Captain, Lieutenant Wenninger, described the lengthy process in graphic detail and talked of excruciating pain in the ears and enormous difficulty in breathing. Two men could not stand it and shot themselves, and Wenninger considered administering himself with a dose of morphine. Eventually, the Captain tried the hatch, and it flew open and out of his hand. He was lifted bodily through it and began to shoot to the surface. To his surprise, he felt no urge to breathe in; indeed, his instinct was to blow out and to slow the

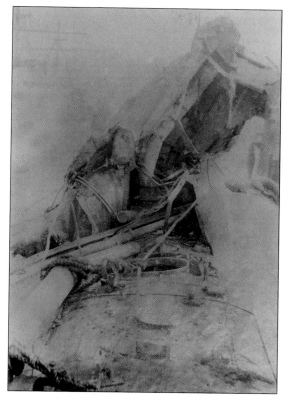

Left: The tangled wreckage of a sunken submarine. In addition to the inevitable trauma suffered as a result of being sunk, the potential escapee would have to battle his way through obstructions and twisted metal before reaching the surface. It is little wonder that, in wartime, few survived.

rate of his ascent. This instinct saved his life, as his last breath had introduced air into his lungs at over 4.2kg/cm² (60psi), and only the process of blowing out had prevented his lungs bursting. Other escapees reached the surface, screamed, and sank again; they had probably held their breath. Once on the surface, the survivors' ordeal was not yet over, for there was no one there to rescue them from the bitterly cold water. It took an hour and a half before the seven (out of 20) were picked up, all by now unconscious, and one of these was to die of exposure.

The only other recorded escape during World War I involved the crew of HMS *E41*, rammed and sunk by her sister HMS *E4* during exercises off Harwich. Seven men were trapped near the conning tower and were able to use it as a trunk and get the hatch open to make the 13.7m (45ft) ascent. However, one man, Stoker Petty Officer Brown, was trapped aft in the engine room. His success in getting out through that compartment's hatch was one of amazing fortitude and determination, and reveals how important above all else is

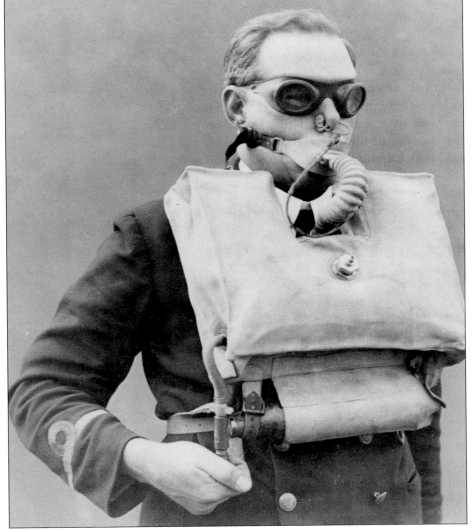

Below: The Davis Submarine Escape Gear is being demonstrated here by Warrant Officer Lacey in 1929. The bottle contained 30 minutes of oxygen, and expelled air was passed through a carbon dioxide absorbent. By blowing against the nose clip, an escapee could 'clear his ears'. Additionally, the DSEA was fitted with a drogue to slow ascent to the surface, which also acted as a buoyancy device and flipped him onto his back once on the surface.

the 'will to live' in an apparently hopeless situation. On top of the usual challenges of survival for two hours in a high concentration of carbon dioxide, he also had to overcome the reverse physics of releasing a hatch that opened inwards. As Shelford put it; 'Throughout he never allowed himself a moment's inactivity, so the deadly mental paralysis due to breathing carbon dioxide never had a chance to creep over and numb his brain. Apart from saving a life obviously too valuable to be thrown away, his escape was of great value in salving *E41*.' Given the fact that there were few, if any, life-jackets available, plus the total lack of special-escape hatches or other escape fittings, it is remarkable that anyone got out alive at all.

There were two examples of rescue by salvage: that is, pulling a section of the boat high enough above the water-line so that men could open a hatch and walk free. The first involved the Danish submarine *Dykkeren,* and entailed the novel but extremely clever notion of providing air to the trapped men from the salvage vessel *Kattegat* via the submarine's external HP air connection while the necessary preparations for lifting were made. A diver connected the hose, and this action saved the lives of the five survivors, because their eventual salvation took over nine hours to achieve.

The second example involved HMS *K13*, which sank in the shelter of the Gareloch during sea trials, after the boiler-room ventilators were accidentally left open. On this occasion, 48 men were trapped, but once again the ability to supply them with air from an outside connection sustained life long enough to effect a rescue.

What is immediately evident from both these successful examples was how vital were the proximity of rescue and salvage assets and their ability to render swift assistance with the provision of air. Without it, those trapped would have died. The rescues also demonstrated that, even with reasonable shelter, salvage ships found it extremely difficult to expedite the operation, as careful evaluation by divers of how the boat was lying, and thus how best to apply lifting apparatus, took a finite length of time. The one conclusion that can be drawn was that no two evolutions were the same and conditions had to be highly favourable to achieve even limited success.

A MORE FOCUSED APPROACH

The attitude towards escape or rescue from a sunken submarine in the 1920s can be summed up by a letter written to his opposite number at the Electric Boat Company by Sir Charles Craven, head of Vickers Shipbuilding and himself a submariner. In this letter, he wrote, 'the best thing that can happen in the event of a submarine sinking is that a full gale should blow and thus render salvage operations impossible'. This negative – but highly realistic – expert view was reinforced during an unsuccessful salvage operation in the United States of the submarine *S4*, despite massive effort. The public outcry that followed demonstrated how far expectation could exceed practicality, a consistent theme!

The failure, however, did inspire action within US Navy submarine circles. Lieutenant (later Admiral) C.B. Momsen was detailed to find some means of individual escape without relying on salvage, and Lt. Cdr. (later Admiral) McCann was to find some means of rescue which did not involve salvage. The former set about applying the principles of Draeger's and Davis's gear, but making the apparatus small enough so that there would be sufficient stowage to service one for every man onboard. The latter set about developing a rescue bell, the basis for which he found in another invention of R.H. Davis, put forward in 1917. This consisted of two compartments, one above the other, the lower one serving as a connecting airlock between the rescue bell and the Dissub. Once connected, the survivors could be transferred to the rescue bell in close to atmospheric pressure and hoisted to the surface.

The 'Momsen Lung' was designed to provide sufficient oxygen to get the survivor to the surface, and, before the escape was made, it was necessary for him to be plugged into a manifold close to the escape hatch. The major drawback of this system was that it tied survivors to a fixed point. The British, having heard of the American breakthrough, went one step further and opted for the Davis Submarine Escape Apparatus (DSEA), which used the same principle as the Momsen device, except that its air bottle contained 30 minutes' worth of oxygen, thereby allowing survivors mobility while they waited their turn to escape. In his report, Momsen emphasized the need for a slow ascent to give men time

to vent their lungs, and his solution was to provide a knotted rope attached to a buoy onto which a survivor could cling to slow his ascent. Sensing that this was an impractical expectation in open-sea conditions, Davis instead fitted his device with an apron which, when extended, acted like a drogue. From 1930, all RN submariners went through DSEA training in a specially constructed, 4.5m (15ft) deep tank in HMS *Dolphin*. The Americans followed with a similar concept, except their tank was 30m (100ft) deep.

The United States Navy pressed ahead with the development of the McCann Diving-Bell, declaring it to be their primary method of getting men out of a Dissub and that the 'Momsen Lung' was a last-resort method. The major modification that McCann made to the Davis invention was that, instead of the bell being negatively buoyant, his would be positively buoyant and dragged down to the sunken submarine by a shot wire attached to the hull by a diver. This would allow it to be used in a tideway and enable it to be fixed to a submarine lying 30 degrees off the upright. A specialist ship was built to

Left: The Mann Rescue-Bell that successfully evacuated the trapped crew of USS *Squalus* in 1939. There are distinct differences between 'escape' (self-help) and rescue (relying on others); until the arrival of the mobile DSRV, the British always favoured the former approach, while the Americans have always favoured the latter.

Right: A young electrician in the motor room of a British submarine. Behind him can be seen the forward of two doors that provide access to an escape tower. The purpose of the escape tower was to minimise the time spent under pressure by those waiting their turn while the two men in the tower made good their escape.

handle it and enable it to be transported to a rescue site, and a team of divers capable of working down to 91m (300ft) was trained.

The British were to make one further refinement to their escape equipment in 1936, from which date all submarines were equipped with the Davis Escape Chamber. This was in recognition of the fact that men waiting for escape in the 'Twill Trunk' scenario would suffer extreme hardship through cold and pressure build-up. The chamber, fitted with an escape hatch, was an airlock big enough to hold two or three men and their escape apparatus. The principle was that the chamber could be flooded and equalized quickly, leaving the remainder of the escape party dry while the men inside the chamber made good their ascent. Once

the chamber was observed to be empty through a glass port, an internally operated mechanism shut the hatch and the chamber emptied into the bilges. The next pair manned the chamber, and so the process continued, with the last man taking with him a special tool that allowed him to flood the chamber from inside. The chambers were sited between two compartments forward and aft, with access from both sides.

The Italian Navy adopted the Belloni 'tub', a water-filled bath connected to an escape tower through which escapees ducked after achieving the required equalization to open the hatch by compressed air. This had the limitation of never having a sufficient amount of redundant HP air to achieve the aim without fitting special air bottles, which in

THE *POSEIDON* TRAGEDY

In 1931, Davis's gear was put to the test when HMS *Poseidon* sank following a collision with a Japanese merchant ship off Wei Hai Wei, the British base off North China. Before she went down, 30 men managed to scramble off her through the conning tower, but eight men were trapped onboard. It took the survivors almost three-and-a-quarter hours to achieve the flooding process that in turn provided them with the $4.6km/cm^2$ (65psi) required to open the hatch, by which time they were almost completely submerged.

Although six of the seven escaped, one died soon after reaching the surface, and all the others suffered from the 'bends', or decompression sickness, a condition induced by breathing under pressure for an extended period which allows nitrogen in the blood to expand too rapidly during the ascent. When the human body is subjected to pressure below one atmosphere for any length of time (e.g. 10 minutes at 55m (180ft)), nitrogen, which makes up 80 per cent of air, is forced into contact with the blood. The blood takes up the nitrogen from the air. So long as the body remains under pressure, there is no effect, but the moment the pressure is reduced, the excess of nitrogen will slowly begin to be bubbled off. If these bubbles come off in the blood vessels themselves, they might fill the right side of the heart with air and cause death in a few minutes. In other cases, they may come off in the spinal cord, causing paralysis and a condition known as 'diver's palsy'; if they come off in muscles or joints, they cause the least serious damage through serious pain in muscles and joints. This condition is known as the 'bends'. The only antidote is immediate recompression in a specialized chamber, followed by a gradual reduction in pressure, allowing the blood to shed the excess nitrogen slowly.

Following the experience of the *Poseidon* survivors, the Admiralty immediately ordered that all submarines be fitted with rapid-flooding valves – a collapsible concertina twill trunk that could be deployed in an escape scenario, but which could otherwise be stowed out of the way in the deckhead – and special accessible escape towers. So confident were their lordships that all was now in place for escapees to look after themselves that they declared the existing fittings supplying air externally redundant and had them removed. From 1935 onwards, rescue by salvage was no longer an option in the Royal Navy Submarine Service.

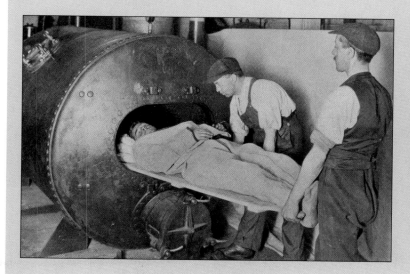

Left: If an escapee or diver is suffering from the 'bends' (trapped nitrogen in the blood), the only way to relieve the danger is to re-pressurize him, in a chamber such as this, back to the equivalent pressure of his original depth, and bring him 'up' slowly.

'Accidents to submarines are ... headline news, and it is unfortunate that ... the imagination of readers is harried by highly coloured stories. The public should be educated on the difficulties ... in escaping from a sunken submarine.'
Rear Admiral B.W. Taylor, Flag Officer Submarines, 1960

turn took up precious room. The Spanish Navy pursued the idea of a single-man escape chamber that operated on the principle of a lift being hauled in and out as each man made his escape in non-pressurized surroundings. It was impractical in other than perfect conditions, with the escapees having many hours of time on their side.

USS *SQUALUS* AND HMS *THETIS*

In 1939, the two escape philosophies were individually put to the test, albeit in vastly contrasting operational conditions.

USS *Squalus* was only 11 days out of her builders' hands when she accidentally sank in 73m (240ft) of water off the east coast of the United States; 33 members of her crew survived the flooding and huddled in the forward compartments. The fact that she was overdue was quickly recognized ashore, and the submarine *Sculpin* sent to look for her found her position by spotting the indicator buoy released by *Squalus*. It was to be another 20 hours before a shot line for a diver was attached to the hull in readiness for the bell to be winched down. This arduous, 25-minute dive by Boson's Mate (Second Class) Sibitzky sealed his place in US submarine history. Two highly trained operators climbed into the bell for the descent and the tricky process of attaching it to the Dissub's escape hatch. Having blown out the water in the lower compartment and equalized this with the surface through the connected vent pipe, they then opened the submarine's escape hatch from the outside. Before recovering the first flight of seven men to the surface, the submarine was fully vented by the rescue ship's (USS *Falcon*) HP air compressors, and hot drinks were supplied to the survivors. When all was ready, the reverse procedure was followed and the first rescue in history achieved. The remaining 26 survivors were brought out in three more trips, with the final transfer being conducted 35 hours after the flooding accident. The ordeal for the last of the survivors was not yet over, as the final ascent was beset by problems;

it took four hours before they finally and stiffly climbed onto *Falcon*. Despite all the conditions being highly favourable (close proximity of rescue forces, good weather, shallow depth, upright submarine aspect, slack tides), the rescue was still a remarkable achievement, and its success owed much to the calm way in which it was conducted.

The loss of *Thetis* only eight days after *Squalus* and the death of 99 out of the 103 men onboard was a sharp contrast to the success of the USN incident, and, although there was a natural reaction to compare the two circumstances, in fact they were very different in nature.

The first major difference was that the *Thetis* was overcrowded, with many civilians onboard who had no experience whatsoever of using DSEA; the second was that 103 men (twice the size of the standard crew) were drawing breath on a volume already reduced by one-third by the flooding, and they started to turn the atmosphere foul after only four hours; the third was that, even if assisting ships responded early, there was nothing they could do in a physical sense because of the earlier decision to remove the external HP air connection. It was thus up to the men trapped inside to get themselves out. The first thought onboard was to get into the flooded compartment to shut the offending torpedo-tube bow cap that had caused the flood, so that it could be pumped out. Three separate attempts were made to get into the torpedo-stowage compartment via the linking escape chamber by fit young men, but they were beaten back by the pressure. The conclusion reached was that the after escape hatch would have to be raised much closer to the surface to give the civilians onboard a fighting chance to escape. This process of raising the stern by transferring water forward took all night and further depleted oxygen levels. They did succeed, however, in raising *Thetis*'s stern above the surface. By the time the first two escapees succeeded, *Thetis* had been down 17 hours, and surface assistance in the shape of the frigate *Brazen* and the Mersey salvage ship *Vigilant* had arrived. It took another two-and-a-half hours before a second pair emerged; their description of conditions signalled that there was little hope left for the dreadfully weakened survivors. At midday, the frigates of the First Anti-Submarine Flotilla arrived. By 1430 hours, 24 hours after sinking, cutting gear was ready to be deployed, but the tide was rising rapidly over the submarine's stern. It was decided to try to raise the stern higher, and so a wire was passed between *Vigilant* and a tug to effect the manoeuvre. At 1510 hours, the wire parted and *Thetis* slipped beneath the waves.

As Captain Shelford remarks in *Subsunk,* 'Much criticism has been directed towards those in charge on the surface from the time that the submarine was found until the stern disappeared from view that afternoon. Even in the light of present knowledge of escape and salvage it is not easy to see what else could have been done. It was the Admiralty's policy for survivors from a sunken submarine to escape without relying on assistance from the surface, and as there were no facilities for rescue from the surface (those involved) had no alternative but to wait for them to escape.' The major issue that was revealed at the subsequent committee of investigation established under Admiral Sir Martin Dunbar-Nasmith VC DSO was the general ignorance surrounding how quickly carbon dioxide built up in a completely shut-down submarine. It was revealed that at four per cent, clear thinking became difficult; at 10 per cent unconsciousness occurred; and at 20 per cent the atmosphere became lethal. The percentage was a combination of absolute levels of the gas in the atmosphere, multiplied by the pressure within the hull. *Thetis* had reached the first level by 2000 hours on the first night; close to the second level by 0800 hours the next morning because of the overnight exertion; and the third level by the late afternoon.

Below: The agony of HMS *Thetis* in Liverpool Bay in 1939. In contrast to the USS *Squalus* success, 99 men died with only four escaping when *Thetis* sank through flooding while on sea trials. Those that perished died as a result of lack of oxygen/surfeit of carbon dioxide, conditions that were accelerated by the number of men onboard and overnight exertions to get the stern above water. Much was learned about the effects of carbon dioxide on the ability of men to think and perform in high concentrations of the gas.

> 'We ... understand the difficulties of escape; we train ourselves to overcome them while fully recognising that, in many circumstances, particularly in deep water, escape is impossible.'
> Rear Admiral B.W. Taylor, Flag Officer Submarines, 1960

LUCK AND THE WILL TO LIVE

Despite the fact that many British wartime commanding officers deliberately clipped their escape hatches (indeed, it was squadron policy in 'The Fighting Tenth' in Malta) in order to avoid the risk of these hatches springing open under the expected retaliatory depth-charge attack, occasional escapes were made from deep. These tended to be cameos peppered in varying doses by an overwhelming will to live, great courage and presence of mind, and pure luck. A near-inevitable result of escape was being made a prisoner of war. This happened to the three survivors from HMS *P32,* who managed to escape from the conning tower of the submarine from a depth of 64m (210ft). It also happened to the six survivors from HMS *Stratagem* in the Far East, who were taken to the notorious Ofuna questioning camp outside Tokyo. Here they bumped into the nine survivors of the top-scoring USS *Tang* and learned of the horrifying treatment meted out by the Japanese to Commander Dick O'Kane.

There were two stories of individuals surviving that sum up the 'luck' and the 'will to live' mentioned earlier. The luck belonged to Leading Stoker Oliver of the World War I vintage HMS *H49* which was sunk off the coast of Holland by a German anti-submarine trawler. He was dishing out DSEA sets in the control room while depth-charges were continuing to rain down. This is the last thing that Oliver remembered before he came round on the deck of the trawler. It would appear that an explosion ripped the hull apart and blew the lucky escapee to the surface!

The 'will to live' belonged to Leading Stoker John Capes of HMS *Perseus.* The submarine struck a mine off the island of Zante near Greece, and Capes was in the after ends and survived the blast. The after-compartment watertight door jammed shut as a result of the explosion; Capes, groping around in the dark, covered in paint and oil, eventually found a torch. He found three companions still alive but injured. They all set to and prepared the compartment for escape, lowering the twill trunk. The only way the compartment could be flooded was via the 'underwater gun', but, because the submarine was at 73m (240ft), the sea came in quickly enough to build up a pressure quickly. Capes climbed into the trunk, released the hatch (which had not been bolted) and climbed back down to feed his companions one-by-one to safety before he made his own escape. None of the injured survived the long ascent to the surface, or if they made it, they were unable to stay afloat, and Capes found himself alone. In the distance, he could see lights and, with the help of his DSEA as a life-jacket, he swam 11.2km (7 miles)! Capes was harboured by the islanders and was eventually recovered to the United Kingdom, where he was awarded the BEM for his extraordinary feat.

There were a number of escapes from deep from German U-boats, but, compared with the number of submarines involved, they were pitifully few. If the hazards of actual escape were overcome, there remained the question of survival. In the grey, cold

Right: Leading Stoker George Oliver was the only survivor when HMS *H49* was sunk by depth charges from a German anti-submarine vessel in October 1940. Oliver knew little about survival, indicating the element of luck needed to survive.

THE RUCK-KEENE COMMITTEE

What was acceptable in war was not acceptable in peacetime. For one thing, public opinion would find the concept of 'no way out' of a submarine totally unacceptable. Immediately after the war, the Royal Navy therefore established a committee of investigation under Captain Philip Ruck-Keene CBE DSO 'to investigate and report on the efficiency and deficiencies of the escape arrangements built into the submarines of the Royal Navy, and to investigate all alternative arrangements'. Based on peacetime accidents from Allied navies, their investigation established some hard facts: 84 per cent of the men known to be alive inside the submarine immediately upon sinking perished before leaving the boat, 10 per cent died during the ascent, and as many survived without breathing apparatus as with. The twill trunk method was satisfactory only down to 45m (150ft), since the build up of carbon dioxide thereafter led to men losing the mental faculties necessary to think straight. The three-man chamber was unsatisfactory, since if one of the trio lost his composure, he put the other two at extreme risk. The Ruck-Keene committee came up with three principal proposals:

(a) Replace twill trunks with single-man escape chambers, narrow enough so that a man could not collapse in it
(b) The chamber would be pressurized by both air and water
(c) Monitoring equipment for carbon dioxide and pressure would be fitted to tell men when to escape, and immersion suits would be provided that gave protection against the elements if escape was necessary before help arrived.

Above: Royal Navy submariners familiarising themselves with the use of BIBS (Built in Breathing System). Each breathing unit is connected via a teat to a dedicated air line supplied by special air bottles external to the hull.

'We realize that we cannot handicap the fighting qualities of our submariners by fitting an excess of escape equipment. ...We appreciate [the] risk... but do not allow it to interfere with the performance of our duty.' Rear Admiral B.W. Taylor, Flag Officer Submarines, 1960

waters of the Atlantic, hypothermia was a real enemy and so much depended on being spotted early by a pick-up vessel (if it was prepared to stop, bearing in mind the risks it faced). Another problem faced by U-boat survivors was that of the escape apparatus itself. The weight of its oxygen bottle and absorbent canister was at the front, and it was excellent as a life-jacket if it remained fully inflated. However, if it was only partially inflated, the oxygen went to the highest point of the bag and tended to push the wearer's face into the water. A number of bodies were discovered to have suffered this plight.

One extraordinary story was that of the temporary ship's cook of *U512*, which was sunk by an aircraft. He was seen to break surface by its crew as they swept over the area looking for evidence of their success, and they dropped him a rubber dinghy. Despite being wounded, he managed to climb into the life-raft, but it was 10 days before he was found. He sustained his life by catching some of the sea birds that constantly attacked him.

After HMS *Untamed* suffered a flooding accident off the Scottish coast in May 1943, resulting in her sinking with the loss of all hands, she was salved. Investigation teams went into her, not only to try to ascertain why she had sunk, but also to examine what conditions existed that prevented the crew escaping. The sample of air in the engine room where the survivors had congregated

Below: Lt. Cdr. Matthew Todd RN, Officer in Command of the Training Escape Tank at HMS *Dolphin*, supervising an escape demonstration to a party of civilians. The escapee has just ascended from 33m (100ft) using the free-ascent method and will have blown out hard all the way to prevent his lungs exploding.

told the whole story. It contained five per cent carbon dioxide which, when combined with the estimated six atmospheres, made the total concentration 30 per cent, well beyond the limit for survival.

IMPROVEMENTS INSPIRED BY TRAGEDY

During the winter of 1946 (one of the coldest on record), volunteers tried out a number of combinations of materials to establish their ability to stave off hypothermia in the freezing waters of the Solent. The eventual solution was two layers of very thin rubber-ized cotton, which became separated by an air-space when the wearer blew into an air-tube stowed in the suit's breast pocket. The air-space provided significant insulation from the cold sea, as well as acting as an additional buoyancy aid, and a flashing light was activated once in the water. The principle of the suit remains as relevant today as it was in 1946.

In addition to this, the committee proposed that men should be trained in free ascent – that is, without any equipment at all. However, to achieve this aim it was necessary to persuade the Admiralty to build a 30m (100ft) high tank. To back up the committee's claims that such training was feasible, a variety of experiments were carried out in a specially constructed decompression chamber at the RN Physiological Laboratory in Alverstoke, England, using both humans and goats, as the latter's respiratory arrangements are almost identical to that of a human being. The purpose of the experiments was to determine the ideal speed that a man should ascend so that he did not rise so slowly as to induce a desire to inhale, nor so fast that the expanding air in his chest would burst a lung. This was eventually determined to be 1.2–1.5m (4–5ft) per second, as it happens the maximum rate of ascent that a body can achieve in water. The money for this project could not easily be found in the short term, and the Admiralty decided that escape towers

would not be retrofitted to submarines already in commission.

From 1948 onwards, tangible results were achieved in the immediate fitting of indicator (distress) buoys, coloured smoke candles, and fluorescent markers to assist search by aircraft. Finally, the system of 'Subsmash' was introduced. In essence, part one, instituted one hour after a submarine

Above: The Royal Navy's 30.4m (100ft) Submarine Escape Training Tank. All submariners have to attend escape training at the start of their careers and at least every three years thereafter.

was overdue in reporting, began to marshal search assets, and part two came into force one hour later. At this point, all available forces would be sent to the search area. 'Subsmash' evolved into the internationally accepted convention of 'Submiss' and 'Subsunk' many years later.

However, progress overall was slow, and, like many other circumstances, it took a catastrophe to provide some impetus to a flagging programme. For the Royal Navy Submarine Service, this occurred in the shape of the loss of HMS *Truculent* on Thursday 12 January 1950.

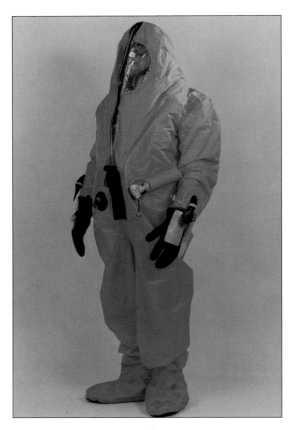

Right: The modern British Mk10 escape suit. This remarkable piece of equipment contains an integral life raft and VHF homing device. Because of its integral nature, the escapee only has to breathe normally inside his hood as he ascends to the surface; however, waiting for him will be the SPAG (Submarine Parachute Assistance Group), who will have dropped onto the scene of the Dissub (distressed submarine) with emergency supplies of oxygen and other first-aid equipment.

The submarine was returning to Sheerness after a day's sea trials and was carrying 18 Chatham Dockyard representatives, in addition to her normal complement of 60 men. She was about to enter the navigable channel when she was in collision with the small Swedish tanker *Devina* bound for Ipswich with a load of paraffin. It was after dark, and confusion over lights worn by the

merchantman caused the submarine to cross the tanker's bow at a range that made ramming inevitable. The resultant crash caused the submarine to be holed and she flooded, settling on the bottom at about 1900 hours. Down below, all but one man managed to make it to either the after ends or engine room, where preparations for escape were made under the control of First Lieutenant F.J. Hindes RN and CERA Sam Hine, respectively. All non-swimmers received priority, as there were not enough escape apparatus to go round. The noise from overhead traffic gave the impression that rescue craft were already on the scene, so the decision was made to escape immediately. Seventy-two men reached the surface in almost copybook fashion, but to their utter dismay there were no rescue ships in the vicinity; what they had heard was shipping passing routinely up and down the river. Although Sheerness could be seen in the distance, the lights began to fade as the survivors were swept out to sea on a strong ebb tide. Altogether 20 men were saved from the numbing waters; 57 were swept out to sea, including the two who had orchestrated what should have been the most successful escape story in history. Hindes and Hine were both awarded the Albert Medal posthumously. The single cause for so few men surviving was simply the failure to produce the Mk1 Immersion Suit quickly enough to supply the submarine fleet: *Truculent* carried none at all.

Improvements after that came rapidly. The 30m (100ft) high escape tower, based on an American equivalent, was built in HMS *Dolphin*'s Submarine Escape Training Tank (SETT); all submarines were fitted with the Mk1 Immersion Suit; all submariners completed SETT training; all submarines were fitted with local emergency air-purification equipment for CO_2 removal and O_2 replenishment during the waiting period; and an external and dedicated supply of air (rather than pure oxygen) for escape known as the Built-in Breathing System (BIBS) replaced the individual breathing apparatus for use

GENERAL ARRANGEMENT OF A DSRV

The rescue diving-bell is extremely limited by weather conditions, so the United States introduced a system that could operate independently of surface conditions – the DSRV, mated to a Mosub (mother submarine).

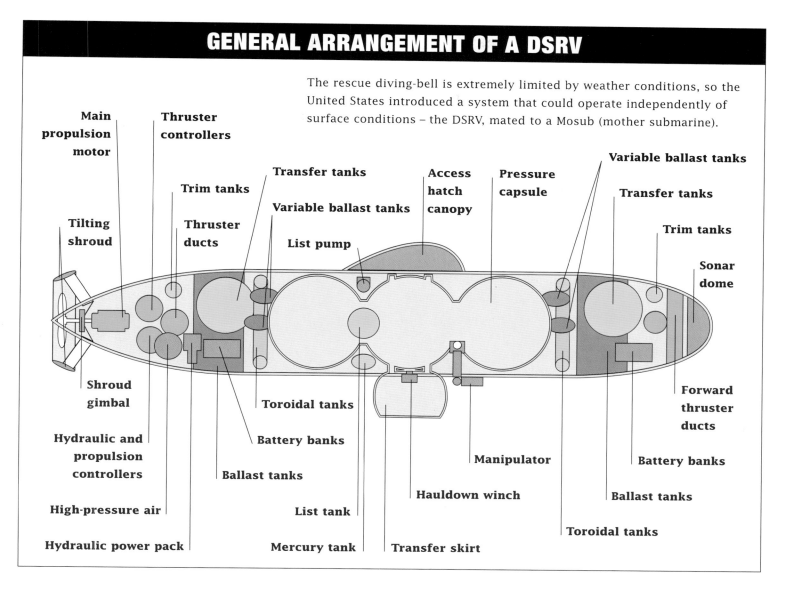

Main propulsion motor

Thruster controllers

Transfer tanks

Access hatch canopy

Pressure capsule

Variable ballast tanks

Trim tanks

Transfer tanks

Trim tanks

Variable ballast tanks

Thruster ducts

List pump

Sonar dome

Tilting shroud

Shroud gimbal

Forward thruster ducts

Hydraulic and propulsion controllers

Toroidal tanks

Battery banks

Manipulator

Battery banks

Ballast tanks

Ballast tanks

High-pressure air

List tank

Hauldown winch

Toroidal tanks

Hydraulic power pack

Mercury tank

Transfer skirt

during the escape evolution. However, there was one casualty in the programme. The first was the abandonment of the British version of the McCann Bell. This had been experimented with from the diving tender HMS *Reclaim,* but difficulties in its speed of deployment to the far-scattered British submarine squadrons led to the conclusion that it was impracticable as a concept.

MODERN ESCAPE METHODS

When the nuclear-powered HMS *Dreadnought* was built in the 1950s, she was fitted with a single-man escape chamber that extended from the hull to the top of the casing, which, because it incorporated a twill trunk, served as a means of rush-escape as well. 'Bottom time' (pressure multiplied by time) determines whether 'stops' are required to avoid a nitrogen-induced 'bend'. The great advantage of an escape tower lies in its ability to avoid pressurizing those waiting to escape, and, unlike the limitations of its predecessors – given the greater strength of watertight bulkheads in an SSN – there was now a greatly improved chance that conditions within the escape compartment could be satisfactorily maintained (no leaks to increase pressure and good control of the atmosphere) to ensure survival for those waiting. These were important considerations, as a tower-escape cycle takes approximately six minutes.

In addition to time under pressure, the other major risk facing an escapee was the essential factor of 'blowing out' to avoid an embolism. This was alleviated by fitting the immersion suit with a hood, thereby making it a self-contained lung; it acted like a bucket over the escapee's head. The air inside the 'bucket' expands as the external pressure reduces and vents to the surrounding water, so the wearer simply breathes normally, as he is now taking in air at a commensurate pressure for the prevailing depth of water. Using this methodology – pioneered by a number of brave volunteers over the past three decades who gradually increased the depth by experimentation – it has been demonstrated that escape from 183m (600ft) is possible. These experiments revealed that the 'bottom time' at this depth is a mere 30 seconds (i.e. once pressurized, escape must start within this time), and that an almost inevitable by-product of the evolution is burst eardrums. The depth of 183m (600ft) is important because that is the maximum depth of the continental shelf before the ocean plunges to the depths, and the waters most congested by a variety of sea-going craft. By extension, they are the most dangerous areas in which a submarine operates because of their vulnerability to collision or grounding.

The miracle of the suit lies is its compactness – roughly 0.09m (1ft) square and 23cm (9in) deep – which allows one for each member of the crew to be stowed in 'escape lockers' in the forward and after escape compartments. The latest version, the Mk10, instead of employing a 'double skin' for insulation against hypothermia, reverts to a single skin, but combines it with an individual life-raft for sustaining life and comfort once on the surface and awaiting the arrival of support forces. To assist yet further in this process, the Royal Navy SETT has a team that can be delivered quickly to the scene of a Dissub to assist those who have

Below: The United States Navy, until recently, had one DSRV stationed on each coast of the United States (*Mystic* and *Avalon* – the latter has recently been paid off). NATO now has a number of smaller ship-deployed DSRVs that can fulfil *Avalon*'s role in the Atlantic, and there are further improvements in the pipeline.

managed to get out. Known as the Submarine Parachute Assistance Group (SPAG), its job is to provide emergency first aid to any escapee requiring it and, recognizing the importance of morale, to ensure that every escapee is made as comfortable as possible until further help arrives.

RESCUE VESSELS TODAY

Tower escape is limited by depth and still carries an element of risk to the escapee because of the considerations of pressurization (albeit for a relatively short period) and survival on the surface. Rescue is thus the preferred solution if it can be achieved in a reasonable time after the submarine sinking. The limitations of a tethered bell to achieve this (sea state, diver assistance, and angle of the Dissub) have already been discussed, so the ideal solution lies in a mobile rescue craft that is able to operate autonomously and 'mate' with a Dissub which is lying at an angle.

The Americans turned their thoughts to this problem following the losses in deep water of USS *Thresher* in 1963 and USS *Scorpion* in 1968. Although there could not have been any survivors from either submarine, nevertheless the 'what-if?' scenario could not have been answered. In 1958, the United States Navy had bought *Trieste* from its Swiss designer Professor Piccard and had then built the improved *Trieste II*, thus building experience in deep-water submersibles. From these and other experimental deep-diving vehicles, in 1971, it introduced the deep submersible rescue vessels (DSRV) *Mystic* and *Avalon*, one of which was stationed on either coast of the United States. The primary mission of these craft was (and remains) to provide a quick-reaction, worldwide, all-weather capability to rescue personnel from disabled submarines (Dissubs) at depths down to 610m (2000ft) and lying at angles of up to 55 degrees. Their potential area of operations covers 20 per cent of Earth's surface. Flown by C5 aircraft to an airport closest to the rescue

site, the craft would be transported to the vicinity of the Dissub by either a support ship or piggybacked on a mother submarine (Mosub). For a rescue operation, the DSRV would locate the Dissub and attach itself to the rescue seat located above the Dissub's escape tower. Once mating was completed and a satisfactory seal achieved between the DSRV and the Dissub by pumping out the skirt space, the hatch of the latter would be opened and the personnel transfer undertaken. A maximum of 24 rescuees can be carried. The release procedure was the reverse of the mating evolution, and the DSRV would then return to the Mosub. If survivors were removed from a pressurized atmosphere, a similar pressure could be

Top: The DSRV, which is transportable by C5 Galaxy aircraft, can be quickly deployed to an airport that is close to a submarine base, where a Mosub can be prepared to accept her.

Above: *An unmanned remotely piloted vehicle, Scorpio is operable from the DSRV. Here she sits on the deck of a recovery vessel, having retrieved Alaska Airlines Flight 261's flight data recorder off the coast of California.*

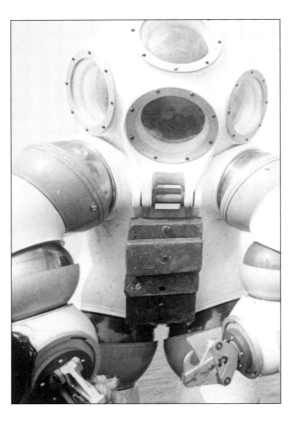

Right: It may be necessary to deploy other assets, such as the armoured diving suit (ADS), before the main rescue takes place. This is JIM 18 of the Royal Navy.

Below: The Swedish Navy's DSRV being deployed. These craft are capable of diving and mating with a Dissub at about 609m (2000ft), beyond which even the strongest watertight bulkhead in a submarine is unlikely to have survived. A critical capability of any DSRV is the maximum angle at which it can mate, as it cannot be guaranteed that the Dissub will have finished in an upright posture on the seabed.

established in the Mosub's escape compartment to avoid the survivors suffering decompression sickness. The DSRV can conduct three of these evolutions in a 24-hour period. Four US submarines on each coast, the four Royal Navy *Vanguard*-class SSBNs, and one French SSBN are all certified to be Mosubs for the DSRVs.

In addition to the DSRV, the USN is also equipped with the submarine rescue chamber (SRC), which is deployed from certified surface vessels. The chamber, which requires atmospheric diving-suit (ADS) support, can operate down to 260m (850ft) and carries five or six rescuees at a time.

The Royal Navy, in addition to its SSBNs being certified to operate with the US DSRV, also maintains its own Submarine Rescue Team, which consists of the rescue submersible *LR5* and its remotely operated 'assistant' *Scorpio*. The 'assistant' is capable of being attached to escape hatches in order to deliver emergency stores and equipment. *LR5* can conduct rescues down to 457m (1500ft) and can carry eight survivors at a time. Constantly available from its base near Glasgow Airport in Scotland, in addition to being able to be deployed from a Mosub, its greatest strength is its ability to be deployed from any suitable A-frame fitted surface ship. This provides it with great flexibility and speed of deployment, as it demonstrated during the *Kursk* disaster in August 2000.

The Swedish Navy is equipped with the URF system, and a new vehicle Swedish submarine rescue vehicle (SSRV) will replace its older sister. This mini-submersible is capable of conducting rescues down to 700m (2296ft) and can carry 35 survivors. It works in conjunction with a mother ship equipped with a recompression chamber, onto which the URF can be lowered for the direct transfer of rescuees.

The Royal Australian Navy operates the remotely controlled Australian submarine rescue vehicle (ASRV), which again is fully integrated with transportable hyperbaric transfer and treatment chambers.

THE *KURSK* TRAGEDY

In August 2000 the world was shaken by the news that one of Russia's 13,900-tonne *Oscar*-class submarines, *Kursk*, had sunk in approximately 91m (300ft) of water with all hands following two explosions onboard. Details of the incident were slow to emerge from official Russian naval sources; however, there were reports that men might still be alive onboard the stricken vessel. The Royal Navy deployed its rescue team, including *LR5*, at the earliest possible opportunity, and it arrived in the area approximately 92 hours later. Despite international concern at the plight of possible survivors, information gradually filtered out indicating there was little hope of finding anyone alive, not least the revelation that the accident had occurred some 48 hours before the official news release. Pessimism deepened when it emerged that the most likely cause of the explosion was a torpedo fuelled by high test peroxide (HTP).

The Royal Navy had suffered a similar accident in 1955 when an HTP 'Fancy' torpedo exploded in one of the tubes of HMS *Sidon* when alongside in Portland Harbour. The devastation created by this accident – despite the fact that a large open hatch had created a vent for the massive blast – was horrifying; 15 British sailors were killed. Without a vent, the explosion of the torpedo in *Kursk* would have instantly sealed the fate of everyone forward. Where hope existed of survivors was in the after machinery compartments, which would have been protected from the blast by a number of

shut, watertight doors. However, even here it was likely that the percussion of the explosion forward would have severely damaged the large water-cooling system valves aft, inducing severe flooding. In such a situation, with a rapid build-up of pressure and CO_2 levels, the only hope of getting out of the submarine would have been by escape, as there was simply no time to wait for rescue. *Kursk* was not fitted with escape apparatus, and there is sad irony in the fact that last letters of victims in the after rescue compartment revealed that they remained alive for at least two hours after the explosion, and the Dissub was lying in water shallow enough for a 'free ascent' escape to have been attempted. The conclusion must be that a submarine requires capabilities for both escape *and* rescue if stricken submariners are to be given the best chance of emerging from a waterlogged tomb.

One theory as to what caused the submarine to suffer explosions in the weapon stowage compartment and sink was that she fell victim to a 'friendly' practice torpedo (as illustrated below). Another theory pushed hard by certain individuals in Russia was that a collision with another submarine was the cause. Neither of these theories has held water, and the most likely trigger to the cataclysm remains a leak of hydrogen peroxide from a practice weapon that was being 'prepped' for firing. The rapid release of oxygen that followed caught fire; after two-and-a-half minutes, the heat generated from this fire caused other weapons to explode.

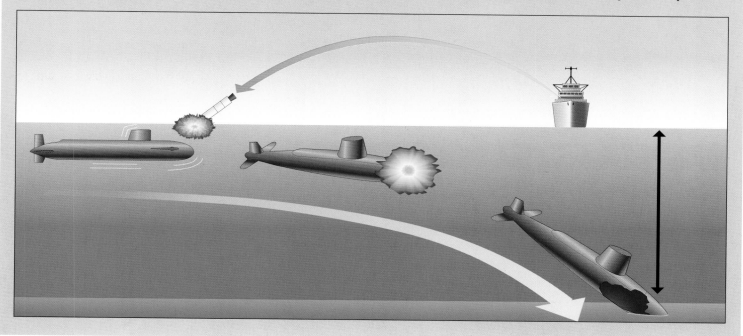

KURSK

The Russian *Oscar II* SSGN is a mighty submarine by any standards – indeed, in size and weight, it approaches the dimensions of the British *Vanguard*-class SSBN. To understand how such a leviathan could be brought low by a relatively small escape of fuel from just one of its many weapons, it must be appreciated how unstable HTP can be unless perfectly controlled. The fluid is 10 times more volatile than fuel oil, and any material other than stainless steel or plastic will act as catalyst, thereby releasing significant quantities of highly flammable oxygen. A single spark (or cigarette end) would set off an uncontrollable chain reaction of blast followed by fire, which would then be fed by high-pressure air and hydraulic systems, causing more weapons (and possibly their warheads) to explode.

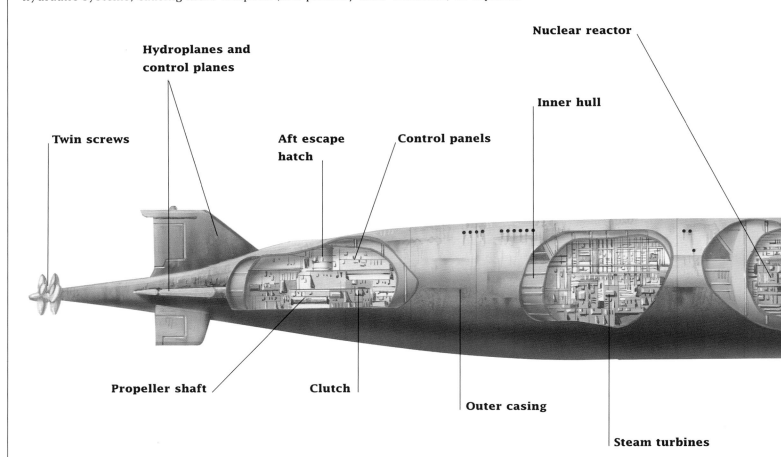

Hydroplanes and control planes

Nuclear reactor

Inner hull

Twin screws

Aft escape hatch

Control panels

Propeller shaft

Clutch

Outer casing

Steam turbines

SPECIFICATIONS

Country: Russia
Launch date: August 1986 (first unit)
Crew: 130
Displacement: 13,900 tonnes/ 16,000 tonnes
Dimensions: 154m x 18.2m x 9m (505ft 2in x 59ft 9in x 29ft 6in)

Armament: 24 SS-N-19 SSMs; four 650mm (25.6in) TTs; four 533mm (21in) TTs
Powerplant: Two shafts, two nuclear PWRs, two turbines
Range: Unlimited
Performance: 22 knots/28 knots

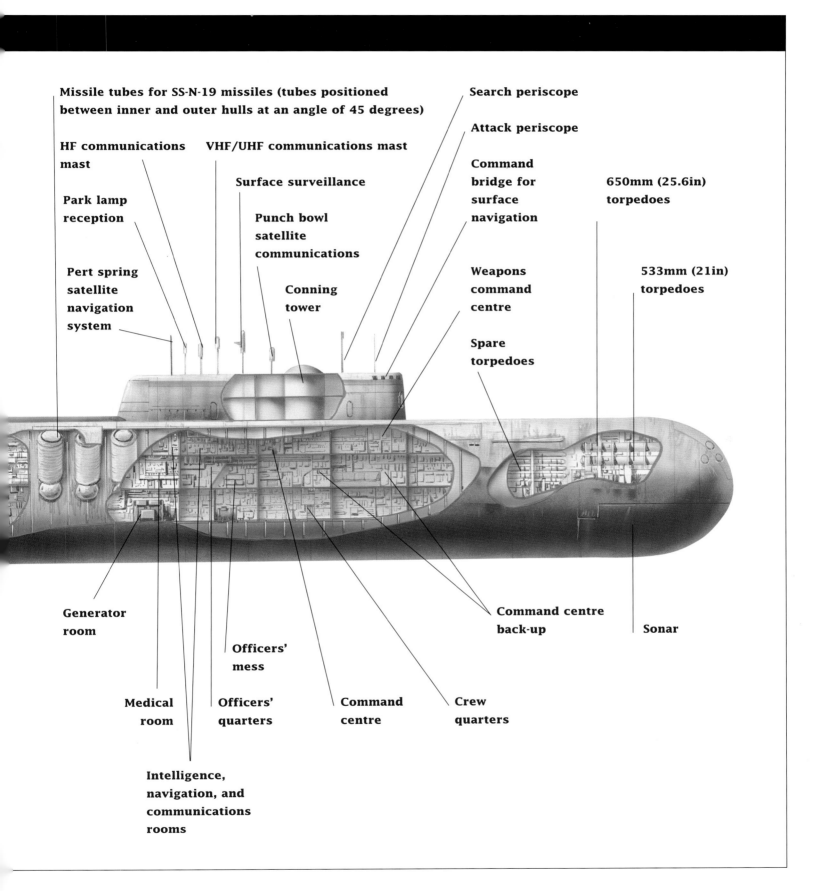

Missile tubes for SS-N-19 missiles (tubes positioned between inner and outer hulls at an angle of 45 degrees)

HF communications mast

Park lamp reception

Pert spring satellite navigation system

VHF/UHF communications mast

Surface surveillance

Punch bowl satellite communications

Conning tower

Search periscope

Attack periscope

Command bridge for surface navigation

Weapons command centre

Spare torpedoes

650mm (25.6in) torpedoes

533mm (21in) torpedoes

Generator room

Officers' mess

Medical room

Officers' quarters

Command centre

Crew quarters

Command centre back-up

Sonar

Intelligence, navigation, and communications rooms

DEEP-SEA VEHICLES

Everyone is aware of the outer space programme, and we receive almost daily reports about projects destined for the Moon, Mars and other planets. Yet we know little enough of the mysteries of our own planet. This chapter is about the 'inner-spacemen' and the important work that is being undertaken to advance our understanding of Earth and its oceans, on which we depend for life.

W e have seen that man's inspiration in taking huge risks in order to conquer 'inner space' was to use it for warfare and to achieve 'command of the sea'. The other great inspiration for battling the underwater elements was for an instinct almost as basic as fighting: salvage and the prospect of riches! For the more altruistic, exploration was the key. For whatever reason, we see the same, plodding progress towards finding the most suitable and safest method of achieving the aim. We also see the pioneers battling against the ocean bottom's natural defences of pressure, darkness and sub-surface currents – and loneliness. The major difference between a submarine and a diving-bell was that the former had to be mobile, while the latter could be static.

Left: Deep Ocean Engineering's *Deep Rover*, with its jointed robotic arms, is a one-man submersible capable of operating at depths of 300m (984ft).

THE DIVING-BELL

The principle of the diving-bell (or 'chest') can be demonstrated by putting an inverted glass tumbler into a bowl of water and pressing it downwards. Air is compressible and water is not; therefore, the more the depth is increased, the smaller the volume of air will become, and the higher the water will rise. At 10m (33ft), i.e. 2 atmospheres, the air will occupy half the volume of the glass. The only way to overcome the phenomenon would be for a diving-bell to be supplied with air from a surface compressor or other source; then the volume occupied by the air would increase and would be ventilated for respiration purposes.

In his *Problemata*, Aristotle referred to Alexander the Great's foray into the depths in a glass diving-bell; in 1250, Roger Bacon in *Novum Organum* referred to 'a machine, or reservoir, of air to which labourers upon wrecks might resort whenever they required to take breath'. Bacon established the principle that a diving-bell could be used as a portable lung.

The earliest dependable record of a diving-bell in actual use was recorded in the *Architettura Militare* written by Francesco de Marchi (1490–1574), the subject of which was Caligula's pleasure galleys that were sunk in the Lake of Nemi. He describes the dress of Guiglielmo de Lorena, the operator, as a diving-bell just large enough to contain the upper half of Lorena's body. The majority of its weight was taken by slings suspended from a surface craft, with the remainder by a yoke resting on the diver's shoulders. One great advantage of this device was that Lorena's arms free to undertake a mission, so whether this was actually an early diving-bell or a diving-suit is debatable!

In 1538, two Greeks exhibited a diving-bell at Toledo on the River Tagus in the presence of Emperor Charles V and several thousand spectators. The bell was shaped like an inverted kettle, and the operators undertook their expedition to amuse and to show off their skill. They amazed onlookers by not only coming out of the river dry, but also with a candle lit earlier still alight. In 1552, some fishermen from the Adriatic gave a similar exhibition at Venice in the presence of the Doge and the Senate. Their bell was 3m (10ft) high, and one of their number remained in it for over two hours.

In 1597, we see the concept of the bell being used as an observation post as a counter to possible underwater invaders. Buonaiuto Lorini of Venice, in his book on 'fortification', describes a rectangular, wooden case fitted with windows, below

Right: The first man to design a diving bell was Guiglielmo de Lorena, who, in 1531, attempted to raise Emperor Caligula's pleasure galleys, sunk in the Lake of Nemi. It is doubtful whether Lorena had sufficient air for the hour's endurance claimed; however, he had a window to look out of and freedom to move his arms, so it was a practical concept in some respects.

which was suspended a platform on which an observer could stand.

The year 1616 saw the development of a mobile exploration or observation bell, when Franz Kessler devised a bell that stretched almost to his ankles, but was shaped in such a way that it allowed him to walk on the bottom. He sat in a harness from which was suspended a ballast weight, and around its top were fitted a number of glass observation ports. It had no overhead suspension; in order to return to the surface, the operator simply slipped the weight and up he popped. History does not record how he would extricate himself from the device once on the surface nor what emergency procedure would have been instituted had he tripped over when on the seabed, thereby losing his 'bubble'!

In 1640, the King of France granted a patent to Jean Barrie for a bell, accompanied by the monopoly of using it for fishing and salvage purposes for 12 years. He used his privilege to good effect and conducted a successful salvage of the cargo of a ship wrecked near Dieppe.

The first British diving-bell was used in 1665 to examine the wreck of a Spanish galleon that had sunk in Tobermory Bay on the Isle of Mull in 1588. Its likely inventor was one Archibald Miller of Greenock, and it employed Bacon's principle of a portable lung. The total weight of the device was 177kg (390lb), and it was suspended on chains from a surface craft. To be recovered by the surface attendants, the diver would bang a hammer against the side of the bell, the noise of which would be easily heard 'on the roof', as water is a very efficient sound-carrier. The speed of sound in air is 347m (1140ft) per second, while in water it is 1494m (4900ft) per second.

In 1538, two Greeks exhibited a diving-bell at Toledo, on the River Tagus, in Spain. They amazed their onlookers by not only coming out of the river dry, but also with a candle lit earlier still alight.

Left: The only purpose of Franz Kessler's bell of 1616 was exploration and observation, as the operator's arms were kept firmly inside the ankle-length bell. If anything, this was a retrograde step from the work started by Guiglielmo de Lorena.

The Spanish Cadaques Bell appeared in 1677. This was an ambitious device suspended on a gallows-frame between two large barges, and was used to recover a large sum of money from two wrecked bullion ships. The bell was made of wood, was 4m (13ft) high, and had a diameter of 2.7m (9ft) across the rim, which was strengthened by iron hoops and attached to which were iron

ballast weights used to make it negatively buoyant. Instead of standing on a platform, the diver sat on a bench as he was lowered. Once close to the bottom, he exited the bell and gathered up as much coin as he could with his lungful of air before depositing his booty into bags suspended inside the bell and taking another breath. This process continued until the air inside the diving-bell became too stale to breathe. On his signal to be brought up, the laborious task of winching the bell to the surface fell to the surface attendants. It is reported that the diver's wages for each trip was as much coin as he could hold in each hand and in his mouth!

Dr Dennis Papin spent most of his working life in England and became a Fellow of the Royal Society. It was Papin who, recognizing the limitations of contemporary diving-bells in respect of breathable air and working space, in 1689 first proposed to provide air under pressure to bells to increase their operators' endurance.

EDMUND HALLEY'S BREAKTHROUGH

Papin never put his theory into practice, but the father of the modern diving-bell, Dr Edmund Halley (of comet fame), did. In 1690, this man of genius defined all the essential elements required of a practical and sustainable submerged workstation. It was made of wood, lead-lined, and shaped like a truncated cone with a standing platform suspended below it. It was 0.9m (3ft) in diameter at the top, 1.5m (5ft) at its rim, perfectly stable, and had an operating depth of 18.2m (60ft). Halley's major breakthrough, however, lay in providing a source of replenishable air, not by a pump, as Papin suggested, but by weighted barrels lowered from the surface. The barrels were ingenious in that they had holes top and bottom; to the top hole was connected a leather hose, while the bottom one was open to the sea. When the barrel was lowered, provided the end of the hose was always below the level of the bottom of the

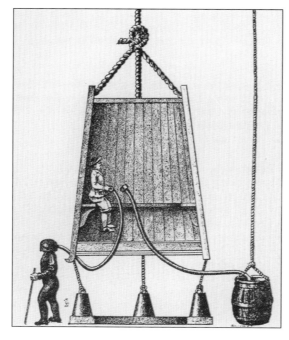

Left: Fighting, exploring, or transporting? This concept of an underwater bicycle (aquapede) by Alvery Templo could have applications in all three directions, although it must have been susceptible to tides and currents.

Below: The Cadaques Bell of 1677 was used to recover bullion from two sunken ships. The divers used were Moors famous for their lung capacity. When they wanted to be hoisted to the surface to hand over their spoils or refresh the air in the bell, they would blow on a horn. It is reported that one blew the horn so loudly he deafened himself and became so dizzy he almost fell out of the bell.

barrel, it served as a source of compressed air. To replenish the air inside the bell, the diver simply raised the hose into it. A further refinement of the Halley Bell was to increase the diver's radius of action, hitherto restricted by a deep breath, by providing an auxiliary bell that covered his head, which was in turn connected by another hose to the 'mother' bell. A window at the top provided light, and, to reduce the ever-increasing pressure in the replenishment area, Halley fitted 'a Cock to let out the hot Air that had been breathed'. Halley claimed that he and three companions spent 90 minutes at 18m (60ft) without feeling any ill effects. Their ascent back to the surface must have taken longer than 19 minutes, otherwise they would have suffered a bend!

Halley's bell was heavy and labour-intensive, so the next generation of diving-bells saw improvements in materials and methods of deployment. The first to emerge was built, in 1728, by Martin Triewald, a Swedish Army officer. It was made of copper and replenished by the 'Halley air method'. One interesting development was the provision of a breathing tube inside the work area that drew air off just above the surface where it was coolest. Halley's successor in significance was John Smeaton, the British engineer who built the third Eddystone Lighthouse, not only because he used a

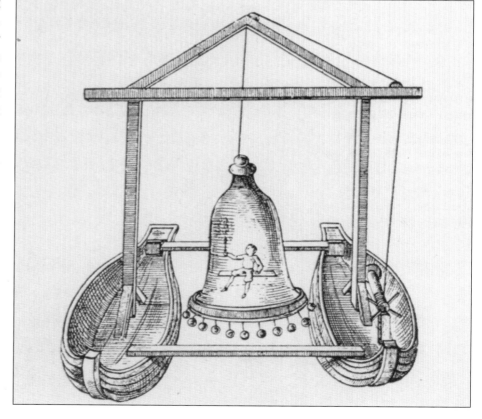

pump, but also because he built it for underwater work, rather than for salvage. Smeaton constructed a cast-iron diving-bell in 1788 for use in the repair of the foundations of Hexham Bridge in Northumberland. It was the first bell to be supplied with pumped air from the surface, allowing its two occupants to work unhindered in its 0.9m (3ft) wide aperture. Its shape was a departure from the traditional bell shape, in that, because of its narrowing towards the top, it had the advantage of maintaining a proportionally deeper air-replenishment area for the occupant. With forced air from above, shape now became irrelevant, with downstream benefits for cost.

In 1812, another British engineer, James Rennie, refined Smeaton's design and made it partially mobile by suspending it from a four-wheel frame running on rails and mounted on a platform. He used this technique on a number of harbour works, most notably at Ramsgate Harbour and Sheerness. The 'Rennie Bell' was borrowed by Isambard Kingdom Brunel to repair the Thames Tunnel in 1827 after it flooded. The Rennie Bell marked the end of the development of the open diving-bell, with only refinements in lighting, communication, and methods of ballasting to follow.

THE CLOSED BELL (BATHYSPHERE)

In essence the 'closed bell' is a tethered submarine, being connected to a surface craft for suspension, power supply, and air, and maintained at atmospheric pressure. The genre has been used almost invariably for inspection or scientific research at significant depths, although one or two were fitted with crude arms and pincers. The vast majority of these vessels through the years have been spherical in shape, as this is strongest to resist sea-pressure.

In 1865, Ernest Bazin, who was the first to use electric lighting underwater in 1864, invented the earliest underwater observatory, designed to look for the famous sunken treasure of Vigo Bay. Although he reached an unprecedented depth of 75m (246ft), his observatory carried no external supply of air, and its deployment was extremely limited by weather conditions.

The next depth to be reached was 130m (427ft) when, in 1889, Balsamello descended

Right: Colonel C.J. Field's concept of a 'viewer' and a 'worker' operating together. This was similar to the device developed by Guiseppe Pino in 1902, which involved a surface hydroscope for viewing the seabed and an electrically propelled 'worker' submarine picking up objects with its arms.

in a cast-iron sphere. It weighed 5.05 tonnes. The design was taken a stage further by another Italian experimenter, Count Piatta del Pozzo, who reinforced his craft with vertical and horizontal rings. It was this shape that was to inspire future designs.

In 1902, Guiseppe Pino developed a unique combination of a hydroscope for viewing the seabed and an electrically propelled 'worker' submarine fitted with arms. The former apparatus remained on the surface, while a series of telescopic optical tubes were lowered to the depths, on the end of which were 12 lenses. The 'worker' was designed to pick up anything seen by the hydroscope.

In 1930, the closed bell came of age in the hands of American naturalist Dr William Beebe and geologist-engineer Otis Barton. The former had made it known that he was looking for a suitable platform to take him *de profundis* and, at first, ignored the overtures of the latter, who felt he had invented the right type of equipment. Eventually, the two got together. Their goal was to reach the incredible depth of 610m (2000ft), so careful design – including the ability to control the ascent as well as the descent of the craft – was essential. To achieve the necessary strength, stainless steel was used, but the first version turned out to weigh 5.05 tonnes – far too heavy! The second effort, 1.45m (4ft 9in) in diameter, with walls 3.8cm (1.5in) thick, although cramped for two men, was half the weight of its predecessor and could be handled by contemporary winches. Three observation windows of quartz glass were fitted, each 20cm (8in) in diameter and 7.6cm (3in) thick. Attached to the 1067m (3500ft) long suspension cable were light and intercom cables, which were fed into the bathysphere (Greek for 'deep sphere') through a double-gland stuffing box. Oxygen for eight hours was replenished from internal tanks, and CO_2 and moisture were absorbed by the chemicals soda lime and calcium chloride, respectively. During their early dives, Beebe and Barton were subjected to a number of alarms and scares,

but the bathysphere and its handling team proved sound. In June 1930, they reached 244m (800ft) and, in the same series, 427m (1400ft) – 0.4km (a quarter of a mile) down and firmly in unknown territory. In 1932, they reached 670m (2200ft), but an alarming oscillation caused by the surface tender bouncing around in rough weather forced them to call a halt. They had seen sights that left them thirsting for more, so in 1934 the team was re-formed, this time with the support of the National Geographic Society and the New York Zoological Society. They dived off Bermuda in August in good weather and reached the incredible depth of 923m (3028ft), over 0.8km (half a mile) down, with only a few turns left on the lowering drum. The blackness outside was almost unnerving, and the pressure on each of the windows was over 19.3 tonnes. Beebe and Barton had done more than their fair share for science!

THE BATHYSCAPHE

During the 1930s, a Swiss scientist called Auguste Piccard secured funding from the Belgian Government to build a large, spherical gondola suspended under a huge gas-filled balloon to research cosmic rays. He piloted *FNRS I* (*Fonds National Belge de la Recherche Scientifique*) to over 55,000m

Above left: Dr William Beebe's steel bathysphere on deck preparing for descent. The cylindrical form can withstand the external sea pressure at great depths, with occupants breathing at normal pressure. Like any explorers entering unknown territory, Beebe and his colleague, Otis Barton, were extraordinarily brave.

(11 miles) above the Earth. In 1948, using the same principles that took him into the stratosphere and back to Earth, Piccard Snr and his son Jacques, an oceanographic engineer, built the first bathyscaphe (Greek for 'deep ship'), the *FNRS II*, to take them to the depths and back again. Father and son recognized that the vulnerability of the bathysphere lay in its dependence on its supporting wire, which might snap and consign them to the depths, so they went for the alternative of a float. They built a 10.16-tonne watertight observation sphere (the gondola) and a float (the equivalent of the balloon) which held thousands of gallons of gasoline fuel and which, as well as being lighter than water, also had the quality of being incompressible at depth. To achieve negative buoyancy, the bathyscaphe carried

tonnes of iron pellets which, when released, allowed the gasoline float to return the vessel to the surface.

Piccard had a falling-out with his French backers, who included Jacques-Eve Cousteau, and so sold *FNRS II* to the French Navy, who had oceanographic research to conduct on its own behalf. In August 1954, the French took the craft to 4048m (13,282ft) off Dakar, Senegal. Following this success, the French Government authorized a second craft, the *Archimede*, specifically to tackle the Challenger Deep off Guam.

Undaunted by the French episode, the Piccards raised further funds from the townspeople of Trieste and built a bigger bathyscaphe, naming it *Trieste* in their honour. Launched in 1953, it weighed 50.8 tonnes without gasoline and 152.4 tonnes

Below: *Trieste*, the brainchild of Auguste Piccard, generated a revolution in underwater exploration and operations. Having established the practicability of conducting work at great depths, she spawned many successors that had, and have, commercial and military applications.

REMOTELY OPERATED VEHICLES (ROV)

The remotely operated vehicle (ROV) at its most simple is a frame to which accessories are bolted, but in more complex forms might be fitted with tracks for bottom crawling. It first established its reputation when *CURV* recovered the B-52 H-bomb in the 1960s. Slowly but surely the ROV has replaced the saturation diver, particularly in dangerous and inaccessible areas, such as inside wrecks such as the *Titanic.* Over the years, they have demonstrated their endurance, dependability, versatility, and economy of operation. Today, using a variety of sensors (cameras and sonars) and manipulators (nippers and grabbers), they are employed on many tasks in the offshore industry; drilling support, pipeline inspection, and route survey, to name but a few.

In civil engineering, they can inspect dams and clean ships' hulls. In a military application, they can search for mines and destroy them, and they are in service with the German, Danish, and Swedish navies; in fact, a submarine wire-guided torpedo can be classed as a combat ROV. In oceanography, ROVs can, at very great depths and without susceptibility to currents, take photographs, record data, and collect samples. One of their great exponents is Dr Robert Ballard of the Woods Hole Oceanographic Institute in the United States and of *Titanic* fame who, while admitting that using ROVs is a different spiritual experience to flying a manned submersible, nevertheless declares that 'robots are better'.

Left: The great benefit of the ROV is that it can operate where human beings cannot – its drawbacks are the relative limitations on how much it can be manipulated and its recovery capacity.

ALVIN

The most famous (and hardworked) manned deep ocean research vehicle is *Alvin*. Her purchase was justified for her role in inspecting the 'Artemis' tracking array in the deep water of the Tongue of the Ocean, Andros Island. She conducted her first (1828m) 6000ft dive in 1965 and since then has voyaged to the depths on thousands of occasions. She sprang to prominence for the part she played in looking for the missing US H-bomb off the coast of Spain in 1966, but is still in operation 35 years later, conducting less spectacular but nonetheless important work for the Woods Hole Oceanographic Institute. Her observation dome has been replaced several times, and she has worked with two support ships, the latest being *Atlantis*, which entered service in 1996.

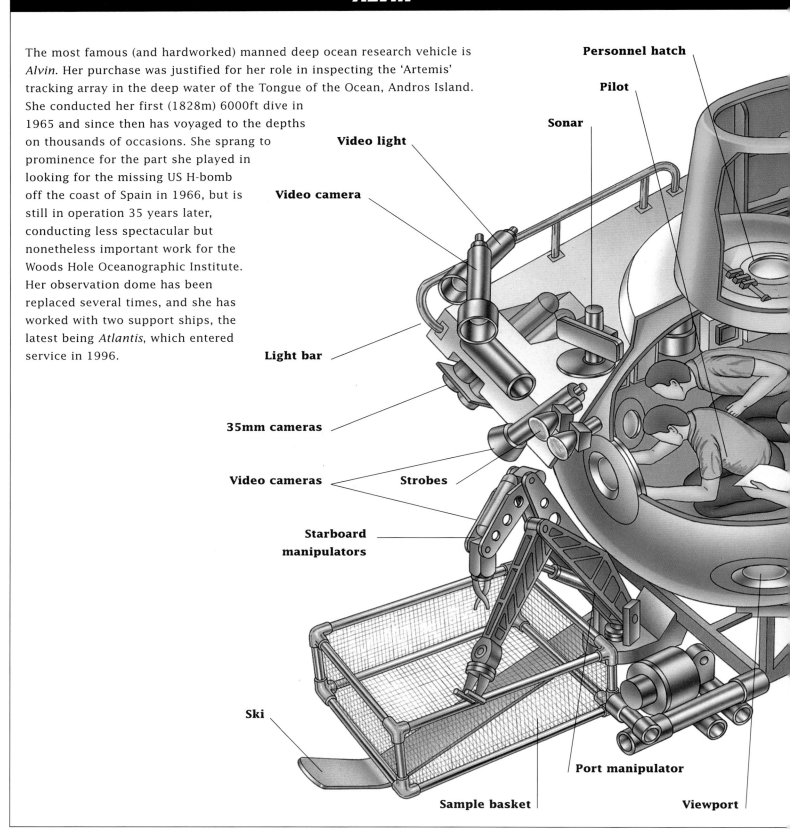

Personnel hatch

Pilot

Sonar

Video light

Video camera

Light bar

35mm cameras

Video cameras

Strobes

Starboard manipulators

Ski

Port manipulator

Sample basket

Viewport

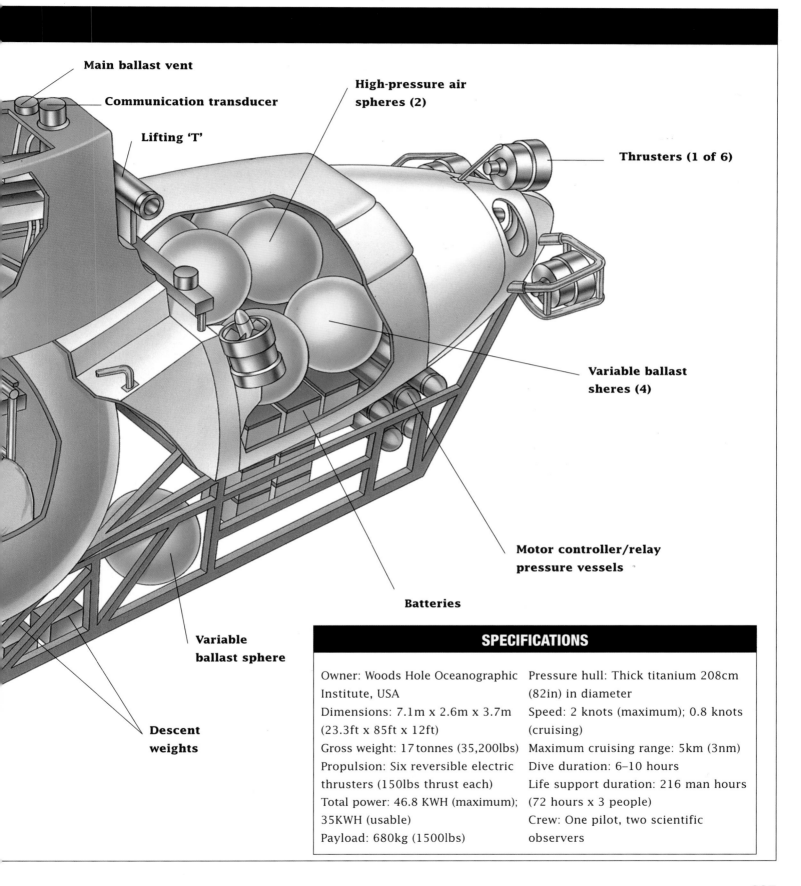

Main ballast vent

Communication transducer

Lifting 'T'

High-pressure air spheres (2)

Thrusters (1 of 6)

Variable ballast sheres (4)

Motor controller/relay pressure vessels

Batteries

Variable ballast sphere

Descent weights

SPECIFICATIONS

Owner: Woods Hole Oceanographic Institute, USA

Dimensions: 7.1m x 2.6m x 3.7m (23.3ft x 85ft x 12ft)

Gross weight: 17 tonnes (35,200lbs)

Propulsion: Six reversible electric thrusters (150lbs thrust each)

Total power: 46.8 KWH (maximum); 35KWH (usable)

Payload: 680kg (1500lbs)

Pressure hull: Thick titanium 208cm (82in) in diameter

Speed: 2 knots (maximum); 0.8 knots (cruising)

Maximum cruising range: 5km (3nm)

Dive duration: 6–10 hours

Life support duration: 216 man hours (72 hours x 3 people)

Crew: One pilot, two scientific observers

In January 1960, *Trieste* entered the Mariana Trench and set the all-time manned-submersible record of 10,911km (35,800ft), the ultimate known bottom of the ocean.

with the float. It was 15.2m (50ft) long and carried two operating crew, and was able to move about on its own using battery power. These batteries also powered the electro-magnets that held the 9.1 tonnes of iron pellets, so that, if there were a power failure, the ballast would be released in a fail-safe mode and the capsule would rise automatically to the surface.

After a 3048m (10,000ft) dive in 1953, the Piccards tried to interest the American National Science Foundation in Washington DC, but without success. Four years later, however, the attitude towards oceanography within the United States Navy had changed,

and so *Trieste* underwent a period of evaluation in the Mediterranean. The trials were successful, and *Trieste* was bought by the US Office of Naval Research and prepared for even deeper dives.

A more robust observation sphere was ordered from Germany and the float's capacity was correspondingly increased. In 1959, the upgraded *Trieste,* crewed by Jacques Piccard and the marine biologist Dr Andreas Rechnitzer, set a new depth record of 5642m (18,510ft) off Guam in the Pacific Ocean. In 1960, following a series of ever deeper dives, *Trieste* entered the Mariana Trench, or Challenger Deep, off Guam; there,

Right: *Alvin* has had an observation chamber change on a number of occasions, both to maintain the integrity of the sphere and to take advantage of technological advances. An early sphere is seen on display at the Navy Yard in Washington D.C.

Left: *Alvin* was named after engineer Allyn Vine. Here, *Alvin* descends to its maximum depth of 4000m (13,123ft) on one of its numerous research missions.

TRIESTE

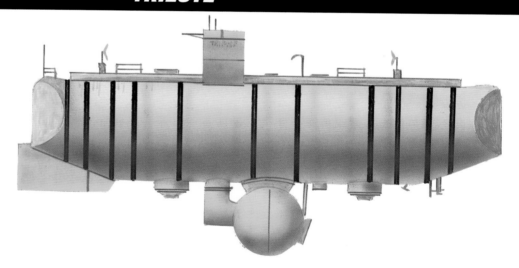

Trieste was a vessel in two parts. The upper was simply a tank containing 106 cubic metres (3745 cubic feet) of gasoline. Being of lower specific gravity than water, this provided a sufficient measure of buoyancy to return the craft to the surface when water ballast held in two small tanks at the extremities was blown out by compressed air. The permanent ballast – nine, later 16 tonnes of iron pellets – was also contained in this section. The lower part was an alloy sphere, large enough for two people, with walls 10cm (4in) thick. *Trieste* was funded in large part by the people of the city whose name she bears.

SPECIFICATIONS

Displacement: 50 tonnes
Dimensions: 18.1m x 3.5m (59ft 6in x 11ft 6in)
Machinery: two-shaft electric motors
Service speed: 1 knot

Constructor: Navalmeccanica, Naples
Material: Steel/steel alloy
Built for: Auguste Piccard
Owner: US Navy

Above: The *PC-8* on the hook. John Perry's interest in the ocean materialized in 1957 with his first plywood and fibreglass underwater vehicle. The US Navy used Perry's 'cubmarine' during its search for a missing H-bomb in 1966.

wreck of USS *Thresher* (lost in 1963) and the recovery of some vital detritus from the seabed being an outstanding achievement.

DEEP RESEARCH VESSELS

While the Piccards were setting extraordinary depth records, a symposium in Washington attended by Allyn Vine of the Woods Hole Oceanographic Institute (WHOI) in 1956 recommended that the United States develop a national programme for manned undersea vehicles. As a result of this recommendation, the US bought *Trieste*, but it was recognized that it was too large and unmanoeuvrable to fit the bill for flexibility. However, it was not until May 1964 that *Alvin*, a battery-driven submersible capable of operating at 1829m (6000ft), appeared on the scene. In 1966, *Alvin* sprang to prominence when, after a two-month search, she found the H-bomb lost from a B-52 bomber off the coast of Spain after it collided with a tanker aircraft. She and the CURV (cable-controlled underwater research vehicle) pulled off a miracle of search and recovery in very difficult circumstances. The search task was described by the Admiral in charge, William S. Gaunt, as 'like looking for the eye of a needle in a field of haystacks in the dark'.

Alvin has been rebuilt many times since her launch, with titanium replacing her aluminium structure that has increased her operational depth to 4267m (14,000ft). She is the world's most productive submersible and has averaged 150 dives per annum, with much of her current work being focussed on 'hot-water vents' and deep-ocean topography.

In 1965, the United States introduced *Halibut*, a highly covert submersible capable of lowering long lengths of cables with lights to examine enemy weapons dumps and lost submarines on the seabed.

In early 1968, Grumman Ocean Systems introduced their *PX-15*, later christened *Ben Franklin*, specifically to study the Gulf Stream and the phenomenon known as the 'deep scattering layer'. *Ben Franklin* was a

in January 1960, she set the all-time manned submersible record of 10,911m (35,800ft), the ultimate known bottom of the ocean. Manned by Jacques Piccard and Lieutenant Don Walsh USN, she spent 20 minutes conducting scientific experiments, and the crew made a phone call to the surface from 11.2km (7 miles) down!

Trieste was to perform a total of 128 dives during her career, with her discovery of the

mesoscaphe, a craft intended to explore the mid-depth regions. The 'deep scattering layer' consists of a mass of light-sensitive plankton that goes deep by day and nears the surface at night. It can play havoc with submarine- and surface-ship sonar, so understanding it in order to exploit its characteristics was an important oceanographic study. The task took 31 days, and years of evaluation followed the collection of data by its crew of six, which included 65,000 photographs of themselves for NASA, who were interested in the effects of isolation on the crew.

Commercial companies began to show an interest in DRVs in the late 1960s, and the Perry Submersibles made a name for themselves. The oil company Shell still uses its *Sea Diver* to inspect underwater pipelines. It can also be used for exploration, fitted as it is with two drills, a mechanical arm, and television cameras.

Deepstar 4000 was designed by Jacques Cousteau and built by Westinghouse in the United States, who in turn leased it to the US Navy. Its mass of sensors for oceanographic research underlines the importance of the science in submarine warfare. The oceans are not homogenous, and variations in temperature, salinity, and depth create 'layers', all of which has an effect on the behaviour of sound in water. The nature of the sound channel so created can diminish – or even enhance – probabilities of detection and thereby generate tactical advice of where and how to search for an enemy submarine, or conversely where best to patrol if you do not want to be found. Given the billions of pounds, dollars, and roubles invested in highly expensive submarines, the money spent on years of oceanographic research to enhance their performance was well spent.

One of the most unusual DRVs to be developed was the NEMO (Naval Experimental Manned Observatory). It overcame the limitations of previous craft of limited vision by providing the two operators with a panoramic view through a 'frog's eye' made of acrylic plastic. Certified to operate at 183m (600ft), it was a bold experiment that established acrylic as a useful material in the DRV game. The *Makakai* was a more manoeuvrable version of NEMO.

The Johnson Sea-Link was brought into service in 1971 and was made up of two spheres: the front observation sphere was

Left: *Makalii* is launched, retrieved, and transported from a submersible barge before transfer to the surface. She is operated by the University of Hawaii, which has a strong interest in marine research.

Above: Johnson Sea-Link (JSL) submersibles are among the best in the world for marine research. The JSL is equipped with an acrylice sphere 152mm (6in) thick, which houses a pilot and an observer. At sea, support for such craft is essential, and it works in conjunction with R/V Seaward Johnson.

The crew of two emerged no worse for their ordeal 75 hours later, although their oxygen supply was almost exhausted.

The French *Nautile* is a manned submersible designed for observation and operations down to 6000m (19,685ft). It is relatively lightweight at 19.6 tonnes, and it is highly manoeuvrable and can be easily supported. It works in conjunction with *Robin*, a multi-camera fitted remotely operated vehicle (ROV) that is controlled by the pilot of *Nautile* via an umbilical. *Nautile* salvaged many artefacts from the wreck of the *Titanic*, and the French also operate *Cyana*, which has a depth capability of 3000m (914ft).

There is a myriad of such craft operating around the world today, all having slightly different characteristics, but all with the aim of understanding the ocean, its floor, and its flora and fauna to best effect. The challenges of exploring 'inner space' will go on for many years to come!

THE STANDARD DIVER

There are various records in the thirteenth century of free-swimming divers being used to drill holes in the hulls, and there are allusions to them wearing hats, possibly as protection against missiles being hurled at them by defenders. There are also suggestions that a breathing tube was attached to these hats to allow the divers to make good their escape underwater. Ludwig von Eybe zum Hartenstein's drawing of a diver's complete kit in 1500 provides an indication of what the well-dressed diver needed in his wardrobe. A similar concept is shown in a sketch from Diego Ufano of 1613 that shows a diver salving a gun.

At the same time as Robert Fulton was trying to persuade the British to buy underwater weapons of destruction, other inventors were giving much thought to the peaceable diving-dress. In 1802, William Forder made a notable advance towards the modern diving-dress when he introduced a helmet and dress that was supplied with air

made of 10cm (4in) thick acrylic, while the rear sphere, a diver lock-in/lock-out compartment, was made of aluminium. She got into trouble in June 1973 when she became entangled with a sunken warship. Various attempts were made to release the stricken crew of four, but, by the time she was finally recovered from the seabed after more than 24 hours, two men had succumbed to carbon dioxide poisoning. A few months later, a similar tragedy almost befell the British *Pisces* submersible when it sank in 419m (1375ft) of water. On this occasion, *CURV III* came to the rescue and recovered the craft.

from a bellows on the surface. The bellows not only supplied the diver with breathable air, but also, to increase diver comfort, they were designed to keep the suit inflated to a pressure equal to the water outside it. The top was made of copper, and to it were attached leather sleeves and breeches. The suit's major drawback was the fact that the bellows used were of the domestic type and were never powerful enough for the job.

The most important step towards modernity was taken by Augustus Siebe, when he introduced his open diving-suit, allowing work to start on removing the wreck of the *Royal George* that had sunk off Spithead, England, in 1782 and was causing a navigation hazard. His dress consisted of a metal helmet attached to a watertight jacket that reached his waist. Under the jacket, close-fitting trousers reached his armpits. The air that was pumped into the helmet forced its way down between the jacket and trousers, and escaped at the waist. Although entirely practicable because of the abundance

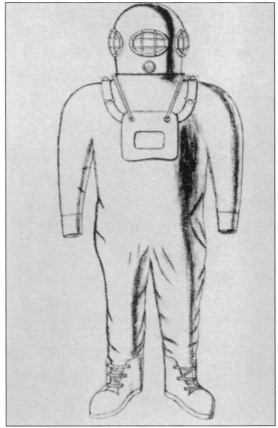

Above: *Pisces V* is another submersible operated by the University of Hawaii, and it is capable of operation down to 2000m (6561ft). Here it can be seen being retrieved by its mother ship *Kaimaki-o-Kanaloa*.

Left: Siebe's first closed dress and helmet of 1837. This was a landmark in diving-dress development in that the diver was enclosed in continuous airtight dress and could bend his neck without losing his air sink. The suit was first demonstrated in 1840 at Spithead, England, during operations to raise the sunken *Royal George* – it was hailed as a great success.

AUTONOMOUS UNDERWATER VEHICLES

The United States Navy definition of an AUV/UUV (unmanned undersea vehicle) is 'a self-propelled submersible whose operation is either fully autonomous (pre-programmed or real-time adaptive mission control) or under minimal supervisory control, and is untethered except for data links such as fibre-optic cable'. In short, AUVs are ROVs with brains. A good commercial example of an AUV is International Submarine Ltd of Canada's *Theseus*, which was developed to lay long lengths of fibre-optic cable under the Arctic icepack and had the ability to replant lays and avoid obstacles. The United States Navy already has UUVs operational in its SSNs with the Near-Time Mine Reconnaissance System (NMRS), a mine-hunting UUV launched and recovered through a torpedo tube.

Above: The Lockheed autonomous undersea vehicle is used by the United States Navy.

of air, the outfit was tricky to operate, particularly as, if the wearer bent down or fell over, the suit then filled with water. This drawback caused Siebe to introduce his closed dress in 1837.

He retained his force pump and helmet practically unaltered, but enclosed the diver in a continuous, airtight dress which was eventually made of sheet rubber sandwiched between two layers of tanned twill. The hands were left free, with tight-fitting cuffs being further secured by rubber bands. A copper breastplate was secured over the shoulders and was fitted to the dress by metal bands fastened over projecting screws. The breastplate was fitted to the helmet by an interrupted screw requiring one-eighth of a turn. Compressed air was fed to the helmet through a pipe from a surface vessel where a pump was operated, and a valve at the back of the helmet expelled foul air. The diver's stability was secured by back and chest weights of 18kg (40lb) each and boots with lead soles weighing 9kg (20lb) each. Without these steadying factors, he was in danger of turning upside down! A lifeline was passed around the diver's waist that enabled him to pass signals to his handlers up top (e.g. three pulls meant ready to come up). Siebe had developed the true working suit that allowed the diver a significant amount of freedom of movement, and the Royal Engineers, responsible for getting rid of the *Royal George*, embraced it with open arms.

The later history of the diving-dress is a history of improvements to the Siebe closed dress of 1837, and the development of decompression tables and decompression chambers, designed by Dr Robert Davis and built by Siebe-Gorman & Co. (the patron saints of divers), made their lives much safer. The dress became known as the standard diver's dress and was ultimately fitted with a telephone and an electric lamp.

THE ARMOURED DIVING-DRESS

The supply of air and protection against sea-pressure to a man working at depth in a suit was always the great challenge, and the first time it was successfully answered was in 1715 by a Devon man, John Lethbridge. His goal was to recover sunken treasure at depth, so he built himself a protective suit based on a barrel with two holes with watertight seals that allowed his

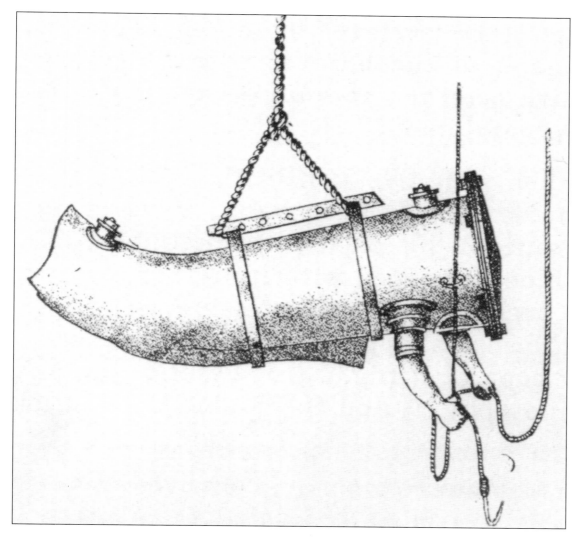

Left: John Lethbridge's apparatus was the first armoured diving-dress and was demonstrated to the world in 1715. His main problem was that, below 21.9m (72ft), the joints on his armholes were affected by pressure and cut off blood circulation. Nevertheless, he is reputed to have made a fortune out of his device.

arms freedom of movement and a glass viewing-port that allowed him to see his booty and therefore do useful work. He could operate down to 22m (72ft), beyond which the watertight seals 'clamped' his arms and stopped his blood circulation – but it was a start. The suit held 'half a hogshead' of air, which gave Lethbridge an endurance of about 30 minutes. His outfit was widely used, and he was reported to have made a fortune.

The first diver's dress with articulated joints, intended to protect the wearer against deep-water pressure, was designed by the American W.H. Taylor, in 1838. Its biggest drawback was the fact that the hands and feet of the diver were only protected by leather, putting the diver at extreme risk if working at depth. However, he had introduced a new technology upon which others could improve. Taylor had attempted to follow the contours of the human body with his suit, whereas the next development, that of L.D. Phillips in 1856, was a simple cylinder to which legs with ball-and-socket joints were attached. He did not attempt to use the diver's own hands for retrieval of material; instead, he fitted four 'nippers' that could be operated internally. The French entered the arena with the Carmagnolle Frères design in 1882. This suit attempted to give maximum flexibility in every direction. It had 22 ball-and-socket joints in the arms, legs, and torso, and there were observation ports at eye-separation intervals all over the helmet. Their ball-and-socket joints consisted of sections of closely fitting concentric spheres kept watertight by strips of watertight linen secured to both parts of the joint and folded in such a way that the linen slid over itself when the joint was in motion.

Spiral wires are particularly good at resisting pressure because the whole length of the wire is resisting compression. An Australian, Alexander Gordon, took out a patent on such a suit in 1897; however, the forerunner of the familiar armoured diving-dress (ADS) of today was the Neufeldt and Kunhke suit introduced in 1920. It consisted of two halves that were bolted together at the waist. The top half carried a self-contained breathing apparatus containing oxygen, while CO_2 was absorbed in a chemical regenerator. The hands were two sets of nippers, and the suit carried a small ballast tank that could be blown out using compressed air from a dedicated bottle. Once again, the inspiration for its development was salvage, this time of one million pounds (about 1.39 million US dollars) worth of bullion lying 122m (400ft)

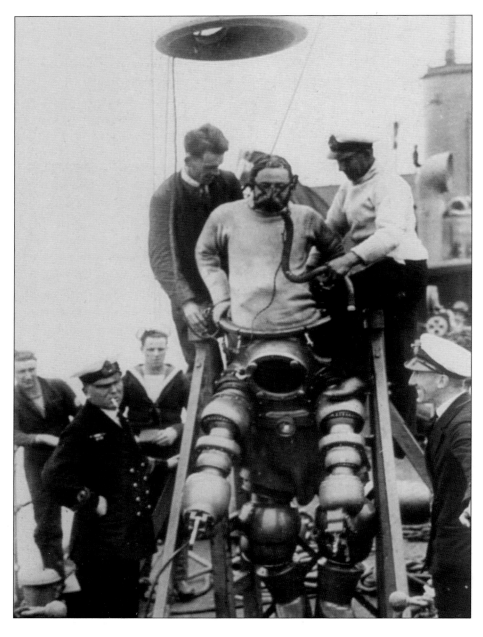

down in the wreck of the *Egypt* lying off Ushant, the rights to which were obtained by the Italian Sorima Salvage Company.

There were problems still to be overcome for the ADS, not least that its joints were susceptible to leaks, and, for a period, the industry had to resort to observation bells, the operator of which then directed mechanical grabs from the surface. This problem of leaking joints was largely overcome by the introduction of liquid-sealed articulated joints that resisted sea-pressure. Forty years later, a British company developed JIM (named in honour of Jim Jarrett, the first operator to make a successful dive), the first truly practical ADS, and it worked in the North Sea oil and gas industry. JIM was developed over the years, with magnesium-alloy bodies being replaced by carbon-fibre reinforced plastic. JIM 18, which can be seen at the Royal Navy Submarine Museum, Gosport, was capable of operating down to 610m (2000ft), with its operator able to carry out a number of quite complex tasks, using specially designed tools, at these great depths. Should the suit become detached from its connecting lines to the surface, it could be made positively buoyant by slipping a ballast weight, and there was 72 hours of life support provided in the event of an emergency. During that time, a backup JIM suit would effect a rescue. As JIM was designed as a seabed system, it made working at intermediate depths extremely difficult, so the 'Wasp' was developed. In essence, this was a smaller JIM with a thruster pack to provide it with greater flexibility. The Newt suit, built by Drager, has taken ADS technology to its current limits. It has improved dexterity and is fitted with a thruster pack consisting of two high-speed motors that allows the operator to work at variable depths and in a significant tideway.

UNDERWATER HABITATS

The late Captain Jacques Cousteau FN, as well as pioneering the Scuba (Self Contained

Left: The JIM suit was a British development named after Jim Jarrett and, from the 1970s onwards, was used in the North Sea oil and gas industry. It was capable of operation down to 609m (2000ft).

Below: The Wasp is a JIM suit with thrusters, which allow the operator much greater freedom on the seabed. Here, the suit is being piloted by Graham Hawkes.

TOURIST SUBMARINES

The first example of a 'tourist submarine' came from Jacques Piccard, after he had returned to Switzerland after *Trieste* had been sold to the United States. He and his father had hoped to build a 'mesoscaphe' for work at medium depths, but they failed to attract sufficient funding. What did attract support was for the design to be used to take visitors to the Lausanne International Festival in 1963 on a submarine cruise of Lake Geneva. The *Auguste Piccard* could carry 40 passengers, each with a personal porthole. The vessel made 13,000 dives without mishap.

Today, tourist submarines abound, particularly in areas of great underwater beauty, many of which are conveniently shallow, so do not put passengers at enormous risk. Atlantis Submarines of Canada has pioneered the industry, and its vessels can be seen operating in the West Indies to the east and Guam to the west. Many such vehicles are positively buoyant and driven down by vertical thrusters, so that, in the event of a power failure, they would bob to the surface, rather than sink to the bottom.

Underwater Breathing Apparatus), was convinced that man could create an underwater habitat in which to live. He expressed his love of the sea through a series of TV specials based on his famous depot ship and floating laboratory *Calypso*, a converted British World War II minesweeper. It was he who popularized shallow-water diving, a pastime now enjoyed by millions of people around the world. There was, however, a much more serious side to his work, and Cousteau as much as anyone pioneered the concept of workstations and underwater habitats to allow the use of Scuba packs at great depths. His first underwater craft was the *DS-2*, nicknamed *La Souscoupe* (Diving Saucer), which became a taxi to his Continental Shelf Stations, the second of which, Conshelf 2, based in the Red Sea, became the first human underwater colony.

Under the guidance of Professor John Holdane immediately before and after World War II, Royal Navy divers had continued earlier American experiments with using the mixed gas of oxygen and helium to sustain life and work at depths below 91m (300ft) – this mixture makes the breather sound like Donald Duck when he communicates! In 1975, working jointly with United States Navy counterparts, a depth of 350m (1148ft) was reached. The team spent 15 days under pressure, 11 of which were in decompression. These experiments, and the work of Jacques Cousteau, led to a technique known as 'saturation diving'. Over a period of time of living under pressure, the gases being breathed saturate the human body, pervading tissue as well as blood. There are no ill effects from the condition; however, decompression is a lengthy business, as there is so much more gas to be expelled. These underwater habitats were built to extend underwater endurance and were therefore not necessarily deployed at great depths. During the 1970s in particular, however, their usefulness for research and exploration was investigated by the Americans through their Sealab 1 and 2 projects which had military applications, and the Hydro Lab which focussed on fish farming, kelp cultivation, and the study of currents, sediments, and other seabed characteristics. The drawback to such 'habitats' is that they rely on surface support and, as well as putting their inhabitants at some risk because of the potential of losing vital services, they are also subject to significant costs.

AQUALUNG

The development of the Scuba diving set, and all its successors for recreational and sporting activities, owes much to Captain Jacques Cousteau. Today, millions of people enjoy water sports of all types, most conducting their business with a respect for the seas and their environment. A scuba diving set, or 'aqualung' works as follows: the first stage of the equipment contains a membrane (1) which on one side presses against the immersion valve (2), which in turn opens onto a flexible tube. The other side of the membrane responds to the water and is blocked by a strong spring (3) which keeps the distributor valve open. The air in the cylinder (4) passes through the open valve and enters into the flexible tube (5). The flow stops when the pressure in the tube overcomes the combined force of the spring and the hydraulic pressure, thus making the membrane move and close the valve. When the diver breathes in, the pressure in the flexible tube is decreased, allowing the valve to open and the air to pass through. When the suction stops, the pressure increases to the point where it closes the valve again. The second stage of the equipment, which includes the mouthpiece (6), also has a membrane (7) on which rests a lever (8) connected to a small piston (9), which keeps the valve hermetically closed. When the diver breathes in, the membrane and the lever move, opening the valve and allowing the air to enter the mouthpiece. The air which is exhaled by the diver is automatically expelled into the water via vents (10) in the second stage.

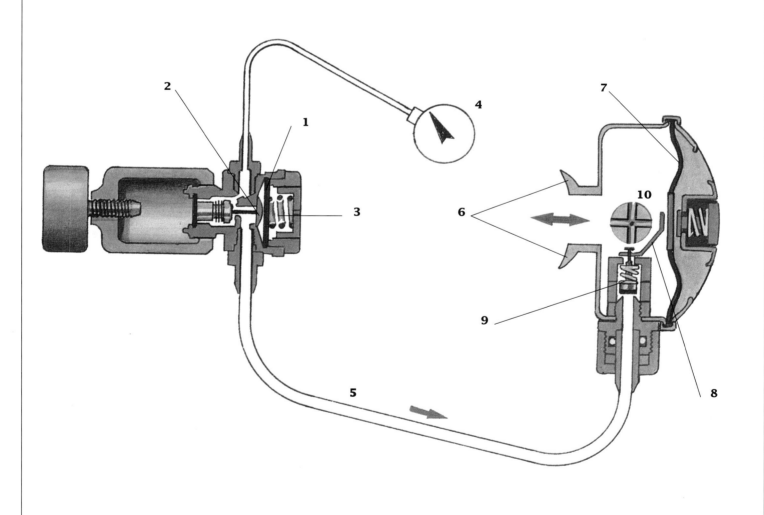